HOW TO
CLEAN
JUST ABOUT
EVERYTHING

HOW TO CLEAN JUST ABOUT EVERYTHING

Reader's
Digest

Published by The Reader's Digest Association, Inc.
London • New York • Sydney • Montreal

CONTENTS

A quick reference guide to 21 cleaning emergencies, from animal accidents and baby sick to water stains and wine spills.

A mini-encyclopaedia of cleaning products, compounds, solutions and utensils, from abrasive cleaners and alcohol to soap and toilet cleaners.

The easiest path to a

CLEAN HOME

CLEAN THINKING

This book covers the full spectrum of topics related to cleaning – from smart routines and the right gear to handling unexpected messes and cleaning specific types of items and materials. But underlying it all is one key idea: the more you know about how to clean and the more organised you are about cleaning – the less effort, time and money you will have to spend actually doing it.

Too many people see cleaning as an odious chore that can't be avoided, but is all too easy to put off. If you have a positive attitude to cleaning and its benefits, then a pristine house becomes something that is much easier to accomplish.

- **This book has lots of advice** on how to clean particular objects in your home. Learning how to get them clean – and doing so more easily and faster than you have done before – can be very satisfying.

- **Too much to do and too little time** is something that unites us all these days. So, on page 64, you'll find a tried-and-tested system for cleaning your house: ZAP – the Zoned Attack Plan – is a truly time-saving strategy for regular, ideally weekly, house cleaning. It is a super-efficient plan that eliminates going over the same ground twice so that you get your house spick-and-span with minimal effort. It will knock hours off your cleaning time and makes it almost fun.

The three kinds of cleaning

There are ten golden rules to follow when cleaning, but before looking at these it's important to understand that there are three different categories of cleaning:

- **Immediate cleaning** prevents small, easy-to-clean messes from becoming big, tough messes that take time and energy to shift. Let's say that after cooking dinner, your hob has a few marks on it. You could leave it, but if you wipe clean the cooker every time you use it, the job will take only seconds, and you will be preventing what could eventually become a multilayered build-up requiring hours of serious cleaning attention. In the immediate cleaning mode, you clean up messes straight away, otherwise spills accumulate and stains and grime set in.

- **Maintenance cleaning** is done regularly, but not necessarily often. For example, you could decide to clean the bathroom splashback tiles once a week (perhaps even set the day) and wash the kitchen curtains twice a year. Maintenance cleaning can be organised as a plan – you might even go so far as to write it down, or block a day off in your diary for particular tasks every now and again.

- **Remedial cleaning** covers cleaning after long periods of neglect, such as tackling the fridge after a year's worth of drips and spills have accumulated on the bottom shelf. This kind of remedial cleaning is preventable. Remedial cleaning also includes what you do after a disaster, major or minor, such as a flood or a pet accident on the carpet.

  The big danger is that remedial cleaning can become abusive cleaning – if a mild cleaner fails to budge the dirt, stronger and more abrasive cleaners and tools are then needed. Abusive cleaning may do more damage than the original dirt did – another good reason for keeping on top of things.

Ten golden rules of cleaning

Your primary goal in cleaning is to remove dirt, whether it be in and around your home or on your garments and other personal possessions. But you do need to determine how far you're prepared to go. You don't want to injure yourself or damage the very thing you're trying to clean. And you also want to get it done as quickly and with as little effort as possible.

Stick to the following ten golden rules and you will achieve safe, effective cleaning that attacks the problem early and with the minimum amount of effort.

1 Clean up immediately. Spills and stains are generally much easier to clean up when you attack them straight away. When you treat the tomato-sauce splatter on your shirt at once, for instance, by rinsing it under the cold tap, it will offer little resistance. If you wait until the next day, you'll expend a lot more cleaning solution and time getting rid of it. As a rough rule, practically all clothing or carpet stains are easiest to remove when they're fresh. The longer you wait, the more chance there is for the stain to have set.

The rare exception to this is mud tracked onto your carpet. This is easiest to clean when you've let it dry first. So hold back until the mud is bone dry and crumbly; then just vacuum it up.

2 Clean from the top down. Don't fight gravity when you clean; you'll lose. Working down from high to low almost always works better in cleaning situations.

When you're cleaning the entire house, start on the top floor and work your way down to avoid tramping dirt through rooms you have already cleaned. When you're cleaning a room, first remove any cobwebs from the ceiling and coving. Then dust light fixtures, followed by window frames and wall hangings. Moving downwards, sweep over the furniture, skirting boards

The benefits of cleaning
• You will be in control of your home instead of out of control.
• You'll feel renewed pride in your environment.
• You can enjoy a healthier and safer home.
• You'll be able to spend more and better time with your family.
• And you can save money – furniture and clothes that are cleaned with care last longer.

and floors. This ensures that any dust shaken loose from on high does not settle on something you've already cleaned below. You don't want to have to dust the room twice.

Similarly, when you clean windows and mirrors, start up high and work your way down, because your cleaning solution obeys gravity and may just drip down. This will save you both elbow grease and time.

However, as with any rule, there are exceptions! The advice for cleaning walls, for instance, is that you start at the bottom and then work your way up.

3 Think dry, then wet. When you're cleaning a room, start with the cleaning jobs that require dry methods (dusting, sweeping and vacuuming, for instance). If you still need to do further cleaning, then move on to wet methods – for example, using an all-purpose cleaner or glass cleaner, mopping and similar jobs. This way, there will be less dirt floating around in the room to cling to wet surfaces.

4 Start with the least harmful approach. Use your gentlest cleaning methods first and move up to more aggressive techniques only if necessary. If you've tried everything you know to be safe, make a rational decision about whether it's worth carrying on. Generally, you may feel it is better to suffer a small spot on your hob, than to ruin the surface by scrubbing it with steel wool.

5 Let time do the work for you. Here's a little time-management trick to make your cleaning easier and faster. When you start to clean a room, spray on your cleaning chemicals first and then find another little job to do while the cleaner does its dirty work. In the kitchen, spray your cleaner on the worktops and appliances, then occupy yourself with removing old food from the fridge while the cleaner soaks in. When you come back to wipe clean, there should be little or no scrubbing to do.

The family that cleans together
Dividing up the chores makes sense, especially if there are two adults. But it's important that everyone shares if you're a family. If you get into the habit of being the only cleaner in the home, then what are you teaching everyone else? That they can be messy, and someone else will take care of it? Instead, make it the job of the whole family to keep your home clean.

Extra help
If you need to motivate yourself to get down to serious cleaning, consider calling in a friend for help – two of you working together will get fast results. You will also be far more ruthless with an audience. It's one thing to keep every birthday card you've ever received, but it's harder to justify why to someone else. And your friend may suggest storage ideas and cleaning solutions that you hadn't thought of before.

6 Carry your supplies with you. Keep your core-cleaning products with you. This will save you from making multiple trips around the house looking for the right tools and cleaners. A simple plastic tool caddy from a DIY store – the sort painters and decorators use – with two deep pockets each side of a handle, is perfect for storing cleaning products. Just grab it by the handle when you start your cleaning routine, and you've got everything you need in one place. You could also use a sturdy, large plastic bucket with a good handle. Or, failing that, an apron with roomy pockets.

As well as cleaning solutions and cloths, you should also carry clean rags, paper towels, and a stack of bin liners for emptying all of the waste-paper baskets around the house. If your home has more than one floor, consider setting up a caddy for each level. However, only do this if you have somewhere safe, away from children, to store cleaning products safely.

If you have room and a secure space in the toilet and bathroom, you might prefer to leave speciality products here, rather than carry them with you.

7 When in doubt, test it out. Before you use a new cleaning technique or product, test the method on an inconspicuous area of the object you're cleaning. This rule also applies when you first clean an object that is delicate and might be damaged by a cleaning compound. Testing will show you whether the object is colourfast and if it might be damaged by the method.

8 Don't soak, go easy on the spray. When you clean an item that could be harmed by a liquid cleaning product – electronics, computer screens, framed artwork or framed photographs, for example – first spray the cleaner on your cleaning cloth and then wipe. Don't spray cleaner directly onto the object you're cleaning. Liquid slopping into your electronics could cause serious damage, and cleaning solution dripping through a frame and soaking the matting could harm your artwork.

9 Read the directions. You've probably heard this before, but the makers of all of the furnishings in your home really do know how best to clean them. And the manufacturers of your cleaning products also know the best way to use them.

So, when cleaning anything, follow the manufacturer's directions whenever possible. This goes for everything from toasters to silk blouses. Keep the directions and cleaning tips that come with any new appliance, rug or other household item and file them away. Unlike guarantees, cleaning instructions are valid for as long as you have the item. Don't discard care labels on clothes, linens and other washable objects – they are there to help you.

10 Get some protection. Last but not least, take care of yourself. Many cleaning products contain acid, bleach, abrasives and other ingredients that can damage eyes, skin, nose and even lungs. And don't let your cleaning products get mixed together. Some combinations – chlorine bleach and ammonia, for instance – will react with each other and produce poisonous gases. When you're using cleaning chemicals, make sure the room you're in is properly ventilated.

And if you're not on mains drainage and have a septic tank, only use those products marked as safe for septic tanks – follow the advice of the professionals who maintain your tank as to which products are suitable.

Your cleaning kit needs to include a pair of rubber gloves and protective safety glasses. If it's not too hot, wear clothes that cover your legs and arms in case of splatters from products. Tie long hair back and, when you're working overhead, consider wearing a light hat, shower cap or headscarf. If you don't get on with gloves, then at least protect your nails. Dab a line of petroleum jelly underneath your nails to keep out dirt. Dot more on your cuticles to keep them from drying out, roughening and splitting from exposure to cleaning chemicals.

Stop dirt at the door

It's much easier to head off a problem before it takes root, than to fix it after the damage is done. So here's some good advice on how to stop dirt in its tracks.

- **Keep dirt on the mat.** Use doormats at every entrance to your home, inside and out. Most of the grime in your house comes from the outside, the bulk of it coming in unnoticed on shoes that don't appear to be either muddy or dirty. If you live in the country, or have a driveway that gets very muddy, keep a wire rack underneath the mat. This will be handy if your family or guests need to scrape mud from their boots or shoes before they enter the house.

- **Doormats need minimal maintenance.** All you need to do is take them outside occasionally and give them a good shake to remove the dust. A good once-over with the vacuum cleaner now and then won't hurt either.

- **When mats are really grimy,** hose them down and scrub them with a squirt of washing-up liquid in warm water. Rinse and allow to thoroughly air-dry. If you prefer, upholstery shampoo is also fine. Make sure the mats are completely dry before you put them back on the floor. Moisture trapped underneath could damage your floors. Replace mats when they get threadbare, as worn ones are less effective at trapping dirt.

Expert **ADVICE**

Thoroughly clean surfaces before applying products that prevent them getting grimy. For example, lemon oil works wonders in preventing residue build-up on shower doors and curtains, but you have to get rid of mildew, soap scum and other gunk before applying it. The same goes for fabrics: the spray-on protectors that repel stains and spills also require that the fabric be clean before you apply the protectant. Fail to take off dirt first, and all you will do is seal it in, beneath the fabric protector.

Stop kitchen grime

The kitchen can be one of the dirtiest rooms in a house, which is alarming considering that it is where you cook and eat. As you heat food, it's inevitable that grease particles will rise into the air, ready to land on all surfaces, especially walls, ceilings and cupboards. But you can minimise this:

- **Suck up some of the airborne grease** by turning on the extractor fan every time you cook on the hob; the time spent washing down grimy kitchen walls will be greatly reduced.

- **Cut down on soup and sauces** jumping out of their saucepans, by using larger pots and pans, with their lids. If you frequently deep-fry, sauté or otherwise cook foods that spit, you could consider fitting an extra line of tiles behind the oven, so that you have a deep splashback.

- **For oven splatters** from a pie or casserole bubbling over, sprinkle the stains with salt to keep the smoke down and make the eventual clean-up job much easier.

- **To protect the fabric on kitchen chairs,** which is always under assault, especially from food spills and sticky fingers, choose laminated fabric (or oilcloth). You could make removable covers yourself and when guests come, remove these and enjoy the clean, non-greasy original underneath. Or choose chairs with a wipe-clean surface.

Take time to clean all your large appliances – dishwashers, tumble dryers and washing machines – and they'll do their job much more efficiently. For example, if your dishwasher's filthy, then you'll be washing your plates and cutlery in dirty water. And if you don't keep the working parts of your appliances in good order, then you've only got yourself to blame if they break down.

Keep tools clean

You won't be able to keep your house properly clean if your tools are dirty, too. They won't work as well and can actually spread dirt and germs around.

- **Wash cleaning rags** regularly in the washing machine, using detergent, hot water and 100ml white vinegar or a scoop of oxygen-boosting additive, such as Oxi Clean, to cut through grease. Throw away rags when they look worn out.

- **Wash cellulose sponges** very frequently in the washing machine or in the top rack of your dishwasher – put them in each evening. After four weeks of use, throw them away.

- **Replace the bag** in your vacuum cleaner at least once a month – more often if you have pets that shed lots of fur. Vacuum bags need air inside to suck properly, so be sure to change them when they are two-thirds full. Keep vacuum brushes clean, too. Take bagless vacuums outside to empty them. That way, you won't tip dust over everything you've just cleaned.

Close your doors

If you keep your doors, drawers, cabinets, wardrobes and other barriers closed, this will keep dirt out in the open, where vacuum cleaners and cloths will be able to deal with it more readily.

- **If you're working** on a messy, dust-producing project in the house, keep the doors to the room you're working in closed. Better yet, hang plastic sheeting across the door and any air vents to confine the dust to one room.

- **Periodically wash venetian blinds** and other dirt-trapping window coverings, such as net curtains. Remember that dirt loves company and acts as a magnet for more.

Smart tricks for pets

Any pet with easy access to the garden will bring plenty of the great outdoors in on its coat and paws. Keeping your dogs and cats clean, and taking preventative measures when you know they have got especially dirty, will reduce the amount of dirt they can bring into your house.

- **Keep a clean rag by the door** so that you can wipe off muddy, wet paws and claws before your beloved animal makes unsightly tracks through the whole house.

- **Once a week, take your dog** outside and give its fur a good going-over with the type of brush suited for its coat. Do this away from the house, so that the hair won't tumble back inside.

- **To lift pet hair from furniture** and other surfaces, wipe with a damp sponge or cloth. The hair will gather in clumps and onto your cloth. An excellent alternative is a lightly dampened rubber glove, rubbed quickly back and forth. It will pick up bundles of hair. Or you could use one of those special rubber brushes with nubs on it that is intended for grooming cats and finer-haired dogs (available at pet shops).

- **Nothing beats your vacuum** for pulling pet hair out of your rugs and carpets. If you have a number of pets or an animal that sheds a lot, it could be worth considering a vacuum, which has been specially designed to deal with fur. They have greater suction for sucking up fur and special filters for trapping potential allergens.

You can machine-
wash 100 per cent
cotton at high
temperatures,
unless the label
says otherwise.
With cotton mixes,
you'll need to
follow instructions
for the less robust
nylon or polyester.
You can use
chlorine bleach on
cotton whites but
don't soak for more
than 15 minutes,
since the bleach
will break down
the fibres. Use an
all-fabric bleach
on dyed cottons.

LAUNDRY ADVICE

Everyone has clothes and linens to clean, but not everyone cleans them as well as they could. This section will help you to do a better, more thorough job on your laundry.

Sorting your clothes

You can't wash all your clothes or linens in the same way. Some things require lower washing temperatures. Some can't even be put in the machine. To avoid laundry accidents, sort your weekly wash into piles, keeping like items together:

- **Separate whites from colours** and light colours from dark ones. This is most important if you want to choose different detergents, for instance a 'colour' product which doesn't contain optical brighteners and so won't dull coloured clothes. Read care labels to be on the lookout for garments that need to be washed separately. This is because the dye colours may run.

- **Separate heavily soiled** or greasy items from lightly soiled ones. Lightly soiled clothes can pick up some of this dirt, making whites look grey or yellow and colours look dull. If you have particularly dirty clothes, put fewer items in the machine than usual and use the maximum detergent dose.

- **Separate out loosely knit** or woven items, or things with delicate trimmings or unfinished seams that could fray. Wash those on a shorter cycle that features more gentle agitation. Also separate lint producers – such as fleece sweat suits, chenille items, new towels and flannel pyjamas – from lint attractors, such as corduroys, synthetic blends and dark things. In the long run, it is quicker to do more loads of washing than spend time getting pale fluff out of a pair of dark corduroy trousers.

Getting ready to wash

It's also worth going through your wash to check for anything that might damage your washing or the machine, or that might actually make your laundry more dirty.

- **Empty out pockets.** Be especially alert for tissues, which can also be wedged up sleeves or stuck in pockets. Keep a small brush handy to brush dirt and lint out of cuffs.

- **Close zips and Velcro.** This prevents snags and keeps Velcro from getting matted with lint and thread.

- **Put tights, stockings and any items** with long ties, such as bikini tops, into a mesh bag to keep them from snagging and tearing, or from getting tangled up with the rest of the wash.

Get tough with stains

It's always best to try to remove stains when they are fresh, but here we look at what to do when you first spot a mark as you go to load the clothes into the washing machine. Modern, premium-brand detergents are actually rather good at shifting most stains these days. The trick is to wash your clothes at the maximum temperature allowed on the care label and not to put too many clothes into the machine at one time. Also, choose the correct dose of detergent. If the staining is particularly bad and you don't feel confident that your detergent will shift it, try the following first.

- **Soak protein stains,** such as egg, milk, faeces, urine and blood, for half an hour in cold water, then run under a cold tap, gently rubbing the fabric together with your hands to loosen the stain. Avoid warm or hot water, which can 'cook' proteins, setting the stain permanently.

- **Pre-treat oil and grease stains** with liquid laundry detergent or pre-treatment spray, applied directly to the stain.

- **Soak tannin stains** such as coffee, tea, soft drinks, fruit and jam for half an hour in a solution of 1 teaspoon liquid detergent (a biological one containing enzymes) per 2 litres warm water. Do not use soap or a soap-based product. Soap can make the tannin stain harder to remove.

- **After washing in the machine,** check to see whether the stain has gone. If it hasn't, do not leave the item to dry and especially do not tumble dry. Try again to remove the stain and then repeat washing.

All about washing machines

There's no point in simply sticking all your dirty clothes and other laundry in the washing machine, bunging in any old powder and hoping the machine will do the rest. There are certain things you need to do if you want to get the best out of your washing machine.

- **Evenly distribute clothes in the machine.** The spin cycle relies on a balanced load. The best mix is large items such as sheets with smaller hand towels and socks.

- **Don't overload the machine.** The wash cycle depends on clothes rubbing together to remove dirt. If the machine is too full, the clothes will not have enough space to rub together. Powdered detergent may not have room to adequately dissolve, and you may end up with clumps of white powder stuck on your clothes. Moreover, there must be enough free-flowing water to carry away the dirt removed from the clothes. Check your washing machine manual for the recommended maximum

Silk safe
Made from protein fibre produced by the silkworm, silk is expensive and delicate and must be treated accordingly. Most silk is dry-clean only, since laundry detergents can harm the fabric. If the care label says that hand washing is safe, use a mild soap and lukewarm water. Never use bleach with silk.

load. Most are between 5-6kg. Considering a
woollen jumper can weigh 1kg and a duvet cover
1.5kg, a full load soon mounts up.

- **Pick the right setting.** Most clothes use the
  normal or regular setting. In fact, even if your
  machine has 22 programmes, you may have
  previously just used this one for everything. But
  do try to switch to the gentle or delicate setting –
  sometimes marked as quick wash. Typically, it has a
  shorter, slower spin cycle and is ideal for lingerie, loose
  knits, washable woollens and synthetic fabrics that can get
  damaged and stretched by over-spinning.

- **Choose the right water temperature.** On many
  machines, the hot cycle draws directly from your household
  hot-water supply, then heats it to the required temperature.
  This is usually a choice of 60°C or 95°C, although pricier
  machines have an override that lets you choose exactly the
  temperature that you want for every wash programme. The
  warm 40°C wash on most machines takes water from the
  cold-water supply and then heats it to the desired temperature.
  Check the care labels in your clothing to set the temperature.

- **Add the right amount of detergent.** It's easy to lose sight
  of just how much to use with each wash. Take the extra minute
  to read the information printed on your packet of detergent and
  use the measure scoop. The main cause of clothes coming out
  yellow, grey and dingy is not using enough detergent.

  Although detergents and powder both work well, liquid
  detergents have the edge with cold-water washes and on oily
  stains. Powders are great for removing ground-in dirt and mud.
  Biological is always best for cleaning, but if you have sensitive
  skin that is irritated by the enzymes in biological powder (these
  actively improve the detergent's stain-shifting ability), then
  you'll have to use non-bio instead.

> **Hot or not?**
> - Use 95°C for 'boil wash' safe items, such as white cotton sheets.
> - Use 60°C for other whites, colourfast fabrics and heavily soiled clothes that can withstand the heat.
> - Use 40°C for non-colourfast fabrics, moderately soiled loads, synthetics, wrinkle-free fabrics, knits, silks and woollens.
> - Use 30°C or less for delicates and for dark or bright colours that you know will bleed.

● **Understand your water.** More than 50 per cent of the UK has hard water. This means there is excess magnesium, calcium and other minerals present in the tap water and detergent has to work harder to combat them. In a soft-water area, soap and detergents will lather up more easily.

If your laundry comes out of the washing machine looking grey and dingy and feeling rough, then you may have a hard-water problem. Other symptoms of hard water are rings around the water line in your bath, a white residue around your taps and drains, and soaps and shampoos that don't lather well. The easiest solution, when it comes to doing the laundry, is just to add a little more detergent.

● **Protect your machine.** You may also want to protect your washing machine's pipes from becoming coated with mineral deposits from hard water – this may lead to long-term damage. A water softening product, which can be added as a tablet with each wash, solves the problem.

Laundry extras

There are many products on the market, other than detergents and fabric conditioners, that you can use in the wash to enhance the look and feel of your laundered items.

● **Chlorine bleach is the most effective** whitener and sanitiser, but the downside is that we all know – mostly from personal wash-day disasters – just how strong a substance chlorine bleach really is. It can fade or alter the colour of fabrics and can weaken fibres.

However, chlorine bleach does have a place as a pre-soak for whites that are very soiled or greying, but use it with care. Never pour full-strength liquid chlorine bleach directly into your washing machine. Always dilute it, then dispense it through a machine's bleach dispenser, carefully following the instructions found on the bleach container – 1 part bleach to 10 parts water is typical. Don't soak cottons in a bleach solution for more than 15 minutes. If the stain remains after this length of time, it means that it's not going to go away using this particular solvent. Don't use chlorine bleach on silk, wool, polyurethane foam, Lycra, rubber or anything that contains rubber or Lycra elastic.

- **All-fabric, oxygen bleaches** are less harsh and are safe for some coloured fabrics. They whiten whites and brighten colours, rather than fading them, as a chlorine bleach would. At the same time, they are not as powerful or fast-acting as chlorine bleach. You'll find oxygen bleach in many of the commercial wash boosters that go directly into the wash cycle of the machine in a dispenser ball.

- **Enzyme pre-soaks** are good for loosening and removing awkward stains before the wash cycle. They work especially well on hard-to-shift protein stains like milk, egg, urine and faeces. When added to the wash cycle, enzymes act like boosters to improve the washing. Many are quite safe for delicate fabrics and contain no bleach.

- **Pre-wash stain removers** contain some combination of concentrated detergents, alcohol, mineral spirits or enzymes. These are especially good for removing oily or greasy stains from synthetic fibres. They are often sold in spray bottles or blocks; their great advantage is that you can directly target the stain and are effective on even low-temperature washes.

- **Detergent boosters** help detergents do their job by increasing stain and soil-removal action, altering the pH balance of water and brightening clothes in the process. However, with a quality detergent and not too many clothes in the wash, boosters aren't generally needed.

Nylon know-how
Relatively easy to care for, nylon clothing and linens can be machine-washed in warm water. To reduce static cling, add a tumble dryer conditioning sheet, such as Bounce, to the dryer and remove clothes from the dryer as soon as they have finished drying. If you need to iron nylon, only use a warm iron – it can scorch easily and quickly at hotter temperatures.

● **Water softeners** are quick fixes if you've got a problem with hard water. Added directly to the wash or rinse cycle of your washing machine, products soften the water, making the detergent work far more effectively.

● **Fabric softeners** in liquid form can be added to the final rinse cycle of your wash load. They also come in sheets that you add to the dryer. These products make fabrics softer and fluffier, reduce static cling and wrinkling, and make ironing easier. However, don't go overboard: if overused, fabric softeners can reduce the absorbency of towels. Dryer sheets, which are placed with the wet washing into the drum of the tumble dryer may, if used too frequently, leave oily-looking splotches on medium-coloured items.

● **Starches and fabric finishes** were popular in the days when people kept their garments for longer, and consequently wanted to improve the look of older clothes. Washing methods were also harsher in those days, and fabrics often became worn and rather limp. Today, starches are rarely used. However, if they're used either in the final rinse or after drying, they temporarily stiffen fabrics so they look crisp and fresh.

Drying your washing

Having a tumble dryer doesn't just mean you can turn round clothes and laundry within a couple of hours, rather than the best part of a day. In winter and on wet days, it also gives you back a home without wet clothes on the radiators or dripping into the bath. But before you get tumbling, spend a moment on the following:

● **Check clothes for stains before drying.** If you overlook a stain you could set it permanently by drying it at a hot temperature. If you find a stain, treat it and re-wash.

- **Take out anything** that needs to be line or flat-dried and has a 'no tumble drying' symbol on it. Woollens may very likely shrink and delicates such as bras and other underwear may 'melt' in the hot dryer.

- **Shake damp pieces before drying,** this loosens them and helps them dry faster and more completely.

- **Don't overload the dryer.** A dryer needs some airflow to do its work. Clothes and other items that are bunched up in a tumble dryer will take much longer to dry and will wrinkle more easily.

- **And don't underload the dryer.** A nearly empty tumble dryer does not work as well as one that is fuller, but not too full. The tumbling effect is reduced in dryers with small loads, prolonging the drying period. If you must dry only one item, find a few towels that are already clean and dry and of a colour similar to the wet garment and put them into the dryer to improve the process.

- **Use the right setting.** Most dryers have the following automatic settings: regular for loads made up mostly of all-cotton fabrics; permanent press for synthetics; and cool or low for lingerie, hand washables, washable woollens, and heat-sensitive items marked 'tumble dry-low'.

  The permanent press cycle typically features a cool-down period after the drying is completed to reduce creasing.

- **Avoid overdrying.** This causes shrinkage, static build-up and creasing. Over-drying can actually set creases into items, making them even harder to remove.

- **To reduce creasing,** remove items from the dryer as soon as they are dry and hang up or fold them as soon as possible. Remove permanent-press items while they are damp and hang on a rustproof hanger. Close buttons and snaps, straighten creases and brush out any wrinkles.

Love that Lycra
Developed in the late 1950s, Lycra (a brand name for spandex) is lightweight, durable and known for being extremely flexible. That's why it's used in swimwear, tights and to add a flattering shape to clothing. You can machine or hand-wash most items containing Lycra. Don't use chlorine bleach under any circumstances. Either let it drip-dry or put in a dryer on a low setting.

- **Clean the lint filter** in your machine after each use. Not doing so is a serious fire hazard. A filter without lint also means a better airflow and improved drying performance.

- **Use a mesh bag for drying tights** and other delicates in the dryer. It will protect them from snagging.

- **For items that call for flat drying,** such as woollens, squeeze out excess water but don't wring, or you may cause creasing. Roll the garment in a clean, dry towel to absorb water.

  If you think that you may have to stretch your garment back into shape after washing, try this tip. Trace round the item onto a piece of paper before you wash. After washing and squeezing out water, place a piece of clear plastic over the paper and put the washed item onto it. Use the traced outline as a guide and pull the garment back to its original shape. Then lay it out flat on a dry towel or drying rack – over the bath is ideal.

Outdoor drying

Even if you've got a tumble dryer, your clothes and bedding always seem to smell better when blown dry by the wind.

- **Turn clothes inside out if it's sunny** – it will stop coloured garments fading in strong sunlight.

- **Peg with care.** Avoid making ridges that will need extra ironing by pegging trousers at the waistband and shirts at the underarm seam, rather than on the shoulders.

- **Check your washing regularly** to avoid over-drying. You will need to bring in synthetics well before cottons.

- **Remember to wipe down** the washing line if you haven't used it in a while, otherwise you will get a line of dirt across your freshly washed clothes.

The best way to iron

Ironing can be a real bind – but you can cut down the time you spend at the board with these tips:

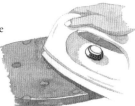

- **Wash and dry your clothes correctly.** Follow the previous advice for reducing creasing during the washing process. Dry things well, and you will cut your ironing time down considerably.

- **Read care labels.** Look out for advice on any parts of the garment that should not be ironed – for instance, a specially finished embroidered section.

- **Keep your equipment handy** – the hassle of setting up will discourage you from ironing and lead to a much bigger job when you do get round to it.

- **Launder the ironing-board cover** regularly and wash the iron soleplate – once it is completely cold – if necessary, using very fine steel wool to remove dirt. Dirt on your iron or board may stain clothes the next time you iron them.

- **Sort items by ironing temperature.** Start with low-temperature fabrics, such as silks and synthetics, and move on to items, such as cottons and linens, that need a hot iron. Iron clothes while they are still damp. This makes the job easier, since creases are not as set in the fabric. When you've finished ironing, hang your garments up immediately to help them stay fresh and pressed.

- **To keep wrinkling to a minimum,** start ironing with small areas, such as cuffs, collars and sleeves, and then work your way across to the larger areas. Iron lengthwise on fabric to prevent the fabric from stretching.

- **Check very carefully for stains** before ironing. The heat will set the stains permanently.

> **Washing acrylics**
> Acrylics can be washed or dry-cleaned; machine-wash using a warm-water setting and fabric softener. Tumble dry at a low temperature and remove from the dryer as soon as dry to avoid creasing. When hand-washing delicate items, use warm water and a mild detergent. Rinse and gently squeeze out the water and dry on a rustproof hanger. Lay knits out flat to dry.

The lowdown on labels

Sewn-in care labels are a legal requirement in all clothing sold in the UK and EC states. Most, but not all, countries have similar laws. In theory, even the ethnic shirt you picked up on holiday should have a care label. The care labels give instructions for the best way to care for a garment, including how to properly clean, dry and iron and what techniques and products to avoid. Here's a handy explanation of the symbols:

WASHING

MACHINE WASH

 Normal
The number shows the maximum temperature for safe washing. Can cope with a full spin.

Use a programme suitable for synthetics. Reduced spin.

 Gentle/delicate/wool programme.

Hand-wash. Look for maximum temperature in the wash bowl.

Warning signs

 Do not wash.

BLEACH

 Any bleach (when needed).

Chlorine bleach may be used.

Warning signs

Do not bleach.

DRYING

TUMBLE-DRY

 May be tumble-dried.

 Tumble-dry on high setting.

 Tumble-dry on low setting.

Warning signs

 Do not tumble-dry.

AIR-DRY

 Line-dry/hang to dry.

 Drip-dry.

 Dry flat.

IRONING

 Hot iron – maximum setting.

Medium iron.

Cool iron – Use minimum setting.

Warning signs

 Do not iron.

DRY CLEANING

 Normal cycle Dry-clean.

Warning signs

 Do not dry-clean.

Problems & solutions

Ordinary dirt and difficult stains are one thing. But sometimes, even when there is no definable stain, clothes just don't turn out right. Here are some common problems and their solutions:

- **Clothes come out grey or yellow.** You may need to increase the amount of detergent in the next load, use a detergent booster or increase the temperature of the wash water. However, the grey could be from dye that has bled from darks to lights, suggesting you need to sort better.

- **Detergent residue on clothes.** If the powdered detergent isn't dissolving properly, put fewer items into the washing machine. Use liquid detergent with 30°C cycles. If the problem is caused by hard water, remove hard-water residue from clothes by soaking them in a solution of 200ml white vinegar per 5 litres warm water. Rinse and re-wash.

- **You have a problem with pilling.** This is most common with synthetic fabrics and makes even new items look shabby. Turn synthetic clothing inside out before washing or wash synthetics together in a gentler, shorter cycle. Using a liquid detergent will help. You can remove pills but it is also very easy to create holes in the fabric at the same time. So, at your own risk, pull fabric tight over a curved surface and carefully shave the pills off with a razor or a battery-powered pill remover, available from haberdashers.

- **There's lint on your clothes.** Separate lint producers, such as fleece and chenille garments, new towels and flannel items, from lint attractors, such as corduroys, synthetics and dark fabric. To remove the lint, use a lint roller or pat with the sticky side of masking tape. Check to make sure pockets are empty of tissues and other paper before you wash. Make sure the washer and dryer lint filters are clean and free of lint.

Perfect polyester
Strong, durable, shrink and crease-resistant, polyester does, however, tend to take on oily stains easily. Most polyester can be washed or dry-cleaned. Wash in warm water and tumble-dry at a low temperature setting. To prevent pilling (bobbling) and snagging, turn knits inside out. To reduce static cling, use a dryer sheet and remove garments as soon as they have dried.

EVERYDAY STAINS

No matter how careful and house proud you are, accidents do happen. This section looks at how to deal with everyday spills and soiling that can happen anywhere.

Take immediate action

Follow the instructions
Most fabric items, including clothes, rugs, linens and upholstery, have care labels. Because fabrics differ in so many ways – type of material, type of weave, colour, style – don't assume that items that look similar can all be treated the same.

Taking swift action can often stop a spill or sudden accident from turning into a stain. Things usually get more difficult when the spill has dried up and become 'locked' into the fibres of the material that it landed on. But even on a hot day, most things will not dry out immediately.

Most stains fall into one of four main categories: protein, oil-based, tannin and dye. The rest are usually a combination of these categories. By understanding what's in a stain, you can determine the best and safest way to remove it.

You also need to consider the material on which the spill has occurred. Some treatments may remove the stain, but if the fabric is delicate, it may be ruined in the process. So you must always make a judgment about whether the stained item can be safely treated, or if the lesser of two evils is actually to live with the stain but keep a favourite item in one piece.

- **There are three main categories** of textiles that can be stained: washable fabrics (clothing, linens and towels), carpets, and upholstered furniture. Below are general steps to follow when trying to remove stains from all three.

- **Washable fabrics.** One of the main advantages with washable items is that you have access to both sides of the stain. That simply isn't possible with a fitted carpet or fixed upholstery on sofas. Pre-treatment often consists of pushing the stain out from the back side of the fabric. Attempt stain treatment on washable fabrics using the following steps:

1 Remove as much of the stain-causing material as possible by blotting with a clean cloth or paper towels, or by scraping it off with a dull knife.

2 Pre-treat the stain by soaking or applying a cleaning solution. It helps to lightly agitate the fabric being soaked or to gently rub together the stained fabric with your hands.

3 Launder in your washing machine according to the instructions on the fabric's care label.

4 If necessary, repeat the preceding steps, possibly using a stronger cleaning solution.

● **Carpeting.** Typically you have access to the top side only for stain removal. But you should never soak carpet stains, because most carpets and rugs have rubber or synthetic-based lining under them. Getting cleaning solutions into those pads can actually attract dirt and lead to other problems, such as mildew and glue deterioration. Try these methods instead:

1 Remove as much of the stain-causing material as you can by blotting or scraping with a dull knife. When blotting up a large stain, always blot from the edge of the stain to the centre to contain it. Standing on the blotting paper will increase its ability to blot up more. Jump up and down if you like.

2 Don't rub; this can push the stain into the pile. Don't use a circular motion, which can destroy a carpet's texture.

3 Use a spray bottle to apply small amounts of water-based cleaning solution and rinse water.

4 To dry patches of carpet that have been rinsed with water, lay a pad of paper towels on the spot and place a weight, such as a brick, on the pad. To prevent transferring colour from the brick to the carpet, put the brick in a plastic bag or wrap it in foil. When the carpet is dry, remove the paper towels. Brush the carpet pile to restore a consistent texture.

Act fast

It's important to remove spills before they become stains. You need to blot up spilled liquids, scrape away solids, and begin your step-by-step stain removal as soon as possible. Factors such as heat and evaporation make stains that are older than about 24 hours much harder to remove.

- **Upholstery** You rarely have a chance to get at both sides of the stain with upholstered furniture. Even if you can remove the covering material, most manufacturers warn against washing cushion covers separately from the cushions because of possible shrinkage and fading. So one small mark can quickly escalate into a big washing job. The trick, as with carpeting, is to remove the stain from the top side without soaking the cushion beneath. So follow the steps for removing carpet stains, listed above, to deal with similar upholstery stains.

Protein-based stains

Baby food and formula milk, cream or cheese-based foods, eggs, faeces and urine – these are all protein stains.

- **Fresh protein stains in washable fabric.** Cold water may be all you'll need to remove them. Don't use hot water, because it can 'cook' the proteins, causing the stain to coagulate between the fibres in the fabric and become locked there for ever. For washable fabrics, soak in cold water for half an hour, put the stain under running cold water and gently rub the fabric against itself to loosen the stain. Launder in the washing machine in warm water.

- **Dried-on protein stains in washable fabric.** With this kind of stain, you may have to take your stain-removal tactics to the next level. Soak washable fabrics for half an hour

Expert **ADVICE**

Your first approach may not remove a stain, so check for any that persist after items have been washed. If the stain is still there, don't tumble-dry the item – the heat could set the stain permanently. Let it air-dry. Likewise, don't iron an item if a stain remains.

in a solution of 1 teaspoon liquid detergent (choose a biological one containing enzymes – the label will say whether it has them) per 2 litres cold water. Follow this soaking by laundering the fabric in your washing machine in warm water.

Inspect the item before drying. If the stain is still there, soak the fabric for an additional half hour and then wash again. If the stain remains after that, your only option may be to add the recommended amount of oxygen bleach to the next wash cycle, especially if the stain was caused by a coloured ice cream, cheese sauce or baby food.

<table><tr><td>Be patient
As effective as stain-removal know-how can be, it is often a multi-step approach, from mildest to harshest treatment. Try one tactic and if that doesn't work, move on to a stronger cleaning solution. If you lose patience and jump ahead, you may make things worse.</td></tr></table>

- **Fresh protein stain in carpeting or upholstery.** Spray with cold water and blot, repeating until the area comes clean.

- **Dried protein stain in carpeting or upholstery.** Lightly apply a solution of ¼ teaspoon mild washing-up liquid (one that doesn't contain lanolin) in 1 litre cold water. Apply the solution to a cloth and use a blotting motion to work it into the affected area. Blot with a clean paper towel to remove the solution. Rinse by lightly spraying the stain with water and then blotting. Do this until all the suds are gone. Then spray again lightly with water. Don't blot this time. Instead, lay a pad of paper towels over the spot, put a weight on it and let it dry. (Refer to step 4 of removing stains from carpeting, on page 31.) If the stain persists, repeat the procedure with a stronger solution: ½ teaspoon liquid detergent (a biological one containing enzymes) per litre cold water.

If that still doesn't completely remove the stain, moisten the stained tufts with a solution of 3 per cent hydrogen peroxide – you can buy this from the chemist where it is sold as a mouthwash. Let it stand for an hour. Blot and repeat until the carpet or upholstery is stain-free. No rinsing is necessary following this procedure, because light will cause the peroxide to change to water. To dry, use the method mentioned above involving a pad of paper towels and a weight. But be careful: hydrogen peroxide is bleach and can drastically fade colours.

Oil-based stains

Oil-based stains aren't as difficult to get rid of as most people think. They include auto grease or motor oil, hair oil and mousse, hand lotion, kitchen grease, lard, butter, bacon, cooking oils, ointments, salad dressing and suntan lotion. Many pre-wash stain-removal products are formulated with special solvents for removing oil and grease.

● **Oil-based stains in washable fabrics.** You should pre-treat both new and old stains with a commercial pre-wash stain remover. Alternatively, apply either liquid detergent or a paste made from powder detergent mixed with water directly onto the stain. Gently work the detergent into the stain. Immediately after this pre-treatment, launder the item in the washing machine in hot water (if that temperature is safe for the fabric).

Before drying the fabric, inspect it. If the stain is still evident, repeat the process until it is gone. For heavy stains, lay the stain face down on a clean white towel or stack of paper towels and press a dry-cleaning solvent – sold in supermarkets as dry-clean stain remover – onto the stain, forcing it out and into the towels. Repeat and launder.

● **Oil-based stains in carpets and upholstery.** Apply methylated spirit to a clean white cloth or white paper towel and blot the stain. Discard the dirty towels and repeat using fresh paper towels and alcohol until the stain is gone. Don't let the alcohol penetrate the carpet backing, as it can destroy the rubber lining.

If that doesn't remove the stain, try the method recommended on page 33 for removing dried protein stains from carpeting and upholstery.

Tannin stains

Alcoholic drinks, coffee or tea without milk, fruits and fruit juices, soft drinks and wine all have tannin as the base of their stains. Most jams also contain tannins, but cherry and blueberry should be treated as dye stains.

- **Tannin stains in washable fabric.** Soak for half an hour in a solution of 1 teaspoon liquid detergent (choose a biological one containing enzymes) per 2 litres warm water. Then launder in the washing machine in the hottest water that is safe for the fabric, using laundry detergent. Don't be tempted to give it a quick go with soap first: natural soaps – including soap flakes, hand soap and hand-wash detergent containing soap – make tannin stains harder to remove. To remove stubborn tannin stains, you may need to wash with bleach. If all the sugars from one of these stains aren't removed, they may turn brown when put into the dryer, as the sugar will caramelise. So check first before you attempt to dry.

- **Tannin stains in carpeting or upholstery.** Lightly apply a solution of ¼ teaspoon mild dishwashing liquid and 1 litre water. Use a blotting motion to work the solution into the affected area. Blot with a clean paper towel to remove the solution. Rinse by lightly spraying with water and blotting to remove excess water. Do this until all the suds are gone. Then spray lightly with water again, but don't blot. Instead, lay a pad of paper towels down, weight it and let it dry, as described on page 31. If the blemish persists, repeat the procedure using a solution of ½ teaspoon liquid detergent (a biological one containing enzymes) per litre of water. If that doesn't completely remove the stain, moisten the tufts in the stained area with 3 per cent hydrogen peroxide. Let stand for one hour. Blot and repeat until the stain has disappeared. No rinsing is necessary following this procedure. To dry, lay down the weighted pad of paper towels as before.

A bottle of red, a bottle of white?

You may have heard that white wine will remove red-wine stains. But if you have the misfortune to spill a bottle of Merlot on your cream-coloured carpet, don't reach for the Chardonnay. While white wine will certainly shift a red-wine spill, so would fizzy mineral water – and which is the cheaper option? As with all fresh stains, you should blot up as much wine as possible first before you try to rinse it out with water. If the stain remains, use the method to remove tannin stains from carpet described left.

Dye stains

Blackcurrant, cherry, grass and mustard are all dye-based stains and can be real nightmares to shift. After all, dyes are meant to stick. But all is not necessarily lost.

● **Dye stains in washable fabrics.** Pre-treat with a commercial pre-wash stain remover. Or apply liquid laundry detergent directly to the stain, work the detergent into the stain and rinse well. Next, soak the fabric in a diluted solution of oxygen bleach (identified as 'all-fabric' on the label), following the directions on the packaging, then launder. If the stain persists, try soaking the garment in a solution of chlorine bleach and water, following dilution instructions on the label. But be aware that you may be putting your item at risk.

● **Dye stains in carpet or upholstery.** You may have to call a professional cleaner or, in the case of a solid-coloured carpet, cut the stained part out and patch it with clean carpet. But before you go that far, try the method described on page 35 for tannin stains on carpet or upholstery. Go very carefully: when you are using hydrogen peroxide, dab a little onto a cotton bud and try to absorb the stain from the carpet into the bud.

Combination stains

Many common stains are a mixture of both oils or waxes and dyes – stains from make-up are always a type of combination stain. They are commonly divided into two categories (Groups A&B) for the purposes of treatment:

● **Group A combination stains** include those from lipstick, eye make-up including mascara, pencil, liner and most kinds of eye shadows, various types of furniture polish and, perhaps worst of all, shoe polish.

Test, testing
Before using a solution for the first time, test it on an inconspicuous part of an item, such as an inside seam or hidden corner. That way, if the fabric or fabric colours react poorly to the cleaning solution, you haven't ruined the whole thing. To test a chlorine-bleach solution, mix 1 tablespoon bleach with 100ml water. Use a cotton bud to apply a drop of the solution to the fabric. Let the garment stand for two minutes, then blot dry with a clean cloth. If there is no colour from your garment on the cotton bud, it's safe to continue with that cleaner.

- **Group B combination stains** include chocolate, gravy, hair spray, face make-up (foundation, powder, blusher), peanut butter and tomato-based foods.

- **To remove these stains,** you must first remove the oily or waxy portion, and then you can try to remove the dye. As with any tough stain, your success is not guaranteed. But by following the steps below, you do stand a chance, especially if you get to the stain while it's fresh.

- **Washable fabrics with stains in Group A.** Start by applying a dry-cleaning stain remover. Next, rub with a liquid detergent and scrub in hot water to remove the oily or waxy part. Then launder, using a laundry detergent and an oxygen or all-fabric bleach. Inspect before drying. If the stain persists, wash with chlorine bleach.

- **Washable fabrics with stains in Group B.** Skip the dry-cleaning solvent. Rub the stain with a liquid laundry detergent and launder in the washing machine in the hottest water possible for the fabric. If that doesn't work, try oxygen bleach, then, if that fails, chlorine bleach (but only on white fabrics).

- **Combination stains in carpets and upholstery.** Begin by removing the oily or waxy part first. Apply methylated spirit to a clean white cloth or white paper towel and blot the stain. Repeat using fresh paper towels and more methylated spirit until the stain is gone. Don't let the alcohol penetrate the carpet backing, as it could destroy the rubber lining.

  If the alcohol treatment doesn't remove the stain, lightly apply a solution of ¼ teaspoon mild washing-up liquid (one that doesn't contain lanolin) and 1 litre water. Use a blotting motion to work the solution into the affected area. Blot with a clean paper towel to remove the solution. Rinse by lightly spraying with water and blotting. Do this until all the suds are gone. Then spray again lightly with water. Instead of blotting

> **Collar treatment**
> To remove lipstick stains from fabric, rub some toothpaste into the stain as a pre-treatment and then wash as usual.

this time, lay a pad of paper towels down, put a weight on it and let it dry, as described on page 31.

Finally, if that doesn't completely remove the stain, moisten the stained tufts with 3 per cent hydrogen peroxide and let stand for one hour. Blot and repeat until the stain is gone. No rinsing is necessary following this procedure. To dry, use a pad of paper towels and weight, as before.

Other stains

Stains produced by perspiration, glue, paint, mud and nail polish don't fall into the previous categories but are still hard to remove. Use the techniques described here to shift them:

● **Deodorant and perspiration stains.** Treat these as you would dye stains. The aluminium or zinc salt build-up from deodorants can make them particularly stubborn.

● **Removing glue.** Begin by scraping off whatever you can with a dull knife (rubbing ice on the glue first to harden it). If the glue is white school glue, treat it as you would a protein-based stain, so don't use hot water – the hot water could cook the proteins. If it is model-aeroplane glue, treat it as an oil-based stain. If the glue won't come out, place the stain face down on absorbent paper towels. To force the stain out, blot the back of the fabric with a cloth moistened with dry-cleaning solvent.

● **Removing emulsion paint.** Treat while it is wet – immediately is best. Soak the fabric in cold water and then

Expert **ADVICE**

To remove stains from dry-clean-only fabrics, first remove as much of the stain residue as possible – by blotting or scraping – and then have the item dry-cleaned as soon as you can (within a day or two).

wash it in cold water with laundry detergent. If the paint has dried, even for as little as six hours, treat it as you would one of the Group A combination stains.

● **Removing gloss paint.** Spot treat while it is still wet, using paint thinner or white spirit and a sponge or cloth, until the paint is loosened and as much is removed as possible. Before it dries, wash in hot water and detergent.

● **Removing mud.** Handle mud as you would a protein-based stain, with one exception: it's best to wait until mud has dried before cleaning it. Once it has dried, scrape off the excess solids. Then follow the protein-stain procedures.

● **Removing rust stains.** If a rust stain remains after removing mud, treat it with a commercial fabric-stain rust remover. Since rust removers can be toxic, follow the directions on the container carefully. A solution of lemon juice and salt sometimes removes rust. Sprinkle salt on the stain, squeeze lemon juice on it, and put the item in the sun to dry. Be sure to test the lemon juice first, since it can bleach some fabrics. Don't use chlorine bleach: it will make rust stains permanent.

● **Removing nail polish.** Blot with a clean cloth moistened with acetone or nail-polish remover until the stain is gone. If possible, lay the stain face down on white paper towels and blot from the back side to force the stain out the way it came in.

● **Removing yellowing from white fabrics.** Fabrics can take on a yellowish tinge for several reasons: not enough detergent in a wash cycle, too much detergent, an insufficiently hot wash, colour transfer from other items or the loss of a fabric's artificial whiteners. Your best bet is to launder with the correct amount of detergent – find one that has both bleach and optical brighteners in it. Most biological powders have the greatest whitening power. If that doesn't work, try oxygen bleach. As a final resort, try a cycle with chlorine bleach.

Mystery stains
Avoid washing unknown stains in hot water, which will set protein-based stains, such as egg or blood. First soak in cold water, which might remove a protein-based stain. If that doesn't work, pre-treat by rubbing with liquid laundry detergent and then wash with warm water. If that doesn't work, try a pre-treatment product or blotting with dry-cleaning solvent. Your last resort is bleaches, beginning with oxygen bleach, with diluted chlorine bleach only as a last resort.

STAIN SPECIFICS

Almost any surface can become permanently stained if you don't know how to deal with the substances that you have dropped on it. Here's how to blitz just about anything that you drop unsuspectingly in your home.

Bloodstains

These are much more difficult to remove once they have dried and set – so act promptly. Keep in mind the following three points when treating a bloodstain on any surface:

- **Always use cold water.** Any heat from water or tumble drying, could set the stain permanently.

- **Be gentle: scrub too vigorously** and you'll dilute and spread the stain into the clean fabric that surrounds it.

- **Work from the outside in** to avoid spreading the stain.

- **Blot bloodstains on clothing** with a clean rag that you've wetted with cold water. If staining persists, mix a few drops of washing-up liquid with a cup of cold water into a bowl and dab the stained item into it, leaving it submerged for 10 minutes. Then blot the area with a dry rag.

- **Hydrogen peroxide** is the next step, but only use it with white or colourfast clothes. (Test on a hidden area first.) Spread the stained area out over the sink, and then pour full-strength hydrogen peroxide through the stain. Scrub with a scrubbing brush or old toothbrush. Rinse thoroughly in cold water.

- **Commercial stain shifters** can also be highly effective. Choose an oxygen-based solution and mix 1 scoop of the paste into a cup of water, scrub into the stain and let it sit for two hours. Rinse in cold water.

- **If you've got bloodstains on bedding,** you can use ordinary shampoo. Make sure the shampoo covers all of the stain, rubbing it in until fully absorbed. Wet with cold water; then, once it has lathered up, scrub with a stiff nylon scrubbing brush. Rinse in cold water. If a ring remains, repeat.

- **Cover fresh bloodstains** on washable upholstery and carpeting with a mix of flour and cold water. Rub gently and dry – either by turning up the radiators or exposing the item to the sun if possible. Brush off the paste once it has dried. You can also try using talcum powder in the same way.

Burns

Burns on clothing may need repairing by a professional but you can significantly improve the appearance of a small burn by cutting out the area and making a patch underneath.

- **First lay the garment on a table** with the lining, if there is one, facing towards you. With scissors, snip a small section of lining loose at the seam. Then cut a small piece of the garment fabric, about the size of the burn, from the inside seam.

- **Locate the burn on the inside of the garment.** Take a piece of gaffer tape, large enough to cover the burn fully, and apply the tape to the burn on the inside of the clothing. With a needle and thread, sew the lining back into place temporarily with long, loose stitches. Turn the garment over to see the burnt area from the outside.

- **Using your scissors,** snip the small piece of garment seam fabric into the smallest pieces you can. You want the cut-up material to look as much like fibres as possible. Then press the 'fibres' into the burn so that they adhere to the gaffer tape underneath. It won't be as seamless as professional reweaving, but you will be the only one who knows.

One way for burns on floors
If there's not too much damage, lightly sand the burn, then wipe away the residue with a damp cloth and polish the floor. Scrape out deeper burns with a sharp knife, then apply putty, which you'll have to disguise by using a crayon the same colour as your floor, or by sticking in a very fine slither of wood. Sand this level and then use a wood stain that matches the floor.

● **Burns on upholstery.** The trick here is to try to disguise the scorch mark. Wet a paper towel with plain water and dab it on the burn. Blot with a dry paper towel. If that doesn't take most of the charred spot out, put a drop of mild liquid laundry detergent on a wet paper towel and blot the spot. Follow up by blotting with first a wet paper towel to remove the detergent, and then with a dry paper towel to absorb the char stain.

● **Burns on fake leather upholstery.** You may be able to fix burns on this type of material with a hole-patching kit, which you can buy from car-supplies stores. This repair will involve spreading a coloured paste over the hole and letting it dry. Follow the package directions to the letter for the best results.

● **Burns on wood floors and furniture.** You may be able to remove enough of the burn to make it unnoticeable. If it's small, use a cotton bud to apply a little turpentine. If the char remains, rub lightly with some superfine (0000) steel wool. If this takes out the burn, but leaves a small indentation, fill it in with clear nail polish. Be prepared to apply several layers.

If the burn is mostly just a scorch, try methylated spirits. Put a little on a soft cloth and dab it on the scorch. It will dry quickly, but take a little of the scorch out each time. Repeat until you are satisfied. Or try bicarbonate of soda on a wet sponge – rub in small circular motions.

If it's burned beyond a scorch but not too deeply, try a thin paste of cigarette ashes mixed with vegetable oil. With a soft cloth, gently rub in the direction of the grain. Follow with coats of clear nail polish to restore a flat surface.

● **Burns on carpets.** Use a pair of nail scissors and snip off the charred pile; vacuum the spot. Snip off few fibres of carpet from elsewhere – ideally, from a spot hidden by a piece of furniture – and glue these into the burn hole.

Chewing gum

Chewed-up chewing gum can harden over time, making it increasingly difficult to remove. So if it gets in your carpet, clothes or hair, act promptly.

- **To remove gum from carpets,** upholstery and washable clothing, first scrape off as much gum as possible with a dull non-serrated knife. Then put one or two ice cubes in a sealed sandwich bag and rub the bag over the spot until the gum freezes. Using the knife, scrape away more gum. Repeat as needed to remove all the gum.

- **If that doesn't work,** try melting the chewing gum. Start by heating it with a hair dryer for a minute or two. Now, with a plastic sandwich bag on your hand, lift off as much of the heated gum as possible. Next, try massaging ½ teaspoon deep-heating rub evenly into the spot. Turn the hair dryer on high and heat the area for 30 seconds. Then use another plastic bag to lift off the remaining residue. Finally, add 1 teaspoon mild detergent to 200ml water and blot the spot with paper towels or a cloth rag to lift any stain. Spot remover or dry-cleaning solvent are also worth trying.

- **Remove gum from clothing** using the procedure described for carpets, but apply the deep-heating rub to the opposite side of the cloth. After 30 seconds of blow-drying, the gum should peel off. Then wash the garment as usual, whether by hand or in a washing machine.

  You could also seal the garment in a plastic bag and place it in the freezer. After it is completely frozen, just scrape the spot with a dull knife to remove the gum and launder as usual.

- **To remove gum from hair,** work peanut butter or oil into the gummy spot for a minute – this should soften the gum. Then gently pull out the gum with a paper towel; finally, shampoo and rinse the area.

Gummy paving

In the UK, more money is now spent clearing up gum than cigarette butts. For removing gum on a massive scale, chemical solvents are the main cleaning method. But if gum on your drive drives you mad, try some non-toxic, high-velocity water. Attach a jet nozzle to your garden hose, the kind used for power spraying, put it on its most powerful setting and fire away at the spot. The quicker you attack the chewing gum, the more easily it will come up.

Crayon & pencil marks

If the marks are on painted walls, glass, metal, tile, marble or porcelain, spray them with a penetrating lubricant (specifically, WD-40), then wipe with a soft cloth. The WD-40 lifts off the stain by getting between the mark and the surface. Spray a little WD-40 in an obscure spot first to make sure it won't harm what you're cleaning.

If it doesn't work, dip a sponge into a solution of washing-up liquid and warm water and wet the crayon mark, rubbing with a circular motion. Rinse with warm water, then air-dry.

● **Pencil marks can be rubbed out** with a rubber, so try it – taking care not to rub too hard – on painted walls and fabric. Remember to choose a white rubber. If that doesn't work: on walls, press a slice of fresh bread into the stain. On clothes, a biological detergent should do the trick.

● **Removing crayon from clothing.** Place the item on paper towels, then spray with a penetrating lubricant (again, WD-40). Spray more on a clean rag and apply it to both sides of the stain. Allow it to sit for two minutes. Then, using your fingers, rub 1 or 2 drops of washing-up liquid into the stain on each side. Replace the paper towels as they absorb the crayon. Wash the clothing in the machine, using the hottest water possible and the heavy soil setting.

● **Alternatively, use a light touch** on the stain with a dry soap-filled steel-wool pad. Or rub the stain gently with baking soda sprinkled on a damp sponge. At a pinch, you could pre-treat with hair spray before washing.

● **Removing crayon on upholstery and carpeting.** Scrape up as much as you can with a metal spoon or dull knife. Then wet the mark with WD-40 and leave for 5 minutes. Scrub with a stiff-bristled brush, then wipe with paper towels. Spray again with WD-40. Dab 1 or 2 drops of washing-up liquid onto the stain and work it in with the brush. Wipe with a damp sponge.

- **On vinyl no-wax flooring,** use silver polish. Rinse well with water and dry with a paper towel.

- **On a wood floor,** place an ice-filled plastic bag on the mark to make it brittle, then scrape with a spoon or dull knife. Or place a clean rag over the mark and heat it with an iron (don't use the steam function). It will soak up the melted wax.

Greasy floors

To remove grease from a concrete floor, sprinkle dry cement over the grease. Once it has absorbed the grease, sweep it up with a broom and a dustpan.

- **Try cat litter if you have** no dry cement. If that fails, wet the stain with water and sprinkle it with powdered dishwasher detergent. Wait a few minutes and then pour boiling water on the area. Wearing rubber gloves to protect your hands, scrub with a stiff-bristled brush and rinse with water.

Hard-water deposits

If you live in a hard-water area, you should know it. Surfaces that get wet frequently will have colourful stains, whitish spots or crusty deposits. Limescale may build up enough to interfere with the function of fixtures like showerheads and taps and washing machines. Soaps will seem to leave a residue and it will take more detergent to get things clean than it has in other places you've lived. The culprits? Minerals in your water, especially calcium and magnesium.

Limescale on enamel baths
Limescale can be very difficult to remove from enamel baths, because the acid-based cleaners you need to shift it can damage the enamel. One answer is to use a solution of half water, half white vinegar. Using a soft cloth, rub only the limescaled area and rinse off the solution frequently.

- **To prevent mineral deposits,** try to keep hard water from pooling on the surfaces it typically damages. You should wipe taps dry, and rinse sinks, baths and the shower base after use; then wipe dry with a towel.

  - **You can remove mineral deposits** with a toilet or bathroom cleaner specially formulated to remove limescale. For small spot areas, such as around the tap and plughole, vinegar or lemon also work well. Fix a half lemon onto a tap overnight (hold with sticky tape). In the morning, scrub away at loose mineral deposits with an old toothbrush.

- **On ceramic tiles and acrylic baths,** use acid-based kitchen or bathroom cleaners formulated for mineral deposits and soap scum, or rinse often in 1 part white vinegar to 4 parts water.

- **On Formica and other plastics,** rub with a wet cloth dipped in bicarbonate of soda. Wipe off with a dry cloth.

- **Soak glassware in undiluted white vinegar** for 15 minutes. Rinse the item and dry.

Ink

A good deal of the ink used in fountain pens is washable. Simply flush the stain out at once, holding the item inside out, so that you push the ink back out the way it came.

- **Methylated spirit works best** for ballpoint pen, but take care as it can be too strong for many fabrics. Use a cotton bud dipped in methylated spirit, then lift up the ink with a fresh dry bud. If you think the fabric can take it (test for colourfastness first), let the solvent sit on it for 30 minutes to give it time to dissolve the ink, before blotting it up. For large areas, use a cloth rather than a cotton bud. Rinse with a solution of 1 part white vinegar per 10 parts water and again with plain water.

- **If methylated spirit** doesn't completely remove ink from fabric rinse with cool water, apply 3 per cent hydrogen peroxide, then rinse the item again. The hydrogen peroxide will bleach what is left of the ink so that it won't be noticeable. Test for colourfastness and don't use on a wool, silk or a Persian carpet.

- **If ink resists removal,** try foam shaving cream (gel shaving cream won't work) or hairspray. Blot larger stains but don't rub – this will break down fibres – and work from the outside of the stain towards the centre, to stop it spreading. Also, protect your work surface from the ink as you don't want to remove one stain to start another. Lay an old white towel underneath.

- **To remove ink from carpeting,** moisten a section of a clean white towel with methylated spirit and gently blot the spot. Wait 30 minutes for the alcohol to dissolve the ink; then press a knuckle into the barely damp rag, working it forwards and backwards over the stain. Change to a clean spot on the towel and repeat, this time working your knuckle left to right. To finish, press your knuckle into the damp towel, twisting your wrist clockwise. (Carpet fibres are twisted clockwise and this motion will help remove stains from between the fibres without causing the carpet to go fuzzy.) Rinse with a solution of 1 part white vinegar to 10 parts water; then rinse again with plain water, applied using a fresh towel and the same knuckle technique.

SIMPLE solutions

The best way to deal with ink is to treat stains immediately. If you're dealing with washable ink, use cool water, but if it's permanent-pen or ballpoint ink, you need methylated spirit. Apply the methylated spirit to the stain with a clean white terry-cloth towel. After half an hour, blot the stain with a fresh white towel.

Mildew

Mildew starts with just a few black dots but it can spread and destroy fabric and upholstery, eat through plasterboard, disintegrate wallpaper and trigger allergies.

Mildew occurs when moisture combines with mould, which is always present in the air. Mildew flourishes in damp, warm, dark places. The moisture that it needs can come from dripping pipes, a leaky roof or simply high humidity, which is why bathrooms are prime sites. When conditions are right, mildew begins to grow within 24 to 48 hours and will continue until you address the problem.

● **To prevent mildew,** dry out those water-damaged areas thoroughly as soon as you notice them. Keeping your house clean, dry and well-ventilated will prevent most mildew problems. Cleaning with soap and water will often take care of mildew stains, but actually killing mildew requires the power of bleach. Don't use straight bleach as it's too powerful and can create toxic fumes.

● **To remove mildew from the bathroom,** mix 1 part bleach with 11 parts water. Wear rubber gloves and use a sponge, cloth or soft-bristled brush to apply the solution. Rinse off with a damp sponge; then wipe down the area with a squeegee mop, to get out every last bit of moisture. Turning on a vent fan before a shower or opening the window afterwards cuts down on moisture.

● **To remove mildew stains from fabric** or upholstery, take the item outside and knock off the surface mildew with a stiff brush. Then air out the piece in the sun. If spots remain, wash the item according to the manufacturer's instructions. Use hot water and laundry bleach if the fabric can tolerate it.

● **To remove mildew from leather,** use a clean cloth dipped in a solution of equal parts of methylated spirit and water.

Wring out the cloth until barely dampened with the alcohol and wipe the affected area. Follow with a cloth dampened only with water and then dry the item in an airy place.

Odours

Odours are tricky to shift because you are trying to clean something you can't see. Masking the smell with perfumes and air fresheners is a temporary solution. To truly quell a smell, you must remove its source.

- **If you have a culinary disaster** and the kitchen fills with smoke, you need to exchange the sooty, smelly air for fresh air. First, turn off the oven or hob, depending on where you had the accident, and if you have an extractor fan, turn this on high. Open windows to create cross-ventilation – windows on opposite sides of the room are ideal. If possible, close doors leading to other parts of the house to confine the smoke.

- **To remove lingering cooking smells,** use a clean sponge or cloth to wipe down kitchen surfaces (other than those that come into contact with your food) with a kitchen cleaner. You are trying to remove tiny, unseen particles and grease, carried by smoke, steam and splatter, in the same way that you would spots you can see. Wipe walls and other surfaces close to the cooker. If the smell is still there, as heat rises and is drawn to cool areas, you'll need to wipe down windows, light fixtures and high kitchen cabinets. If it's still smelly, wash kitchen curtains and exposed dishcloths.

- **To deodorise your waste-disposal unit,** grind bits of lemon or orange peel into the unit every so often.

- **If you want to cut down on fridge odours** don't let old food linger, unnoticed, at the back of shelves. Wipe inside the fridge with a sponge and plain water. Be sure to clean the

For sweet-smelling hands
To reduce an onion smell on your hands, rub them before and after you cut onions with the sliced end of a celery stalk. A little vinegar rubbed on your hands before or after cutting onions has the same neutralising effect. If that's too late, use a stainless-steel hand-washer, from hardware and kitchen equipment stores. The onion residue simply clings to the stainless steel as you wash your hands with this soap-shaped piece of metal.

rubber door seal as it can attract mould. Keep an open box of bicarbonate of soda on a shelf and another in the freezer – this will absorb odours. Replace both boxes several times a year. Cat litter and ground coffee work just as well.

● **To remove musty smells in a basement,** first ventilate the room. The musty smell comes from mould and mildew, which thrive in dank, dark environments where the air is stale. Open windows and doors, use fans to circulate the air. If it is a persistent problem, consider buying a dehumidifier – from DIY and electrical stores.

● **To remove musty odours in an unused room,** simply sprinkle cat-litter granules over the floor. Leave these for a day and then sweep or vacuum them up. If you use a vacuum, dispose of the bag. If you sweep up the cat litter with a broom, collect the residue in a dustpan and dispose of it outdoors.

● **To reduce rubbish-bin smells,** clean the bin regularly – once a week is ideal. Take it outside and hose it out. Then scrub thoroughly inside with a nylon-bristled brush and a solution of 50ml bleach to 5 litres warm water, plus a couple of squirts of dishwashing liquid. Air-dry until it is completely bone-dry.

Pests

To prevent pest invasions, you need to tighten up entry points into your home, especially for crawling insects. Fill gaps between the wall and floor with plaster and inspect boxes and gardening equipment for ants, wood lice and spiders.

- **Cut off the pests' food and water supplies.** Repair leaky taps and make sure the tiles behind the sink aren't coming away. Keep food in tightly sealed containers. Wipe down worktops and remove food spills on the sides of and behind the cooker. Also attack pest breeding and living areas by filling holes in walls and floors, removing piles of cardboard and paper bags inside or around the house, and eliminating general clutter.

- **To kill ants, avoid sprays** and instead use a long-life insecticide that ants take back to their nest. As a prevention, use an insecticide 'pen' (sold in supermarkets and DIY stores) to draw a line through the point that ants usually enter your home: they won't cross the line.

- **Killing the fleas on your pet,** whether you use a flea collar, shampoo or other remedy, is just part of preventing a flea infestation. Keeping your home clean counts just as much, because 90 per cent of a flea's life cycle is spent off the pet and in its bedding or your rugs – in its egg, larva and pupa stages.

  Designate a pet sleeping area, such as a tiled utility room, that is easy to clean and clean it regularly – more often than the rest of the house if necessary. Cover your pet's bed with a machine-washable blanket. Then all you have to wash is the blanket, not the bed. When you pick the blanket up, carefully lift all four corners, so flea eggs don't roll off. If you have fleas, vacuum rugs and upholstered furniture, then empty the cylinder or dispose of the bag outside the house. Steam-cleaning carpets is even more effective.

> **Killing pet fleas**
> Flea collars are one way to kill fleas on your pet, but you can also bathe your animal with a specialist flea shampoo, available from your vet. Alternatively, a product such as Frontline (also available from your vet) can be applied to the back of your pet's neck with a dropper.

- **To eliminate clothing moths,** you need to thoroughly clean clothes before storing them out of season. Moths are attracted to the food, perspiration and urine on soiled fabrics, rather than to the wool or cotton itself. So if clothes are totally clean, there should be no problem. For long-term storage, put clothes (except leather, which needs to breathe) in airtight bags or plastic containers. Those with a vacuum seal will take up significantly less space. Steer clear of commercial moth repellents which may contain naphthalene, which is harmful if swallowed. Instead, apply a few drops of essential oils – cedar, eucalyptus and lavender – on a handkerchief or piece of cotton that you can store with your clothes.

- **If you need to get rid of mice,** your best bet is a standard snap-back mousetrap. Poisons can be dangerous to your pets and can leave dead mice out of reach, where they can become a food source for other household pests. Buy traps at hardware stores and bait them with peanut butter, rolled oats, cheese or, if you'd rather not leave out food, cotton-wool balls (mice use these for nests) and spread them strategically around the house. Put them perpendicular to walls that mice run along. Mice are renowned for their powerful noses, so wear gloves when baiting the traps to avoid leaving your scent.

Pet clean-up

As much as we love our pets, they can bring a lot of dirt with them into the house. And then there's always the nasty surprise of the odd pet accident!

- **To remove pet hair from furniture,** start with the vacuum cleaner. Buy a lint-brush attachment for your vacuum if you don't already have one. This gadget first prises up and then sucks up short, wiry hairs that have imbedded themselves in your upholstery. As an alternative, wear a damp rubber glove and rub your hand across the sofa cushions; the hair will clump together for easy removal.

● **If you have to clean up pet vomit,** first pick up the solid stuff; wearing rubber gloves, remove with a paper towel or spatula. If the vomit is on a hard surface, such as a vinyl or wood floor, simply wipe up the liquid with moist paper towels and then thoroughly mop the spot with clean water.

● **To clean pet vomit from fabric, carpet or rugs,** first pick up any solids and then blot up as much of the liquid vomit as possible using paper towels. Next, apply a cleaner with active enzymes, designed especially for pet mess. These cleaners actually digest the proteins found in the vomit. They usually take a while, so let the cleaner stand for as long as the product's directions suggest. Wash and rinse clothing, or dry-clean according to label instructions. For carpeting or furniture, blot with clean, cool water to rinse (but avoid using too much water, especially if there is a pad under the carpet or stuffing in the upholstered furniture). Remove excess liquids by either repeatedly blotting with fresh, dry paper towels or using a wet vac. As with any pet accident, the key to success is to clean the mess up immediately.

SIMPLE solutions

To cut down on the amount of hair your pet sheds, use the brush attachment on your vacuum to literally hoover your pet. If you are careful and your pet doesn't mind it, this is a good way to clear up hair before it even falls out. You might find that your dog, or even your cat, loves the attention. It feels like a pet massage. But if your pet is afraid of the vacuum, regular combing or brushing will do. Don't try this if you have a particularly strong vacuum cleaner; the powerful suction may hurt your pet.

- **When cleaning up pet faeces,** first pick any solids with toilet tissue and flush down the toilet. If there is little or no residue, clean with soapy water and paper towels. Then rinse with clean water and paper towels. If there is residue, follow the steps listed for cleaning up vomit (see page 53). Wash and rinse according to the type of material affected.

- **Wipe up fresh urine** straight away, using paper towels: once urine has soaked in and dried, its odour can be hard to remove.

- **To remove urine from a carpet,** soak up as much of it as possible with paper towels. Then cover the spot with a thick layer of dry paper towels, with newspaper on top of that. Stand on the padding for a minute or so. Remove the soaked padding and take it to your pet's toilet area – the cat's litter box or the dog's designated outdoor area – to lure your pet there the next time. Repeat the blotting process. Apply a specialist pet cleaner, then rinse the accident zone by blotting with a cloth soaked in clean water. Remove excess water by blotting with paper towels (as above). Don't use fragrant chemical cleaners, vinegar or ammonia. As with the urine smell, these odours may draw a pet back to the scene of the crime.

Rust

Rust is unsightly and destructive. The natural reaction of metal to water and air, it affects iron, steel, chrome, baths, toilets, sinks, concrete, garden tools, metal outdoor furniture, carpeting and fabric, among other things. But if you step in and deal with it before it gets too bad, rust is relatively easy to shift.

- **On baths, toilets and sinks,** use rust-remover designed for cars. On stainless-steel sinks, lighter fuel will get rid of the rust but this is a job to be done with extreme care as lighter fuel is highly flammable. Wash thoroughly afterwards.

- **On iron and steel items,** remove the rust by rubbing it with fine glasspaper or steel wool.

- **On metal baking dishes** and other cookware, sprinkle powdered detergent onto the spot and scour with the cut edge of half a raw potato. Or pour cola on the rust and let it work overnight. Wash off in the morning.

- **For rust on concrete,** sprinkle dry cement powder on the stain and use a small piece from a broken patio slab to rub it out. The combination of powder and stone acts like pumice to rub away the rust.

- **Bind a cloth soaked in WD-40** around rusty spots on metal furniture and leave for a few days. Wipe off, then sand with medium glasspaper. Wash, rinse and dry thoroughly, and then paint with a rustproof paint.

- **On carpets and rugs,** apply a paste of water and bicarbonate of soda to the stain, allow it to sit for three or four hours, then follow with a commercial carpet shampoo.

- **On clothing,** apply a paste of lemon juice and bicarbonate of soda to a hidden spot, to make sure the colour holds. If all is well, apply the paste to the rust stains. Let it sit an hour before hanging the garment outside to dry, then wash as usual.

  For white clothes, mix cream of tartar with lemon juice and apply it to the stain. Allow the garment to dry and then rinse thoroughly before washing.

SIMPLE solutions

Garden tools are among the most rust-prone items in any home. To stop them from rusting, mix some fine sand with just enough old motor oil to make a clumpy constituency in an old bucket. When you put them away, push the head of each tool down into the sand. Wipe before using.

Smoke

There's nothing appealing about the stale smell of smoke in your house or on your clothing. Whether the smoke comes from cigarettes or cigars, which have left their own special odour in your home and clothes, or whether you've had a more serious cooking accident or fire, it is possible to get rid of smoke smells and staining.

● **To remove the odour of smoke** from clothing, whether the smell has come from a fire or from cigarettes, hang the clothes outside in the sun. Sunlight breaks down smoke molecules and fresh air is great for the fabric. You may want to attach a fan to an extension cord and allow the fan to force air across the clothes. Check the clothing every two hours and leave the garments outside until the smell dissipates. You'll have more effective results in the wash – your next step.

● **To wash smoky clothes,** first pre-soak the garment in a sink filled with 100ml bicarbonate of soda and 10 litres water. Then place the item directly into the washing machine, using a detergent with oxygen bleach. These detergents remove the odour completely, and don't merely mask it with perfume. Wash smoke contaminated clothing separately from the rest of the laundry.

SIMPLE solutions

To remove the smell of smoke from just a small area in your home, such as a wardrobe or chest of drawers, use an open box of bicarbonate of soda. Or try placing a dish of sliced apples nearby – it really does work.

If smoke has penetrated a large part of your home, understand that you have an extensive clean-up job on your hands involving a variety of materials that require different cleaning techniques. Your safest bet is to contact your insurance company and professional cleaners.

● **After washing, hang the clothes** outside to dry or, failing that, on a clothes horse or rail in a room with an open window. Using a tumble dryer is not recommended, because the heat can set the smoke odour into any fabric from which it hasn't been completely removed. Using a fabric deodoriser, such as Febreeze, will neutralise any residual smoke odour.

● **If the clothing label** says 'Dry-clean only', then that's what you should do – take it to a professional. It's worth checking first that the dry cleaner specialises in smoke removal. Don't forget to air the clothing out first. Your dry cleaner will appreciate the gesture.

● **Removing protein-generated smoke** – from cooking bacon or chicken, for instance – can be more difficult to shift because these items produce heavy, greasy smoke that fabric readily absorbs. (Wood smoke tends to be flaky and easier to clean.) Air clothing affected by protein smoke on a hanger near a source of fresh air.

● **To clean smoke from walls and ceilings,** first vacuum up any visible residue. Wipe down the walls with a chemical sponge (available at chemists and on-line). Then dilute a special smoke-removal cleaner (available at cleaning supply stores and conservation suppliers), according to the directions on the packet.

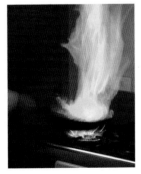

Fill a spray bottle with the cleaner. Spray and wipe one section of the wall or ceiling at a time, using a clean cloth. When you're doing walls, start from the bottom and work your way up to avoid streaking. You may have to repeat the process several times. Oil-based paint will hold up well to washing. Be careful as emulsion paint can wear off if you scrub aggressively or wash it too many times.

Soot

A by-product of smoke, soot is a combination of oil, carbon and tar and it can settle into microscopic cracks in myriad objects in your home. Run your finger across a wall with soot on it and the oils in your finger, combined with the soot, will permanently mark the surface. Even after you clean the wall, the soot mark will remain.

● **Before you start, test in two or three rooms** in an inconspicuous, high area: take a paper towel folded into a pad, dampen it with water and wipe across the surface. If the towel turns grey, you've got dust. If it turns black, you've got soot. If there's a lot of soot, it's worth calling a specialist cleaner.

You can treat light surface soot if it isn't widespread. But you'll need to systematically plan your cleaning. The general rule is to work from the top to the bottom of an area – except when using the wet method described below. Then you'll need to work from the bottom up.

● **Start by using a dry method** to remove as much soot as you can. Wear old clothes, rubber gloves, a scarf or cap, dust mask and safety goggles, especially when removing loose particles. Sweep or feather-dust using a quick, flicking motion, or vacuum keeping the head about 1cm from the surface to avoid scratching. Don't rub, as this will make a big smear. Place newspapers under affected surfaces to catch falling soot. Vacuum upholstery: if this doesn't work, call in a professional who specialises in soot removal. Take small but sturdy objects such as lampshades outside to blow off the soot.

Use a special soot sponge or chemical sponge (available at hardware stores, industrial-cleaning supply stores and conservation suppliers) on walls and ceilings or on unfinished wood (but not vinyl wallpaper). Apply to the surface in methodical lines so you can see where you have cleaned. Attach the sponge to a pole for ceilings or walls.

● **The wet method for cleaning soot** is the last resort after you've removed as much of the soot as possible by vacuuming (or dusting or brushing) and using a soot sponge. Put down a plastic dust sheet and wash the surfaces with a solution of warm water and a couple of drops of all-purpose cleaner. Apply liberally to the surface with a sponge, rag or hard-bristled scrubbing brush. Rinse with water and wipe dry. If necessary, repeat this procedure.

If a small stain remains after repeated washing, apply turpentine carefully with cotton swabs made by tightly rolling cotton balls around the end of a wooden skewer – solvents can dissolve the plastic stalks of cotton buds. Lightly moisten the swab with the turps and gently roll it across the object. Don't rub or wipe, since this might ingrain the soot and carbon in the surface of the object. Never fully immerse an object in solvent. Work slowly and methodically. Test this method on an inconspicuous part of the object first.

Expert **ADVICE**

Specific soot-removal jobs, such as the ones below, require specific techniques:
● On objects with a glossy finish, such as coffee tables and vinyl surfaces including wallpaper, vacuum first. Use a damp cloth to wipe up carefully.
● To clean ceilings, vacuum and use the soot sponge. Then use the wet method.
● To use the wet method on walls, clean from the bottom up. Start in small sections, wipe the wet sponge onto the wall in circular motions, then wipe dry with an old towel or rag. Wipe up any soot drips immediately.
● Clean floors first and last: before attacking any other part of the room, vacuum thoroughly to get up any loose material so it won't be ground in. Then protect the floor with dust sheets while you clean the rest of the room. Return to the floors again for a thorough cleaning at the end. Try water first on wood (but don't over-wet) and tiles. For carpeting use a regular carpet shampoo applied either with a carpet-cleaning machine or a wet vac. If a wood floor won't come clean, you will have to refinish it. If small soot stains remain on the carpet, apply turps with a cotton bud, scrub, rinse, and then shampoo the carpet again.

Stickers

Gummy, hard-to-remove stickers and price tags are plastered all over many things we buy. Even when they're designed to be easy-peel, if left in place too long all stickers can be very frustrating to remove.

- **To remove stickers with water-soluble glue,** soak the item in a basin of warm water until the glue dissolves and the sticker comes off. If you can't immerse the object in water, soak a towel in water and apply that to the sticker.

- **To remove pressure-sensitive adhesive labels** – these are the ones that are peeled from a backing and then pressed into place – first peel off as much of the label as possible. Rub the remaining adhesive off with your fingers. Coax off difficult bits with your fingernail or a dull knife.

- **To take off old or dried-out sticker adhesive,** try removing it with warm, soapy water or a 50-50 solution of vinegar and warm water. You might also try salad oil, WD-40 or acetone (or an acetone-based nail-polish remover). If these tactics don't work, you'll have to move up to solvents, such as paint thinner, but bear in mind that you may damage the surface of your object. It may be easier and less harmful to just leave the sticker where it is.

- **To remove peelable stickers from wood,** first heat the object with a hair dryer to melt the glue, then rub off.

Vomit

If you're a parent then you'll know all about vomit. There can't be a child in the world that hasn't brought up a bit of something once in a while.

- **Pour clean cat litter** onto fresh vomit on a hard floor or similar surface. It will absorb most of it and can then be swept up. Follow by wiping with a damp sponge or cloth. If you don't have any cat litter, use bicarbonate of soda.

- **To clean vomit from carpet or upholstery,** lift off any solids with paper towels and then sponge with cool water. Cover the spot with plenty of bicarbonate of soda; allow to dry, then vacuum. Later, sponge the stain with a sudsy solution of washing-up liquid. Rinse and blot dry.

- **With fresh vomit on clothing,** bedding or table linens, shake the item over the toilet and flush. Then hold it under running cold water, with the soiled side down. Don't use hot water – it will cook the protein and set it in. For dried vomit, scrape off any solids and then soak in cold water, using a biological pre-soak, for several hours. For both new and old stains, follow by rubbing a little undiluted liquid detergent into the stain and washing in warm water and detergent. If any stain remains, repeat or use chlorine bleach on white fabrics or oxygen bleach on coloured ones. If possible, dry on a clothesline, rather than in a dryer.

SIMPLE solutions

To remove old vomit from a hard surface, scrape off as much as possible with a putty knife, kitchen knife or spatula. Wash the surface with a little undiluted washing-up liquid applied to a sponge or cloth. Then rinse and dry. If the acid in the vomit has eaten away wax or an underlying finish, renew it with a spot application.

Water stains

It seems ironic that the most abundant cleaner of all – water – is itself capable of leaving one of the toughest stains to remove.

- **For white water stains on wood,** unless advised otherwise, rub with a cloth dipped in a wood cleaner, going with the grain of the wood. Follow by buffing with a clean cloth and applying furniture polish. You could also try a 50-50 mix of bicarbonate of soda and white toothpaste (not coloured or gel); mayonnaise – let sit for an hour; petroleum jelly – let sit for a day; a solution of equal parts of vinegar, boiled linseed oil and turpentine; and olive oil, applied with superfine (0000) steel wool. If none of these works, refinishing may be the only cure.

- **For black water stains on furniture,** strip off the finish using a paint or varnish remover. Let the piece dry; then treat it with oxalic acid bleach. This is highly toxic: follow the directions on the label.

- **For water stains on painted walls or ceilings,** dab with a mixture of 1 part chlorine bleach to 10 parts warm water. If several applications don't work, you'll need to repaint. But first apply a sealant so the stain won't bleed through.

- **For water stains on carpets or upholstery,** try a 50-50 solution of water and white vinegar. Wet a cloth with the mixture and gently blot the surface.

SIMPLE solutions

Water stains on washable cloth are water soluble to some extent, especially when recent. But detergent isn't much help because the water stain isn't dirt; it's caused by a change in the fibres. Bleach helps, but caution is in order. Chlorine bleach can damage fibres and leave a residue. So use an oxygen-based bleach. Treat the whole item, not just the spot. Use 100ml bleach per 2 litres water, and rinse several times.

Wax

If you burn candles, some wax is bound to spill. Minimise damage in advance by burning only white candles. The dye in coloured candles is much harder to remove.

- **For white wax on carpets or upholstery,** try the hot-and-cold method. First put some ice cubes into a plastic bag and place this on the wax for a few minutes to make the wax more brittle. Then scrape off the wax with the dull side of a table knife. Use a hair dryer on high to soften the remaining wax and scrape again. Put a layer of paper towels or white rags over the wax and pass a warm iron over the area. Keep moving a clean area of the towels or rags onto the spot. Test some dry-cleaning solvent on an inconspicuous area, and if it does no damage, blot a little into the remaining wax stain.

- **For white wax on table linens or clothing,** you still use the hot-and-cold method but with some variations. Put the item in a plastic bag and then into the freezer for half an hour before scraping. On washable items, saturate the final stain with a solution of 1 part methylated spirits to 2 parts water and let it sit for half an hour. Rinse and then launder in the washing machine. Send non-washable items to the dry-cleaner.

- **If you're removing coloured wax,** after freezing and scraping, use turpentine on the rest of the wax. Test first and work on only tiny areas at a time, blotting with a rag. Only you can judge whether the treatment is worse than the disease, because it may damage some materials. Some dyes may not be removable. Treat washable colourfast fabrics with bleach, following directions on the packet. Then launder. For fine rugs or upholstery, consult a professional.

- **To remove wax from dishes and glass,** heat with a hair dryer and then wipe with a cloth. Then keep wiping and polishing with used fabric-softener sheets.

Wax on wood

If you get wax on a fine piece of wooden furniture, don't worry – wax comes off fairly easily from wood surfaces. If you get at the wax while it is still warm, wipe up all you can with a clean cloth. If the wax has hardened, soften it first with a hair dryer set on medium and then wipe it away.

THE ZAP TOP-TO-BOTTOM CLEANING SYSTEM

Here's a foolproof way to get your weekly house cleaning done, top to bottom, as swiftly and efficiently as possible. Professional housekeepers say you need just two things to do a speedy but thorough job of cleaning your home: focus and organisation.

Ground rules for cleaning

Before we get down to how to use the Zoned Attack Plan (ZAP) in your home, it's worth setting out some ground rules:

- **Clean from left to right and top to bottom** in each room. A systematic, clockwise approach to a room eliminates any retracing of steps. And a top-to-bottom system lets gravity work for you and avoids duplication of effort.

- **Keep cleaning supplies together** and close at hand, so you don't have to interrupt cleaning while you track down supplies.

- **Deal with the clutter in your home separately.** The ZAP approach assumes belongings are tidied up and put away.

- **Move furniture towards the centre of the room** when it is time to dust. Once you've vacuumed the outside of the room, push furniture into place and vacuum the rest.

- **Set a deadline for completing your cleaning.** Knowing up-front how much time you'll spend cleaning can make the list of chores less daunting.

- **Learn to multi-task:** if you must answer the phone, do some low-concentration tasks at the same time.

Focus
For the three hours or so that you will spend cleaning your home from top to bottom, strip the distractions out of your life. Don't dawdle over magazines you should be putting in the recycling bin. Don't pick up the phone if it rings. And don't watch television – listen to energising music instead.

- **Use both hands while cleaning.** Dust or wipe surfaces with one hand while lifting objects with the other. Squirt spray cleaner with one hand and wipe the surface with the other.

- **If you have pets,** use rubber gloves and a circular motion to collect pet hair from chairs and sofas. Throw the hair on the floor and suction it up when you vacuum the floor later.

- **Spray a lint-free towel with window cleaner** and keep it handy for cabinets or tables with glass inlays.

- **Pull an old, clean cotton sock** over your dusting hand and lift objects with the other hand as you clean.

- **Get a 6m extension cord** for your vacuum cleaner so you won't have to plug it in, in every room.

- **If it's truly not dirty, don't clean it.** Don't waste time on a rarely used room. Dust lightly and forget it.

Assemble your arsenal

Effective cleaning starts with good tools and products. Use a plastic or rubber cleaning caddy with dividers, stocked with everything you'll need as you make your rounds (see page 66).

Arrange items in the caddy so that it is well balanced. Avoid specialised items that accomplish only one job; when you do need such products, such as toilet cleaner, store them near the place that you're most likely to need them.

- **For a house with several floors,** it's worth keeping a caddy on each floor, providing that you have somewhere safe to store it out of children's reach. Also keep basic tools, including a broom, dustpan and mop, on every level.

- **Alternatives to the caddy,** especially if you have a smaller house or flat, are a large bucket, or an apron with large pockets.

Organisation
You need a clear cleaning plan. This establishes a pattern, and because you work in the same order week in, week out, leads to speed. The Zoned Attack Plan (ZAP) is so-named because you concentrate on one portion of your house at a time. It's the ultimate time-saving strategy for weekly house cleaning.

The cleaning caddy

Fill your caddy with these items:

- Glass cleaner
- General-purpose cleaner; choose one in a spray bottle
- Heavy-duty degreasing cleaner
- Wood polish
- Powdered scouring cleanser (not shown)

You'll also need a few extra tools
Some of these may not be mentioned in the weekly ZAP routine, but you will need them for some of the cleaning jobs you'll be doing:

- Lamb's-wool duster
- Nylon scrub pad

- Stiff-bristled toothbrush for scrubbing around taps
- 1cm soft-bristled paintbrush for dusting lampshades and removing cobwebs
- Toilet-bowl brush
- Rubber gloves
- Clean cotton rags
- Microfibre cloth (E-cloth)
- Large rubbish bag
- Plastic squeegee for bathrooms
- Safety glasses to protect your eyes from splattering cleaner or airborne dirt
- Plastic bin for collecting items that belong elsewhere (not shown)

Divide & conquer

The ZAP system divides your home into four zones and you completely clean each zone before moving on to the next. With ZAP, you've an efficient step-by-step process that couldn't be easier to follow:

- **Zone 1** Bedrooms, bathrooms and halls.
- **Zone 2** Kitchen, informal dining area and family room.
- **Zone 3** Formal living room and formal dining room.
- **Zone 4** Laundry room, home office and other spaces.

Zone 1

Go into each bedroom, strip the sheets and throw them into the hall. Go in the bathroom and throw towels, facecloths and bath mats into the hall, too. Gather all of these up and put them near the washing machine. Start a wash load with the bath mats and a couple of towels.

Get the cleaning caddy you keep upstairs and go into the upstairs bathroom. Squirt toilet cleaner inside the toilet bowl. Spray all-purpose cleaner or bathroom mousse, if you prefer, on the basin and basin surround and bath.

Empty the rubbish bin into the bag that's in your caddy.

Spray a clean rag with window cleaner and clean the mirrors. Scrub the inside of your toilet bowl with the toilet-bowl brush, then flush. Wipe down the basin, bath and surrounds. Rinse basins and baths. Spray all-purpose cleaner on the toilet seat and exterior and on the shower walls. Wipe everything down. (Note: this prevents mixing two cleaners in the toilet.)

Mop the floor, backing out of the room.

Go into a bedroom and empty the waste-paper basket.

Move any light furniture or other obstructions towards the centre of the room, away from the walls.

Dust the entire room, starting at the entrance and moving from left to right. Using your lamb's-wool duster, take one wall at a time, working from top to bottom.

Now vacuum around the entire outside of the bedroom. (That's why you moved the furniture.) Return the furniture to its original position. Starting at the far corner of the room, vacuum the rest of the room, backing out the door.

Go into the other bedrooms and repeat steps 6 to 9.

Give the upstairs hall a quick dusting, moving left to right, top to bottom, one wall at a time.

Put away the upstairs cleaning caddy. Vacuum the upstairs hall, moving backwards towards the stairs. Taking rubbish with you, back down the stairs, vacuuming as you go.

Dust and vacuum the downstairs hallway.

Unload the washing machine. Put everything but rubber bath mats into the tumble dryer. Load the washing machine with dirty sheets and towels. Hang the bath mats out to drip-dry.

SIMPLE solutions

When you really need to speed-clean, try these work-faster tips:
- Time yourself. One week, set the stopwatch, and you'll discover that you spend 8 minutes in a bedroom. Next week, challenge yourself to do it in 7.
- Listen to favourite, upbeat music on an iPod or other portable system.
- Share the work: the four zones of ZAP divide neatly into two. One week, your partner or flatmate does the harder first sections, next time you swap.
- Plan a treat for immediately after your cleaning is finished. You'll want to hurry along to get to a favourite snack, TV show or hairdresser/beauty-salon appointment.

Zone 2

Go into the kitchen and pour some water into a microwave-safe bowl. Heat in the microwave on High for 3-5 minutes.

Meanwhile, spray on a cleaner that's safe for your hob (make sure it's cool first); then also spray an appropriate cleaner onto the oven and fridge doors, and the worktops.

Take a cleaning cloth and move from left to right around the kitchen, wiping down work surfaces and appliances from top to bottom. Wipe up any food spills from the hob. Wipe under worktop appliances, such as the toaster. Make sure the water in the microwave has cooled, then pour it away and wipe down the steamed interior of the microwave.

Pick one section of cabinets to clean each time you do the kitchen. Spray that section with an all-purpose spray and wipe. In a month or so, you'll have worked right round the room.

Throw out spoilt food in the fridge and pick one shelf or drawer to clean; wash carefully with sudsy water. Rinse very thoroughly. Dry glass shelving using a lint-free linen tea towel.

Clean the sink with an appropriate cleaner; if in doubt, simply use a cloth and washing-up liquid. For shiny, polished taps, dry with a microfibre cloth.

Mop the floor.

Go to your casual dining area. (In a kitchen-diner, take care of table and chairs in step 3.) Dust around the room, left to right, top to bottom. Pull the chairs out and wipe up spills or crumbs from the table and chairs. Mop or vacuum under the table and move the chairs back. Clean the rest of the floor.

Go to your family room and move light furniture into the centre of the room. Dust the room from left to right, top to bottom, one section of wall at a time.

Vacuum the outside of the family room. Put furniture back in its original position. Vacuum the rest of the room.

Take the towels, facecloths and bath mats out of the dryer or off the line and set them on a worktop. (Don't bother folding.) Take the sheets and towels out of the washing machine and put them in the dryer. Load any remaining sheets and towels in the washing machine.

Zone 3

Go into your formal living room. Move any light furniture, including lamps, into the centre of the room.

Dust the room, moving from left to right, top to bottom, one wall at a time.

Vacuum the outside of the living room. Return the furniture to its original position.

Vacuum under the seat cushions of the sofa and armchairs with the brush attachment. Vacuum the centre of the floor.

Go to the dining room and repeat steps 1 to 3.

Dust the dining-room table and chairs.

Pull the chairs away from the table and vacuum under the table. Return the chairs to their original positions and vacuum the rest of the room.

Expert **ADVICE**

If you live alone, you may be able to get away with less frequent cleaning – there will be parts of your home that are less used than those of a larger household. But this doesn't apply to areas where we all spend lots of time – whether the kitchen and loo are used by one person or six, bacteria left on surfaces will multiply just as fast.

Zone 4

Remove the sheets and towels from the dryer or line and add them to the unfolded pile on the worktop. Move the last of the laundry from the machine to the dryer or clothesline.

Empty the rubbish bin into your plastic bag.

Since this is not a high-traffic area, a quick dust will do; move around the room left to right and top to bottom. Wipe up any spills with a damp rag.

Mop the floor.

Continue the pattern of dusting and then vacuuming or mopping in the other miscellaneous spaces of your home – such as a conservatory or office.

Empty the vacuum-cleaner cylinder (or check on the bag level), then put it and your cleaning caddy away.

Take your bag full of rubbish out to the dustbin.

While you're outside, take your doormats and shake them out thoroughly, into an unobtrusive spot.

Take all your dirty cleaning cloths to the kitchen or laundry room and put them in the washing machine.

Once all the sheets, towels and other household laundry items are dry, spread out one of the sheets and put all the other laundry on top, along with the bath mats that were drip-drying. Pull the corners of the sheet together to make a sack. Take it all to the bedrooms and put the sheets back on the beds. (This is why you didn't bother folding them.) Return the towels, facecloths and bath mats to their usual places. Of course, if you have several sets of bedding and you like to rotate, you'll need to fold the sheets up, then take fresh supplies from the airing cupboard.

A-Z of
EVERYDAY CLEANING

Air & allergens

Trapped in our centrally-heated, double-glazed homes are dust mites, airborne chemicals, cooking fumes and, for some of us, cigarette smoke, carbon monoxide from fireplaces, pet allergens (fur, skin and saliva) and many other irritants.

- **Good ventilation** will do more than anything else to freshen the air in your home. When you get up in the morning, open a window in each room for five minutes no matter what the temperature is outside. If you absolutely can't bear to do this throughout the whole house then at least air the bedrooms.

- **Smooth surfaces** – tile or hardwood floors, for instance – will keep the air cleaner, too, because allergens collect in upholstery, curtains and carpets. So if you have a condition, such as asthma, that means you really do need clean air then consider swapping to hard floors and venetian blinds.

- **Don't rely on smells** to tell you that the air is fresh. Using bicarbonate of soda or vinegar to absorb odours may reduce smells, but they do little to clean the air. The same is true of aerosol spray air fresheners, which pump more chemicals into your environment.

- **Clean any fan vents** in the bathroom regularly.

- **Controlling the humidity** in your home can go a long way towards helping improve air quality. Central heating systems can create extremely dry air, which can be corrected with a humidifier or much more simply and cheaply by placing bowls of water near your heat source, for example on windowsills above radiators. You might think houseplants would do great things to clean up the air in your home, since they gobble up carbon dioxide and expel oxygen. But very moist pots of soil can be splendid breeding grounds for mould. So it's a question of getting the right balance.

For serious allergen control

If less expensive approaches haven't worked, consider buying an air filter unit – especially if allergens are a medical problem. A HEPA filter traps microscopic particles by drawing air through fine disposable filters and returning the purified air to the room. However, you will need one in every room.

- **To control allergens in the air** in your home, you have to go directly to the source. To minimise pet allergens and mites in the house, wash dogs frequently – this should be about every two weeks if someone in your home has allergies. Few cats are likely to tolerate this, but some may allow damp combing which cuts down on shedding.

- **To keep smoke to a minimum,** limit the number of times you have fires in the fireplace and, if you or anyone else simply must have a cigarette, always smoke outside.

- **To keep dust mites under wraps,** put an anti-allergen mattress cover over the mattress on your bed. You spend a third of your life here so it's worth keeping it clean.

Aluminium

Much of the aluminium that enters your life these days is extremely easy to care for.

- **Cleaning coated aluminium** window and door frames is straightforward. Use only a smooth cloth and avoid cleaners with abrasives – aluminium can scratch. A sudsy bowl of washing-up liquid is best. Afterwards, be sure to dry thoroughly.

- **Clean older bare aluminium** that has oxidised with some WD-40. Spray it on or apply with a rag and then go over the aluminium with fine steel wool (00). Move the steel wool back and forth (not in circles) and don't rub so hard that it scratches. When you're finished, wipe the WD-40 off with a clean rag. Test this method on an inconspicuous area first. If you're still not happy with the appearance of the aluminium, consider giving it a coat of outdoor emulsion paint. (Oil-based gloss paint might crack due to the expansion and contraction that aluminium goes through as outdoor temperatures change.)

Pollution stained aluminium
If aluminium frames outside have dark streaks, these were probably caused by pollution and there's a chance that they will not simply wash off. In that case, you have nothing to lose by using a mildly abrasive cleaning cream. Dampen a cloth, dab on some of the cream and rub it into the cloth. Then rub the cloth just on the streaks, very lightly. Rinse immediately with a garden hose.

Animal bedding & cages

The fabric used for bedding for cats and dogs is likely to be machine washable – but do check the labels. Ideally, wash pet bedding at 60°C to kill fleas and other insects and their eggs, and then dry on a washing line.

- **Washing pet bedding in the bath** is an option if it's too big for the machine (but remember to thoroughly clean the bath afterwards, with very hot water and bathroom cleaner). Or use either wicker or plastic beds – then place a cushion pad or quilt inside that can be easily washed.

- **The easiest, and most hygienic, option** is to use a cardboard box. Change it once a month and simply throw away the old box with your other recycling.

- **Wicker beds should be vacuumed** each week. Every few months hose them down outside, on a sunny or blowy day, to ensure that the basket dries relatively quickly.

- **All cages need to be cleaned regularly** so make life simple and have a second, spare cage for your bird or rodent to stay in while you are doing the cleaning. With rodents, replace soiled wood shavings with fresh daily. Each month, thoroughly disinfect the cage, using a specialist cleaner from the pet shop: do not use kitchen spray cleaners. Apply to the cloth and wipe each rung of the cage. Wipe again with a just damp cloth.

Antique clothing

When cleaning antique clothing it's worth avoiding most modern conveniences, which are generally too harsh for fragile fabrics. Before you start, fix any tears – the stress of cleaning may make them worse.

- **The safest way to clean fragile garments** is with a sponge bath. Stir a squirt of mild non-biological liquid detergent into a washing-up bowl full of water and dab the solution on gently with a sponge. Rinse by sponging on clean water, taking care not to get the garment sopping wet.

- **To remove stubborn stains** that don't respond to a sponge bath, mix a few drops of 3 per cent hydrogen peroxide (sold in chemists, as a mouthwash) into a washing-up bowl full of room temperature water. Place the garment in the bowl and let it sit – don't agitate – for one to three days. Then rinse with fresh water until it rinses clear.

- **Never wring out an antique garment.** Lay it out flat to dry and be careful when moving whilst wet – just the weight of the water can tear the fibres. To move the garment, lay it on a bed sheet and carry the sheet.

- **Don't starch fragile antique** garments before storing. Starch attracts insects and also stresses the fabric along folds. If possible, store the garment spread out flat. If space doesn't permit this, roll it up. Don't place garments directly in wood drawers or cardboard boxes – these could brown the fabric – but protect the cloth from such materials with sheets of acid-free tissue (available at sewing shops). Don't store your antique garment in a plastic bag – it needs to breathe.

> **Hands off hand-me-downs**
> Always wear gloves when you touch delicate antique clothing. Acid from your hands can get onto the fabric and, over time, cause it to rot. Also, take off watches and jewellery which could snag fabric.

Expert **ADVICE**

When cleaning antique clothing, here are the basic guidelines to follow:
1 Avoid regular dry-cleaners – find one who specialises in antique textiles.
2 Mend any rips before you clean.
3 Don't use your washing machine or tumble dryer.
4 Sponge items clean, don't get them too wet.
5 Never wring out garments or hang them up – leave to dry flat.
6 Don't starch before storing.

Antique furniture

Some of the cleaning methods you'd readily use on everyday furniture can ruin the look and reduce the value of an antique.

- **The safest approach to cleaning antiques** is to simply dust once every week or two with a soft, dry, non-abrasive cloth or chamois. Avoid furniture polishes – they will just leave a film that will attract more dirt and polishing can damage the finish, the patina of your piece, and diminish its value.

Keeping fine furniture
- Don't store antiques in a very dry room.
- Keep out of direct sunlight.
- A room with fluctuating humidity or temperatures can cause antique furniture to crack.
- Don't place drinks on antique furniture.

- **If a more aggressive cleaning method** is necessary first make sure that the finish isn't too fragile. If it's in good condition, wipe down with a slightly damp cloth and follow up immediately with a dry one. (Never saturate an antique with water – that would ruin even a stable finish.)

  If you need stronger cleaning power, mix 1 teaspoon of mild washing-up liquid in a litre of water. Dip your cloth in the solution, wring it out and wipe the furniture down quickly. Follow up right away with a dry cloth. Test this method on a hidden spot first, to ensure the finish holds.

- **Wax antique furniture** no more often than every three years – and again only if the finish is stable. A dark paste wax is good because it won't leave a whitish residue in crevices, which lighter waxes do. Apply a thin coat with a soft cloth and follow up right away with a clean cloth, rubbing the wax off until it's dry.

- **If an antique has a water stain** – and it's not very valuable – you can try waxing the mark. Start by applying a paste furniture wax to the stain with a soft cloth to see how much the surface darkens. Work your way outward from the stain, trying to create a match with the surrounding surface. If your antique is valuable, however, don't try this yourself. Get help from a professional restorer.

Appliances

To find out how to clean a specific item – a washing machine for example – look under the name of that type of appliance.

- **To clean a small electrical appliance** first unplug it – and let it cool if it's been in use recently. Wipe down with a damp cloth. If it has food splatters on the outside, mix a solution of warm water and washing-up liquid to dip your cleaning cloth in. Keep the water and suds away from the electronic workings. Never put an appliance in water unless instructions say it's safe to clean it that way. Some appliances have washable parts that should be removed from the electronic base to make cleaning easier and safer (can openers and slow cookers, for example).

Aquariums

Proper cleaning is a life-or-death issue for fish and should begin on the day you buy a new aquarium. Clean all of your new gear – tank and accessories. Soap and detergent are not suitable as the residue will hurt the fish. For new equipment, just use plain warm or cold water.

- **Check your aquarium's water** once a week for its pH, ammonia, nitrate and nitrite levels, using testing equipment sold at the pet shop. Read up on the chemical tolerances of your particular fish so you will know when it's time for a change of water. How many fish you have, how big they are, the species, the tank size, the kind of filtration you're using and the lighting, all affect how often you must change the water, so get expert advice, right from the start. You should never change all the water at once; just change 10 to 25 per cent of the water in your aquarium and expect to do it about every two weeks.

Aquariums

- **To change the water** in your aquarium, round up enough buckets to handle 10 to 25 per cent of the water in your tank. Use a siphon hose to draw the water out. A clear hose is best, so you can see what you're sucking up.

Don't refill the aquarium with water straight from the tap. Nearly all tap water has chlorine added and that will hurt your fish. Many pet shops will test a sample for you or you can use a home water chemical test kit. To remove the chlorine, either use a dechlorinating product, or let the water sit in a fresh bucket

SIMPLE solutions

The gravel at the bottom of your aquarium doesn't have just a decorative purpose. It also acts as a biological filter that traps gunk in the water. Keep it clean and it will work better. You can give it a gentle vacuuming each time you change your aquarium's water with a device that you can easily make yourself.

- Attach a clear plastic siphon hose to the top of a small plastic soft-drinks bottle. (The hose needs to be wide enough to fit tightly over the neck of the bottle and long enough to run out into a bucket at the other end.) Cut the bottom off the bottle.

- Place the bottle on the bottom of the tank. When the siphon starts drawing water out of the tank, it will suck up the dirt, waste and old food without disturbing the gravel. Move the bottle from one patch of gravel to the next, working your way across the aquarium floor.

- Since you'll be using this technique at water-changing time, you'll have to stop when you've removed your target amount of water. It may take you two sessions to cover the entire aquarium floor.

- Alternatively, you could install a special filter under the gravel, which will reduce the need for vacuuming.

for 24 hours before pouring it in to the tank – this will have given the chlorine time to dissipate naturally. In any case, make sure the new water is about the same temperature – within one or two degrees – as the water left in the aquarium.

- **To remove algae** use algae scrub pads (available at the pet shop) and clean the inside walls of your aquarium whenever the green stuff becomes visible. If you don't want to put your hands in the water, try a magnetic cleaning system. One magnet, attached to a scrubbing pad, goes on inside the tank. Another magnet, on the outside, drags the pad around. Algae thrive on light, so the more light your aquarium gets the more algae you will to have to clean up.

- **Clean the filter** in your tank once a week – or more often, depending on the feeding habits of your fish and how many you have. Most tanks have a mechanical filter and models vary; follow the manufacturer's instructions. A clean filter means better water and healthier fish.

  Another filtering tool is carbon; it removes the yellowish cast caused by food and waste. Carbon may already be a part of your mechanical filter. If not, you can buy a carbon holder or even make your own. Put the carbon (available at the aquarium store or pet shop) into an old pair of tights, tie a tight knot to secure and cut away excess fabric. Place the carbon filter where it will get good water flow in the tank.

- **To thoroughly clean an old tank** – especially if fish have died in it – remove any fish to another water-filled container and empty everything out. Refill with fresh water and add 2 teaspoons of bleach for every 4 litres of water. Let it sit for at least 30 minutes, then empty, rinse well and refill. Now neutralise any bleach residue by adding a chlorine neutraliser (available from pet shops). Empty the water once again and rinse. Then fill your aquarium with water that you have let sit for a day and pop the fish back in.

Nature's cleaners

Why not use some live-in workers to clean your tank? Some aquatic creatures will happily gobble up algae and save you the job. Just make sure that they're compatible with the other creatures in your tank. You want them to eat algae – not be eaten. In freshwater tanks, try mollies, whiptail catfish, bristlenoses and Siamese algae eaters. In saltwater tanks you can use turbo snails and some hermit crabs.

Aquariums

- **Try to maintain a clean fish tank** and so cut down on how often you need to clean it. You can do this in several ways.

- **Keep it out of direct sunlight** and you'll grow less algae. You should also be sure not to leave your aquarium lights on for too long, as artificial light also causes algae to grow.

- **Start with freshwater fish.** They're less sensitive to variations in the chemical levels in the water so even if you get it slightly wrong, they should still be safe. Besides, tracking the salt levels of a saltwater tank is yet another thing to do and it could put off a beginner.

- **Don't give your fish too much food.** Fish don't have anywhere to store food, so the leftovers float around, driving up the levels of harmful chemicals. Watch your fish at feeding time. When they begin to slow down their rate of eating, the meal is over so don't add more food.

- **Inspect your fish every day** to see whether they have any injuries, infections or parasites. When you buy new fish, let them stay in a 'guest room' for a month – a separate quarantine tank – so you can monitor them for any diseases that could harm the rest of your fish.

Artwork

Unframed paper-based artwork, such as prints, etchings and drawings, can be damaged easily by cleaning and any medium used is likely to remove the art as much as the dirt and dust. Prints, etchings, drawings, watercolours and pastels just can't be cleaned, except professionally (which may involve another artist re-filling in colour that's been cleaned off). So preserve artworks under glass and frame them. That way, you are cleaning the exterior casing, not the artwork itself.

- **To clean a framed work** lay it flat and wipe all surfaces – front and back – with a soft, dry cloth. Don't use a feather duster or a paper towel, which could scratch the glass or frame. Lightly moisten a soft cleaning cloth with glass cleaner and wipe the glass. Don't spray cleaner directly onto the glass; it may get behind the glass and damage your artwork.

- **Don't attempt to dust an oil painting.** Feathers from a feather duster or fibres from a cloth can snag on the paint surface and damage it. Nor should you use a vacuum cleaner with its brush attachment. You can blow away dust by waving a feather duster at it, making sure it doesn't actually touch the surface; the resulting wind will do the job. Don't blow on your painting – saliva in your breath can be damaging.

Expert **ADVICE**

It has been suggested that you can clean a painting by simply rubbing it with a cut potato or a slice of bread. The theory is that mild enzymes or acid in the potato will clean the artwork and that the bread will absorb dirt particles. But don't be fooled: while both tricks can work with robust wallpaper, they are not suitable for delicate artwork. In fact, painting restorers spend more time fixing the cleaning mistakes of well-intentioned amateurs than cleaning up age-old dirt.

Artwork

● **Don't use feather dusters** or cloths on valuable picture frames – although they're safe for modern frames. Remove any attachment from your vacuum hose and put a soft flannel cloth over the end, secured with a rubber band, to reduce the suction. Dislodge dust from the nooks and crannies of a delicate frame with a soft watercolour brush and use the covered hose to catch the airborne particles.

● **Clean plaster-of-Paris sculptures** with a cloth lightly dampened in distilled water. For harder, more durable sculptures you can use plain tap water, but make sure you dry it carefully to avoid any watermarks.

● **To dust a wood sculpture** spray a few drops of eucalyptus oil onto a soft cloth (old T-shirts are ideal) and gently wipe the entire surface once a week, pulling dust out of crevices. You can use a very slightly damp cloth, but take care that no moisture is left behind to damage the wood. Don't use silicone-based products which will soak into the wood and build up. You can also use the dusting method described for picture frames to clean sculptures. If your sculpture is stained, get expert advice and don't attempt to deep clean yourself.

● **To wax a wood sculpture** first remove any build-up from furniture polish or furniture cleaning soap. As a test, dip a cotton bud in white spirit and dab it on a hidden spot to see whether it damages the finish. If not, apply white spirit to a soft cloth and gently stroke over the sculpture. (Don't breath in: inhaling dust could cause lung damage.) Be careful not to snag the cloth on the wood and pull off chips and splinters. Then apply the wax to another soft, clean cloth and gently rub it into the surface. Carnauba wax works well and comes in a variety of colours or clear. Talk to a conservator before waxing stone, marble, plaster of Paris, or a painted surface.

Asphalt

Without a doubt, asphalt is tough and hard-wearing, but there are a surprising number of cleaning considerations where the rubber meets the road.

- **To clean your driveway** or other asphalt surface, give it a good wash once a year. Remove leaves and dirt with a broom or leaf blower. Mix 4 tablespoons of detergent in a bucket with 4 litres of water. Splash some onto the driveway as needed for spot cleaning and scrub with a stiff broom. Then give it a good rinse with a garden hose. Avoid high-pressure hoses or steam washing, which could damage the asphalt.

- **Clean petrol and oil spills** as quickly as possible. Asphalt is a petroleum-based material. This means a puddle of petrol or oil could eat a hole in your driveway. Soak up a spill with paper towels and spray away any of the remainder with a garden hose. For a little more cleaning power, mix detergent in water as described above and work at the spot with a stiff-bristled scrubbing brush. Also, it's worth taking preventive measures. Lay down some cardboard, newspaper or plastic when you add oil or petrol to your lawnmower or oil a bike chain on the drive.

SIMPLE solutions

If you don't have any paper towels outdoors when you spill any petrol or oil on your asphalt surface, don't overlook these other handy absorbents.
- Cat litter works well on outdoor oil spills. In addition, it can be used to solidify very small quantities of paint and other liquids.
- Sand or soil also work well for oil spills outside or in the garage.

Asphalt

- **To remove asphalt stains on clothing** pre-treat the stain with a biological stain removing product, then machine wash. If you get asphalt on your shoes, spray them with WD-40 and then scrape the asphalt off with a paint scraper or putty knife. Make sure that you rinse your shoes well before you wear them in the house.

- **To remove asphalt from your tools** again the WD-40 trick works. Spray it on, wait a few minutes and wipe it off. Turpentine, paint thinner and white spirit also work but we don't recommend them here, because they're highly flammable.

- **To remove asphalt from a car** or other motor vehicle go to a garage or car supplies store and buy an asphalt or tar-removal product designed for that purpose and follow the directions on the packet carefully.

- **Keep an asphalt driveway** looking better for longer by maintaining the surface regularly. Reseal with a commercial sealant every two or three years to protect it from the weather and to maintain its looks. If you reseal more often, you will get a thick build-up of the material, which can start to crack.

  Eventually your driveway will crack though – heat and cold alone will cause this – so seal up any breaks in the asphalt without delay. Use an asphalt-patching product (available at

hardware and home improvement stores) that will cover cracking and also prevent weeds from growing in the fissures. Weeds will accelerate problems with your driveway because, as the plants grow bigger and take root, the asphalt surface will become even more cracked.

Attics & lofts

Neglect your attic or loft space and you could be harbouring a source of dust and mould right over your head. Give it a thorough clean once a year and you'll not only remove a source of these irritants from your home, but you'll also have a valuable storage space that you won't dread going into. So you'll use it more often and the rooms in the rest of the house will be less cluttered.

- **Before you start** – especially if it's been several years since you even went into your attic – you should gear up to protect yourself. Wear a full mouth-nose dust mask (available from DIY stores) to protect your lungs from dust, allergens and other nuisances. You may need an apron or overalls to protect your clothes, goggles to protect your eyes and heavyweight rubber gloves. If your attic is already used for storage, make sure everything up there is organised before you attempt cleaning. This means storing small items in labelled boxes, grouping together boxes that contain like items and opening up walkways so that you can get to any box in any part of the loft space.

- **To actually clean the attic** use an extension lead, so that you can vacuum and start sucking up dust from the top down – ceiling, beams, walls and floor. If your attic already has things stored in it, don't just clean around the boxes – clean under them, too. Once the major grime has been vanquished, you're ready to give the area a light once-over with a damp cleaning cloth dipped in a solution of water and mild washing-up liquid.

Attic mould
You may find mould growing in your attic if you have a leaky roof or poor ventilation. Get these problems fixed and then vacuum up as much mould as possible. Wear a mask and use a stiff brush to loosen any mould that remains then vacuum again. Finally, paint with a mould-inhibiting preparation.

Baby equipment

Babies require a lot of equipment and you will spend more time than you might imagine meticulously cleaning every item that your newborn baby comes into contact with. Your baby's new immune system is just developing and needs to be carefully protected from 'everyday' germs that you'd shrug off without noticing.

Healthy hands
A newborn's immune system starts working at about six weeks. Before that, immunity comes from whatever the mother supplied during pregnancy and continues to provide through breast-feeding. To fend off bacteria, make sure anyone holding a newborn has washed their hands thoroughly.

- **It's important to find the right balance** between cleanliness and germ phobia. With a healthy baby, it isn't necessary to scrub and sterilise everything in sight, but you should be careful with anything that may end up in your baby's mouth: bottles, teats, dummies and utensils used for feeding.

- **Sterilising baby bottles** is a first-year essential. Some bottles may be dishwasher safe but you will need to rinse them out again anyway, to ensure there are no traces of detergent. In reality you'll only get a thorough clean by hand washing. Wash the bottle and teat in hot water with sudsy washing-up water. Use a bottle brush and a teat brush to get right inside and so remove any caked-on milk in the interior corners. Force soapy water through the hole in the teat. Rinse thoroughly with running water. Now sterilise, according to what kind of steriliser you have. A microwave one, which fits inside the microwave, holds up to eight bottles and takes only around five minutes, is easily the top choice. If you don't have a microwave, a bulkier, plug-in steam steriliser works just as well. Do not touch the sterile teats when you go to make up the formula: use teat tongs instead, to manoeuvre them back onto the bottle.

- **To keep a changing table clean**, use an antibacterial cleaning spray after each nappy change. These don't need rinsing off so you can give it a simple spray and wipe, and you're done. Antibacterial wipes are faster still: but at 2p–5p per go and with as many as ten nappy changes a day in those first, frantic weeks, using them can become very expensive.

- **To clean prams and buggies** sprinkle bicarbonate of soda on a damp paper towel or clean cloth and wipe down the item, then rinse with warm water. (Bicarbonate of soda is a mild alkali that can make dirt dissolve in water. It acts as a mild abrasive when not totally dissolved.) If that isn't strong enough, use the suds only from a solution of washing-up liquid to dab away at the dirt.

- **Highchairs can become covered** with a surprising amount of food. It's as if your baby or toddler has smeared something over almost every surface of the chair. So after each meal, give a thorough wipe down. A blunt knife is useful for getting up dried in deposits. Use cleaning wipes and then follow with an antibacterial cleaning spray. Use soapy water on any wooden surrounds and then dry promptly.

- **Clean a cot** by using bicarbonate of soda (as described above) to wipe the cot rails. Wash baby bed linen in a washing machine, using hot water, ideally at 60°C to kill bacteria.

- **Some plastic and rubber baby toys** can be cleaned by placing them in the dishwasher. Do this regularly to keep microbes or organic material on the toys to a minimum. Wash stuffed animals in a washing machine, using hot water (60°C) to kill dust mites. If you feel this is too tough a treatment – many soft toys say surface wash with a sudsy cloth only – then use the freezer as a dust mite killer. Put a soft toy in a sealed plastic bag and pop in the freezer for 48 hours: no creature can survive that.

Banisters

A beautiful staircase and banister can be the centrepiece of a home's entrance, so don't let an accumulation of everyday grime diminish its wow factor.

● **Dust a painted banister** with a soft, water-dampened cloth. If it's especially dirty, make up a solution of a couple of drops of mild washing-up liquid in a bucket of warm water. Dip a clean cloth in the solution and then wring it out well. Use to wash down a small section of banister at a time, then wipe with a dry cloth. Oil polish is best avoided on painted wood, since it can cause discolouration. Wax is rarely needed, but if you use it, choose a light-coloured wax for light-coloured paint.

● **Dust a wooden banister** with a soft cloth and a little furniture polish. That will restore moisture to the wood and prevent any dust collected on the cloth from floating back onto the balusters (the posts or spindles that support the handrail). When dust collects in the intricacies of turned or carved balusters, use a cotton bud to get into any crevices and clean out the really tight spaces.

Barbecues

Cooking outdoors is great fun and you can create delicious meals, but before you start the barbecue, make sure it's ready – clean equipment makes for tastier, healthier food.

● **To clean a barbecue** start by removing the grill grates and then clean it inside and out with 2 parts hot water to 1 part washing-up liquid. (With gas barbecues, you'll need to cover the gas receptacles with aluminium foil to stop water leaking inside.) Scrub with a nylon brush to prevent scratching the barbecue (or use just a cloth, if you're concerned that even a brush might be too much). Follow by rinsing off with hot water and then wipe dry with a clean soft cloth. Finally, apply vegetable oil, using a clean cloth, to the barbecue's outside surface. This will keep the body of the barbecue shining and lubricated against the elements.

● **If your barbecue instructions** say the racks are dishwasher safe you're lucky. If not, several methods work well. First scrub them with a wire brush and the hot water and washing-up liquid mix described above. If they're too encrusted, spray them with oven cleaner. Place the treated grates in a rubbish bag lined with paper towels, tie the top closed and stash the bag in the garden shed, out of reach of pets and children for a couple of hours or even overnight – powerful chemicals are at work. When you re-open the bag to remove the grates, point the opening away from your face to avoid inhaling potent fumes. Thoroughly hose off the grates, wipe them down with hot water and washing-up liquid and rinse.

If you are fortunate enough to have a self-cleaning oven in your kitchen, your barbecue clean-up couldn't be easier. Just put the barbecue grill grates into the oven and let the intense heat do the work for you.

cleaning a **BARBEQUE**

1 Use a stiff wire brush to remove most of the burnt-on food and grease.

2 Sponge both sides of the grate, as fat droplets often congeal underneath.

3 Re-season and protect the grate by spraying it with vegetable oil.

Barbecues

- **When cleaning a gas grill,** first make sure that the gas bottle is disconnected. Then inspect the burners for cracks and corrosion and if damaged, replace them. Use a pipe cleaner or non-metallic bottle brush to clean the tubes which carry gas to the burners. Brush around the connections between the gas bottle, the regulator and the hose with soapy water and turn on the gas. If you smell gas or see bubbles, turn the gas off, tighten the connections and repeat the test. If the gas is still leaking – a potentially dangerous problem – you need a new hose.

- **Try to eliminate some of the grease.** When you've finished cooking, leave burners turned on for 10 to 15 minutes with the cover closed. Let the grill cool and then scrape away the residue with a wire brush. This job will be even easier if you coat grates with a non-stick cooking spray each time you cook.

Basements & cellars

Before cleaning a basement or cellar, knock down cobwebs with a long-handled broom, then thoroughly sweep the floor and brush away debris from the walls.

- **Mix hot water with all-purpose cleaner** and wash the walls first, using a strong-bristled floor brush with a long handle. Rinse with warm water from a second bucket.

- **Next, scrub concrete floors,** using hot water and household detergent. After cleaning, open any doors or windows to air out the room and help the drying process.

- **If mould or mildew is a problem,** mop the walls and floors with a solution of 100ml of chlorine bleach to 8 litres of water, then rinse well. The bleach will kill existing mildew, but it will return unless the source of the moisture is addressed.

Baths & sinks

For everyday care, wipe down the bath after each use with water and a cloth or sponge to keep soap scum under control. Staying on top of the problem like this goes a long way, especially considering that most acrylic baths come with dire warnings about the danger of abrasive cleaners because their layer of acrylic is now so thin. And it's certainly true that if you scrub your way through the tub's protective finish, you'll soon have stains that are embedded in the glass fibre, porcelain or enamel.

- **To clean porcelain baths** you can use most bathroom cleaners. Polish stainless steel on fixtures by rubbing with bicarbonate of soda on a damp sponge. Rinse well with water.

- **Remove rust stains** by squeezing lemon juice over the spot and rubbing gently with an old toothbrush in a circular motion. Be aware, however, that there may be permanent damage to the bath surface underneath, especially if the rust has been there for some time. Rinse with water and repeat if necessary.

- **To remove blue-green stains** caused by water with a high copper content, combine equal amounts of cream of tartar and bicarbonate of soda (usually a tablespoon of each is enough) and add some lemon juice drop by drop until you have a paste. Rub it into the stain with your fingers or a soft cloth. Leave it for half an hour and rinse well with water. Repeat if necessary.

Watch out
When using any new cleaning product that you are at all unsure about, always test it first on an inconspicuous area to see that it doesn't cause damage to the material you are cleaning. And don't combine bathroom cleaners, in case you create a toxic mix with noxious gases: chlorine bleach and ammonia make a dangerous mixture. It's safe to use more than one type of cleaner as long as you rinse well between the applications.

Baths & sinks

- **Before cleaning an enamel bath** check that your cleaning product says it is 'safe for enamel'. If it doesn't don't use it. With enamel that has started to wear, cleaning products hit on the weak spots, taking off the sheen from the surface.

- **Cleaning acrylic tubs** can be difficult because mild cleaners have little impact on serious soiling but abrasive cleaners applied with too much pressure will quickly dull the finish. For everyday cleaning, spray on a bathroom cleaner designed for acrylic and wipe with a soft sponge. If absolutely necessary, use a mildly abrasive cleaner and a light-duty scrubbing sponge. Rinse off with water so the chemicals don't stay on the surface.

Beams

To dust beams, get out your vacuum cleaner and its extension wand and snap on the brush attachment. Alternatively, you can attach a lint roller replacement tube – one of those rolls of sticky paper that you use to lift dust off clothing – to a paint roller and run it across the exposed surfaces.

- **If your beams are really dusty and dirty,** you'll need to wash them, so you may need to use an extension ladder. For wood that has been varnished, mix a mild detergent with water, then wipe down and rinse a small section at a time using flannels or, for harder-to-reach areas, a sponge mop. Go easy with the water solution – you are just wiping the beams, not drowning them. If beams are unfinished, don't use water. Or if you absolutely feel you must, restrict it to a damp cloth, but with no detergent.

Beds

It's worth cleaning the divan or wooden slats of your bed regularly, to increase its working life. Mattresses are covered in a separate section, as are stains that might be found on beds.

- **You should clean wooden slats** several times a year. Use the crevice tool on the vacuum cleaner to lift up dirt and dust from each slat. While doing this, take the opportunity to check the holding screws. They may need tightening to keep the base of the bed sufficiently supportive.

- **Wipe wood headboards** and support posts with a cloth wrung out from a solution of sudsy washing-up liquid to remove grease and dirt. Rinse, dry and polish with a dry cloth (a microfibre one will give the best shine). Avoid using polishes as you'll smell the residue at night.

- **Fabric headboards** can trap grease and dust so you'll need to clean them often. Get into the habit of giving the headboard a quick vacuum at the same time as you do the bedroom. To revitalise a headboard, use upholstery cleaner. Protect the mattress with a towel before you spray on the cleaner; it's important not to get chemicals into the mattress, which could inhibit the action of the springs. Do this in the morning and then open the windows to air the room.

- **Vacuum divans regularly** to remove dust. If you get a greasy patch try wiping it off with a wrung out cloth, as for wood headboards – but take care not to over-wet. If the divan is still dulled with grease, try to absorb particularly bad patches by rubbing in baby talcum powder, then brushing off with a stiff brush. Using a mattress protector and a valance help will shield your divan from dirt.

> **The bed habits of single men**
> A survey by *Guardsman,* the UK's largest provider of mattress protectors, found that single men typically change their bed linen every two months. Practically everyone else nips the bedding off to the washing machine weekly including single guys once they get partners.

Bedspreads

Laundering a bedspread, particularly if it's large or padded, can be difficult to do at home. Most washing machines and dryers just aren't big enough. So you may need to take your bedspread to the local launderette, where the washers and dryers are bigger than most home varieties.

● **Before washing check the care label** to make sure that your bedspread is in fact washable and weigh it to check that your washing machine will be able to deal with the load – if not, you may need a trip to the launderette. Pre-treat any heavily soiled areas with a pre-wash stain-removal product. Set the washing machine to a delicates programme with a normal spin cycle. Add the bedspread and some detergent.

● **To dry a bedspread** transfer it to the dryer and select the setting appropriate for its fabric type. Add a couple of clean, dry towels and then toss in two or three clean tennis balls; these will knock against the bedspread and keep its filling from clumping together. Stop the dryer twice during its cycle to make sure it 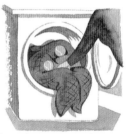 isn't getting too hot. Shake the bedspread out once, too, in order to make sure the filling doesn't jam in one corner.

● **To fluff up a candlewick bedspread** – the durable, still-popular knotted or tufted kind your grandmother probably had – try this clever approach. Wash as described above, then hang it outside in a stiff wind, folded over the clothes line with the knotted sides facing. The knots will perk up as they rub against one another. Or, once your candlewick spread is dry, spread it on a clean floor and sweep with a pristine broom.

Bicycles

A clean bicycle is also a safe one, because each wash provides an ideal opportunity to inspect the tyres for wear and tear. Bent rims can create small pinches that grow over time if the tyres aren't properly inflated. So be sure to inflate your tyres to the recommended levels suggested by the manufacturer.

- **To make cleaning easier,** consider buying a bicycle work stand. It will stabilise the bike as you wash it and let you take off the wheels if you want. They cost from around £20 for a budget, folding stand to more than £200 for a solid, professional support. Another alternative is to suspend your bike with ropes from a strong, low-lying tree branch. If you're concerned about the mess that caked-on mud might make beneath you, spread a groundsheet underneath. Leaning the bike against a wall is another option, but makes your work more cumbersome and your bike more likely to topple over.

- **Start cleaning your bike** by gently knocking off any visible dirt with a brush. Then use a garden hose on low pressure to rinse it. You want the water to trickle out, rather than spray with force, because water under pressure can force grime into the chain and other moving parts. For the same reason, never use a power washer or put your bike through a car wash.

- **Next, degrease the drive train.** The hardest parts of a bicycle to keep clean are always the chain and linked, moving parts – the pedals, derailleur, rear hub and such – so tackle them first. It's a good idea to protect your hands with work gloves. Then apply a degreaser, such as WD-40, to a soft cloth and clean the chain, a few links at a time. Move the pedals forwards to work on a new section of chain. Once you've cleaned the chain, carefully remove it from the chain ring (also called the chain wheel) – the metal wheel with pointed teeth that

> **Board riders**
> If you own a skateboard, keep in mind that most are made of wood and shouldn't get wet: dry them if they do. You can scrub the grip tape with a soft-bristled brush dipped in clean water. Rinse by wiping with a wet cloth and dry well with a clean cloth. If the bearings get wet, remove them from the wheels and wipe them dry as soon as possible.

Bicycles

keeps the chain in place. Using a small screwdriver, carefully remove any caked-on dirt caught between the teeth. Then slip a cloth between them, gently rubbing it back and forth as if you were flossing your teeth.

Still cycling
If you have an exercise bike then it's important to keep that clean too. After you've finished using your equipment wipe off the perspiration – the salt from sweat is corrosive – and wipe down control panels to keep moisture from seeping in. To make it easier, keep a roll of paper towels handy in the room at home where you exercise.

- **Now wash the entire bike** using a big sponge and a bowl of strong, sudsy washing-up water. Don't forget to clean the seat and its underpinnings, handlebars and handgrips and be sure not to miss the brake levers and under the fork that connects the handlebars to the frame. Wash the wheel rims and tyres. Gently soap the drive train to remove any residue from the degreaser. Rinse the bike completely with a garden hose and then ride it in the work stand to slough off excess water. Towel off the bike and ride it around to shake off more water. Then towel it off again completely.

- **Lubricate the chain** with more WD-40 or a specialist bike lubricant. Turn the crank backwards as you spray. As lubricant attracts dirt, wipe off any excess with a soft cloth.

- **Wax a clean bicycle** to protect it and deflect dirt. Bike waxes are sold at any cycle shop. Following the instructions, apply wax with a soft cloth, being careful to hit the bike's various tubes, joints and other hard-to-reach spots. Or simply spray your bike frame with an ordinary furniture polish that contains wax.

Binoculars & telescopes

Don't let dust or grime spoil your birdwatching, stargazing or special safari. Keep your binoculars and telescopes in good working order with these simple procedures.

- **Remove loose dust or debris** from binocular lenses by blowing gently on each one, without spitting. Or use a lens cleaning pen, which has a soft natural brush at one end and a cleaning tip on the other, to get right into the crevices.

- **Spray each lens lightly** with lens cleaning fluid, then wipe with a clean sheet of lens tissue, using a gentle circular motion; rubbing too hard can remove the protective coating. With a new sheet of lens tissue, remove remaining fluid. Never wipe lenses with edge of your clothes or a tissue; the fibres could scratch the delicate lens coating. Also resist the temptation to use commercial glass cleaners; most contain ammonia that will eat away the lens coating.

- **Wipe clean the outer casing** of binoculars with a soft cloth dampened with water. Keep rubber eyecups and focus knobs lubricated with a vinyl or rubber preservative.

- **Clean telescope optics** no more than twice a year – their reflective coatings are easily damaged. In fact, if you use canned air (sold at camera shops) instead, to blow away dirt, you should never have to move onto contact cleaning at all. If you feel you must, remove the mirror from the tube and use a camel-hair brush – sold at most camera stores – to remove surface dust and dirt. Dampen a sheet of lens tissue with lens cleaning fluid. Wipe the mirror, eyepiece and lenses from the centre to the outer edge, using minimal pressure. Should the optics collect dew outside, don't wipe dry. Instead, let them air-dry, then clean with distilled water and a lens tissue: distilled water leaves no spots.

Birdbaths, feeders & birdhouses

Just as our baths, kitchens and sleeping areas need constant attention to keep them clean, so do the same spots we set up for our feathered friends. Keep birdbaths, feeders and houses free of fungi, algae and bacteria and the birds will happily return for more. Simply use a scrubbing brush and a tired toothbrush.

Bleach and birds
You can use bleach to clean outdoor bird equipment – it will not harm the birds, as long as you use it in a weak concentration. Because it breaks down quickly in the environment, there will be no chemical residue either. However, do shy away from treating wooden birdhouses and feeders with preservatives that contain petroleum compounds. The fumes they emit could harm birds.

● **Clean a birdbath** once a week during warm weather. Stale standing water can turn into breeding grounds for mosquito larvae, so dumping out old water and cleaning inside is essential. First, use a scrubbing brush with stiff bristles and warm water to scrub out the birdbath. If the bath has a telltale ring from algae or other deposits or feels slimy to the touch, mix a solution of 1 part bleach to 10 parts water in a clean bucket and use that to scrub the bath. Wear rubber gloves to protect your hands. If you don't like the notion of using bleach, mix equal parts of white vinegar and water and scrub. Rinse with fresh water and air-dry.

● **Clean bird feeders** every two weeks all through the year. This is because birdseed and other bird food gets damp and mouldy in humid conditions and the birds feeding at your trough may get sick. If you can, take your wooden feeder apart. Dust off the pieces with a wire brush and then scrub with warm water and a stiff-bristled scrubbing brush. If the feeder is really dirty, wear rubber gloves and mix 1 part bleach to 10 parts  water in a clean bucket. Vigorously scrub it, both inside and out. Rinse thoroughly and then dry. For plastic or metal feeders, brush them out, then rinse with warm water and dry with a soft cloth, or simply leave to air-dry.

- **Clean a birdhouse during cold weather** when birds aren't feathering their nests inside. If the birdhouse has a removable side or top panel, take it off and dip the pieces into a solution of 1 part bleach to 10 parts water. With an old toothbrush, dig into the cracks and crevices – this is where feather mites, which feed on bird feathers, often lurk. You don't want these bugs infesting the next generation to take up residence in your birdhouse. To guard against mites, as well as fleas, flies, larvae and lice, use an aviary dusting powder, from pet shops.

Blankets

It's a myth that you can't wash blankets, because they'll shrink and distort. These days, most blankets, including some made of wool, are machine washable. Check the care labels and make sure that your washing machine and tumble dryer will hold the blanket comfortably. Weigh the blanket first, if you're unsure and check it against your machine's maximum weights. Don't just cram it in and go – the blanket won't rinse or dry properly if there isn't really enough room. In that instance, take your blanket to a self-service launderette with a commercial-size washing machine and tumble dryer.

- **Before washing a wool blanket,** check the label to make sure it is washable. If it isn't, have it dry-cleaned. If you are going to wash it, measure the blanket and save the measurements for later – you may want these as a guide as to how far you want to stretch the fibres out to afterwards. Pre-treat any spots or stains with stain remover, following label directions. If the binding (the narrow fabric along the edges) is really filthy, use a nylon-bristled scrubbing brush to gently scrub it with washing-up liquid or make a paste of equal parts non-biological detergent and water and apply it carefully.

Blankets

- **To machine-wash a wool blanket** use a non-biological powder that's safe for wools and choose the gentlest cycle, with a minimal spin. Most machines have a specific wool programme that you should choose.

- **To hand-wash a wool blanket** – if your blanket won't fit into the machine, or you're worried that it will be too harsh – fill the bath with cold water and add 1 measure of a hand-wash detergent that is suitable for wools. Put the blanket in the tub and press down into the soapy water to wash.

    To rinse, fill the tub several times with fresh, cool water. Don't wring. Instead, squeeze out excess water by rolling up your blanket in two or three large white towels.

- **To dry a wool blanket** you have several drying options. The first is to use your tumble dryer, but only if you have a 'No heat' or cold setting.

- **Alternatively, spread out dry towels** on a clean garden table, flatten the blanket out on top and stretch it to its original shape, using the measurements you took previously.

- **Hang the blanket over two** tightly strung clothes lines that won't droop under its weight. If you chose this or the previous approach, you can also plump up the blanket afterward in the tumble dryer on the 'No heat' or cool setting.

- **To clean a cotton or acrylic blanket** simply wash as you would other cotton or acrylic items – in the washing machine, following the maximum temperature on the care label. Dry a knitted cotton blanket in a dryer on low heat so it won't pill. For other cotton blankets, the regular setting is suitable. Or hang a cotton blanket from a taut clothes line to dry. Tumble-dry an acrylic blanket on low heat.

Blinds

Blinds – and especially the slatted versions such as venetian blinds – are like miniature dust-collecting shelves. Ignore them and you'll have a full-scale dust library in no time. So make giving them a really thorough clean and dust a regular part of your routine.

- **To dust blinds** fix the brush attachment onto your vacuum cleaner and adjust the blinds to expose the flat surface. Then, from top to bottom and left to right, vacuum the entire surface. Adjust the blinds again to reverse the slats and repeat.

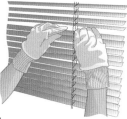

- **Alternatively, run a lamb's-wool duster** or an old paintbrush along each slat to wipe away dust.

- **Wear an old pair** of thick absorbent cloth gloves and simply run your fingers along the tops and bottoms of the slats. The gloves will pick up the dust and dirt as you wipe.

- **You could try using** a Venetian blind duster. This useful piece of equipment is specially angled so you can move up and through the slats with speed.

- **Parchment, paper or rice-paper blinds** should not get wet at all. Clean them as you would non-washable wallpaper – with commercial cleaning putty or an art gum eraser. Or find a spot remover that claims to work on the material at hand and test it on an inconspicuous area first.

SIMPLE solutions

Try cleaning washable blinds outside. Spread an old shower curtain or piece of plastic on a level surface, open the blinds and spray with a garden hose. Then use sudsy water to clean the slats with gloved fingers. Rinse thoroughly and air-dry.

Blinds

- **Wood and bamboo blinds** should not be immersed in water. Wipe them down with a damp rag soaked in a solution of washing-up liquid and water. Then dry them off quickly with a fresh rag.

- **Washing aluminium and vinyl blinds** is fine, but don't use harsh cleaners or abrasives on them. And don't use any cleaner with ammonia on aluminium, because it will damage the finish. To clean aluminium or plastic blinds, you have a couple of choices. You can wash them where they hang, using water and a squirt of washing-up liquid, then rinsing off afterwards, or you can take them down and wash them in the shower or tub.

- **To give blinds a bath** raise them and remove from their fixings. Run enough warm water in the tub to cover the blinds and stir in around 100ml of washing-up liquid. Wearing rubber gloves, place the blinds in the water and extend them. Dip the blinds several times to loosen grime. Then let them soak for five minutes. Use your gloved fingers to clean both sides of each slat. Drain the dirty water and either rinse the blinds in a fresh tub of water or spray them with a shower attachment. Spread out the blinds on a clean towel and blot with another towel. When they are completely dry, wipe a fabric softener sheet along each slat. This helps stop the blinds attracting more dirt.

Boilers

Having your boiler cleaned is an annual job for a professional. So never open it up. Your should only ever clean the cover. Wipe it with a just damp cloth, then dry. To remove any scratching on the painted metal, rub petroleum jelly, in a circular motion over the mark. Wipe off, then buff to a shine.

Books

Books can be real dust magnets – and they're also often victims of spills and greasy hands. It's usually best to just dust them, using a vacuum cleaner with the soft brush attachment or a feather duster. Assuming that you're dusting books in situ, just go over the exposed spine and top of each one.

- **If the cover of a book** is smudged with fingerprints or smeared with food, use a damp rag to remove spots. If you need more cleaning power, mix ½ cup of mild detergent in a bucket of cool water and test on an inconspicuous spot. If the cover appears durable, wipe with a rag slightly dampened with the detergent solution, then dry with a soft cloth. Use a soft eraser to clean up a grimy paperback. Be careful, too much pressure can rub off some coloured inks.

- **Simply wipe leather-bound books** with a clean cloth or use the vacuum cleaner to remove dust. Avoid treating with products that contain oil – this can make books go mouldy.

A book fan
To rid a book of its musty smell, open up the book near an oscillating fan which will dry out any dampness. Then, if some smell remains, sprinkle the pages liberally with unperfumed talcum powder. Shake, then brush off any excess with a soft brush.

Boots

Many boots come with a protective coating that keeps them shiny and bright until they take their first step outdoors. In most cases the coating will wear off and then dirt and grime can work their way in, clogging the pores that allow the boots to breathe and dry, and breaking down seams as well as the leather or fabric itself.

- **To dislodge dirt** first bang your boots together. Then wipe off surface grime and dust with a damp cloth, paying special attention to creases and wrinkles. Go into the stubborn stitched areas with a dry, stiff nylon brush or an old toothbrush.

Boots

- **To clean a boot zip,** close it first. Wet a nylon brush and rub it on a bar of soap. Then scrub down the zip channel. Wipe it dry with a soft cloth. Then undo the zip and, using a dry corner of the soap bar, rub down each side of the zip to lubricate it for an easy slide. Wipe off the excess with a soft, dry cloth.

- **If your boots are very stained** use either saddle soap or a fabric cleaner, such as Woolite, on a dry cloth and rub the whole of the outside in small circles until the stains disappear. Then stuff the boots with crumpled newspaper and let them dry at room temperature before repolishing. Remove salt stains with a specialist shoe stain remover. Alternatively, dampen the salt stains again, so that they dissolve in the water, then brush your boots firmly to remove them. Rubbing leather with milk can also help to restore an even colour.

Tough scuffs
Use a pencil eraser to get scuff marks off boots. If they're bad, but still won't shift, use a wax crayon in a matching colour to restore the appearance of the leather.

Bottles

Cleaning the outside of an ordinary bottle is as simple as any other glass-cleaning task. The real challenge, of course, is removing dirt from the inside.

- **To clean the outside of a bottle** use warm water and washing-up liquid. Mildly abrasive washing-up pads are fine for use on modern glass. For antique glass, stick to a smooth cloth.

- **To remove hardened residue inside** let the bottle stand full of soapy water (warm water and washing-up liquid) for several hours, until the residue softens and can be loosened by shaking or by use of a bottle brush.

- **Alternatively, fill the bottle** with white vinegar and leave it to stand for a day before rinsing out.

Brass

There are two kinds of brass to consider when cleaning: brass with a protective lacquer coating – this is most common today – and raw brass. Raw brass is the bigger challenge to care for, since this copper-and-zinc alloy oxidises when it is exposed to air, resulting in tarnish. Removing tarnish requires elbow grease.

- **On lacquered brass,** mix mild washing-up liquid with warm water and apply it with a soft, cellulose sponge or cloth. Rinse with fresh water and dry thoroughly with a soft cloth. Buff with an extremely soft cloth.

- **On raw brass,** use a metal polish like Brasso, which contains cleaners to eliminate the tarnish, abrasives for polishing and oil to protect the brass from the air. Follow the instructions on the package and use only a thin layer of metal polish.

- **To brighten up soot-grimed brass** fireplace equipment rub with extra-fine steel wool (0000) or a very fine emery cloth in one direction only – not with a circular motion. Once the brass is clean, follow up with a commercial brass polish.

---

natural ways to clean **brass**

- Like many natural methods, it's a bit messy, but think how satisfied you'll feel that just half a cut lemon and a dash of salt has restored your brass to its former glory. Sprinkle the cut lemon with salt, then squeeze it over dirty, unlacquered brass. Wipe off with a cloth, then buff up with a second, clean cloth.
- Alternatively, make a paste of bicarbonate of soda and water (or just use non-gel toothpaste, also a mild abrasive). Apply the paste to a soft cloth and then rub the brass. Wipe clean with a fresh cloth.
- Once clean, rub the brass with a light coating of mineral oil, olive oil, or lemon oil to protect it from further tarnish. Lacquered brass doesn't need this protection.

Brick

Exposed interior brick can be cleaned by simply putting the brush attachment on your vacuum cleaner and running it over the wall. The brush will loosen the dust and dirt and the vacuum will suck it up.

- **On exterior brick,** particularly in a damp and shady spot, mould, mildew and algae are often a problem. To kill and remove the growth, mix 50ml of bleach with 5 litres of water in a bucket. If you find you need more strength, increase the bleach or try a specialist moss and mould killer. Wearing rubber gloves, dip a stiff-bristled brush (not metal) in the solution and scrub the brick. To rinse, hose the brick down with fresh water.

- **You can use caustic soda** to clean dingy brick. Because it is so powerful (it will cause burns instantly) always get the water bucket filled first, then add the caustic soda to the water. This minimises the risk of getting splashed with the concentrated product. Wear rubber gloves, long sleeves and protective goggles. Apply the solution with an old rag – only apply if you can be sure that children or pets won't have access to the wall while it is sitting in this extremely strong solvent. Let the cleaner sit on the bricks for 15 minutes and follow up with a scrubbing brush. Apply the cleaner again if necessary and scrub once more. Rinse with water. You could also use a powerful cold oven cleaner – which contains caustic soda – but this might prove expensive over a large area of brickwork.

- **To brighten soot-stained brick** try this trick. Mix a can of a cola soft drink (its acid adds cleaning power), 100ml of an economy all-purpose household cleaner and 4 litres of water in a bucket. Sponge this onto the brick and let it sit for 15 minutes. Scrub with a stiff-bristled brush to loosen the soot. Rinse with a clean sponge and fresh water. If you are working outside, use a hose. To make the solution more powerful, add more cola.

Cleaning under pressure

A high-pressure hose can work magic in cleaning brick, but be careful – the pressure can damage both mortar and bricks, especially bricks with a sand finish. Use a low setting and keep the nozzle 60cm from the wall. Keep the spray moving; it's the concentration of water on one spot that will lift off loose brick particles. Aim for the brick, not the mortar.

Bridal gowns

Unless your gown specifically says that it can be machine washed, never try to clean it yourself. If you've bought a second-hand gown, take it to a professional dry-cleaners. If yours is new and you're just panicking about on-the-day disasters, this emergency know-how will keep you calm.

- **To fix a last-minute stain** do not use spot cleaner on your gown. Instead, use talcum powder as a disguise. Just sprinkle some talc onto the spot and let it absorb the moisture. Brush off lightly. If your dress is slightly too long and a rehearsal has left scuff marks along the bottom of the gown, mark over them with a piece of white chalk.

- **For liquid spills** try fizzy mineral water. Depending on the location of the stain, you might have to undress and dress all over again. Working from the inside out, use a clean, white handkerchief to blot up as much of the stain as possible. Be sure to dab, not rub. Then wet the handkerchief with the mineral water and dab again, working again from the inside.

SIMPLE solutions

Chances are that you'll get some make-up on your wedding dress on the big day. It may be your own or you might get smudged with someone else's lipstick after all those congratulatory kisses and hugs.

Luckily, there is something you can do: a light mist of WD-40, the all-purpose lubricant, will lift up the stain. Only the most well-prepared bride will have a can handy but it's possible that your wedding photographer might have some in his kit bag; WD-40 is also used to clean up tripods and grubby metal.

Removing lipstick is just one of many uses for WD-40: you'll find a list of 2000 ideas at www.twbc.org/wd40.htm, ranging from cleaning piano keys right through to polishing mother of pearl. The suggestions come from consumers and are untested by the manufacturers, but if WD-40 worked for someone else, it may also work for you.

Bridal gowns

- **If your gown needs a final touch-up** on the day, press only on the inside of the gown. And don't use steam. If the fabric hasn't been pre-washed, steam can create spotting or a colour change. Place a dry handkerchief between the iron and the gown. Then press in a downward direction. Don't move the iron back and forth – this will destroy delicate fibres. Press one area and then move the cloth to another.

- **When the honeymoon is over** don't put off taking your gown to the dry-cleaner. You might want to hand it down to someone or sell it and, without the proper care, it will become yellow and useless to anyone else.

  First, take off any easily removable trimmings or shoulder pads. Then search out any spots you may have ignored during the wedding day. Dry cleaning usually removes the obvious – make-up, grass stains, food – but you may also have acquired some invisible spills – champagne is a classic – that only show up later. If you can remember where they are, you will give the dry-cleaner a head start. Otherwise, when your gown is preserved and stored, the champagne stains will be too.

  When you store your gown, don't encase it in plastic or expose it to sunlight. Instead, ask the dry-cleaner to wrap your gown in acid-free tissue and store it in an acid-free box to slow the ageing process.

Briefcases

To clean the inside, empty the briefcase and shake it over a rubbish bin to get rid of broken pencil leads, paperclips, scraps of paper, old crumbs and the general grit and grime that accumulates in offices, airports and car boots.

- **Vacuum out everything else,** using a hand vacuum cleaner or the crevice attachment of a regular vacuum cleaner. Use a spray bottle of water (the sort you use to mist over plants) to lightly spray the lining. Pour a little washing-up liquid on a small cloth and rub lightly on any persistent stains. Immediately wipe down the lining with a dry cloth. Don't close the briefcase – let it air-dry.

- **Clean the outside** with a liquid saddle soap or put a couple of drops of detergent in a small bowl of warm water. Swirl to create some bubbles. Dip a face flannel in the water and quickly wipe down the briefcase. If your briefcase has a zip, take a dry bar of soap and rub it down the zip. It will clean and loosen the zip at the same time. Remove excess soap with a dry flannel.

Brocade

Brocade is a combination of fabrics woven into a raised design. When cleaning brocade, you must consider the fabric contents of the weave. It can be made of wool, cotton, silk, synthetic fibre or a combination of these. If there is no care label, then clean according to the most delicate element. So with cotton and silk, clean as silk.

- **To remove a stain from brocade** first remove as much of the stain as possible by lifting it off with a dull-edged knife. Then start to force the stain out from the wrong side of the fabric (you may have to remove the fabric from furniture to do this). Place the fabric, stain-side down, onto an absorbent tea towel. Fizzy mineral water will help lift the stain, but if you don't have any, use lukewarm tap water. Pour a little on a paper towel and dab it on the stain, forcing it onto the tea towel. Dab a spot, then move to another spot and dab again. Keep dabbing until the stain disappears.

Bronze

Artists using special paints can re-create the look of weathered bronze in a faux finish called verdigris. But real bronze will do the job all by itself if you're patient. With time, bronze creates its own protective patina – an earthy green colour. But even with the no-cost natural process, you still have to clean it and you must be careful to remove water residue. Lingering moisture and even grit can degrade bronze. If you lose a little of the patina while cleaning, don't worry – it will come back again.

- **When cleaning bronze** you're essentially cleaning two different metals at once. An alloy, bronze is a mixture of copper and any other metal except zinc. Like any decorative surface that is exposed to the environment, bronze can gather a layer of film or dust (or dusty film) that needs removing. First, wipe away any loose or surface dirt with a soft cloth, then use a soft toothbrush to get into crevices and ornamental work.

- **For a more thorough cleaning** carefully wash the bronze with a solution of 1 tablespoon salt dissolved in 3 litres of water. For the toughest grime, dissolve 1 teaspoon of salt in 150ml white vinegar, then add enough flour to make a paste. Let it sit on the bronze for 15 minutes to an hour. Rinse with clean, warm water. Be sure to towel-dry the piece thoroughly, because moisture and salt by themselves can degrade the bronze.

Expert **ADVICE**

You can buy bronze with a factory-finish lacquer, which will protect it from changes in colour as well as corrosion. Never apply a chemical cleanser to lacquered bronze. A weekly swipe with a damp cloth will keep it in good shape. Linda Cobb, author of *Talking Dirty with the Queen of Clean*, recommends using a damp microfibre cloth, which polishes as it cleans. Although you can buy cheaper imitations, E-Cloths remain just about the best. Buy them direct from haberdashery sections of department stores.

Calculators

To clean a calculator thoroughly, dust both sides with an eyeshadow brush, being careful to brush away lint and any dust or dirt that have accumulated. If there is a great deal of lint, brush it off with a soft, dry toothbrush.

- **Keeping the keys clean** can be difficult. Because fingers transfer all kinds of dirt – such as newspaper ink or sticky sugar – the keys are like magnets for lint and grime. To get rid of anything that doesn't belong, dip a cotton bud into a small amount of methylated spirit. Press the bud onto a paper towel to eliminate excess liquid. Dab each key lightly. For the bigger surfaces, such as the back of the calculator, you can use a cotton ball dipped in methylated spirit to get rid of unsightly dirt.

Cameras

Cleaning cameras without causing damage in the process is a daunting task. What you use to clean them is also somewhat controversial. One method uses just air (canned) and minimal contact; the other uses contact cleaning and solvents. But the real trick is in preventing dirt and damage in the first place.

- **To clean the lens** first examine it with a magnifying glass. Any foreign material, including dirt you can't see with the naked eye, will mar your pictures and may damage your lens.

- **To get rid of dust or dirt on the lens** start with air. Camera shops sell a blower brush, but the blower on most of them are actually ineffective. A better alternative is a bulb syringe, available at chemists, which shoots out a puff of air. Still more effective is a can of compressed air. Also known as 'canned

Cameras

air', it's an aerosol can containing air under pressure, with a nozzle extension. If your lens is removable, check the back end occasionally and clean it in exactly the same way as the front.

- **To remove persistent specks** that don't respond to the air treatment, brush them away with a blower brush or soft watercolour paintbrush. You can also use a cleaning cloth. But you don't want to move specks around – this will only damage the lens or its coatings. The best cloth is a microfibre lens-cleaning cloth, which can also be used on the body of the camera and can be washed and reused. These cloths trap particles among their fibres rather than on the surface.

- **To remove fingerprints** or really persistent specks, you may need lens-cleaning fluid. Check your owner's manual for recommendations; there are many types on the market. If you have a plastic lens, make sure the lens cleaner is suitable for plastic as well as glass. Use a few drops of lens-cleaning fluid on a microfibre cloth – never directly on the lens – and clean with a light, circular motion. Fingerprints should be cleaned immediately in this way. If left for a long time, fingerprints can actually etch themselves into the glass. Fingerprints can also cause glass mould, which doesn't need as much moisture as most other moulds. The mould also feeds on dust, and can destroy the surface of a lens. Using your camera in the sunshine every so often will usually be enough to prevent it. If you aren't going to be using your camera for a long time, store it out of the case; camera cases can build up moisture and grow mould quite easily.

- **To clean inside a traditional film camera** use compressed air and a soft watercolour brush to banish dirt from the film chamber, followed by a gentle wiping with a microfibre cloth.

Cameras

- **When cleaning a digital camera** slip the battery pack out to make sure it is powerless before you start. A new product for use with a digital camera is a lens pen, which combines a retractable brush on one end with a cleaning tip on the other.

- **Protect a camera's lens** with an ultraviolet filter (even if you remove it for picture taking) and lens cap. With many new cameras, you can't lose the lens cap because it just slides aside.

- **Don't store a camera** where it will be exposed to direct sunlight, high humidity, rapid changes in temperature (which may cause condensation) or temperature extremes.

- **Wipe off the batteries** of a digital camera and the contact points in the battery chambers before inserting new batteries. This will help to prevent corrosion.

- **Consult the owner's manual** for hints about preventive maintenance and specific information about your camera.

Expert **ADVICE**

Ed Romney has made a career of restoring really filthy cameras. His advice to the average amateur photographer is always the same: 'Don't clean it – keep it clean.'
- For everyday maintenance, Romney subscribes to the basics of cleaning a camera, but that's about it. 'It's a pity to do unnecessary things to a camera', Romney says. 'More lenses are destroyed by cleaning than anything else. Over-polishing a lens is an awful thing to do.'
- Romney is also worried about the mould that can attack lenses and literally eat them. To kill it, he wipes the lens with a rag dipped in a 50-50 mixture of ammonia and hydrogen peroxide.
- More cameras are thrown away because they are dirty than because they are broken, he maintains. So keep your camera clean and it will repay you with a long and effective working life.

Can openers

It's a wonder that we are not poisoned by our can openers. When you consider the mixture of substances – chicken soup, tuna fish, dog food and other debris – that congeal on the blades, a can opener's potential toxicity isn't surprising. The juices left on the blades have been shown to harbour the bacteria that cause food poisoning, skin infections, pneumonia and other ailments. To avoid trouble, always wash the blades carefully after each use.

- **Cleaning a hand-held can opener** is simple. Just wash it with the dishes, either by hand or in a dishwasher.

- **Most electric can openers** have blades or cutting assemblies designed to be removed and washed with the dishes. With older models that do not have detachable blades, carefully clean the cutting parts with a cloth dampened with water and a little washing-up liquid. Scrub away accumulated dirt with an old toothbrush. To clean the machine's body, wipe it with a clean damp cloth with the unit unplugged. Never immerse an electric can opener in water.

Candle care
If you place candles in the freezer for a couple of hours before using them, they'll burn more slowly and with less dripping. But don't freeze the entire candlestick – the cold could harm some metals.

Candlesticks & candelabra

The easiest way to clean wax from candlesticks is to wipe the wax off while the drips are still warm and soft. But this may seem overly fastidious in the midst of a dinner party.

- **To remove hardened wax** try this general-purpose method. First, remove all you can with your fingers or with assistance from a soft wooden stick – one from an ice lolly is ideal. You could also use warm water to soften the wax. Never use a knife or other metal object.

Candlesticks & candelabra

- **If there is still some left** after this, try to get the wax harder still. Wrap ice cubes in a plastic bag, then push them onto the wax to freeze it solid. When you've got it all off, polish the candlesticks with nylon material – an old pair of tights is ideal – and finish according to the sections on copper, brass or silver as relevant.

Caning

Used on antique and contemporary chairs, stools and other small pieces of furniture, caning is made of woven bamboo or reeds. Historically, caning often supported cushions, which also helped protect it, and using cushions is still a good idea.

- **To clean caning** use the brush attachment of a vacuum cleaner regularly to suck out loose dirt, or dust it with a brush such as a paintbrush. To wash dirtier caning, use a little mild detergent in water applied with a sponge, cloth or medium-stiff brush. Rinse with clear water and dry with a towel or soft cloth. Don't use harsh detergents or cleaners.

- **To prevent stains on caning** clean up any spills promptly with a wet cloth or soap and water. A stain may be impossible to remove. If you do get a serious stain, your best bet may be to paint or stain the cane.

- **To fix a sagging cane seat,** provided the material isn't broken, wet the seat thoroughly from underneath. The underside is more porous than the top and will absorb better. Then let the caning dry in the sun.

Carpeting

For routine carpet cleaning, a vacuum cleaner is the best tool; it will remove about 85 per cent of carpet dirt. But to get down to the deep dirt, you will need to give your carpeting a more thorough cleaning than a vacuum cleaner can provide. How often depends on your lifestyle, but the recommended range is every 6 to 18 months.

Three rules for carpet spills
1 Scoop up any solids and soak up any liquid that hasn't sunk in yet.
2 Then blot the spill with white towels or rags. Work from the outside in so you won't spread the stain.
3 Use water to dilute any spill that remains, and then continue to blot.

● **Vacuuming your carpeting every day** would be ideal but most people settle on once a week, even if it doesn't appear dirty. If you can, vacuum heavily trafficked areas a little more often. And be sure to vacuum up any obvious soiling before it gets ground into the carpet fibres.

The more powerful your vacuum is the better. You can use either an upright machine, which has the advantage of having a brush bar to beat more dirt up out of the carpet, or a cylinder with a power nozzle, which relies on suction alone but can come in handy if you lack the strength to push an upright, or find it awkward on stairs.

● **Persistence is essential** for effective vacuuming. You may need to have to go over a piece of carpet up to seven times to remove all the dust and dirt you'd like to.

● **Set your vacuum** for the pile level of the carpet – unless it has an automatic adjustment.

● **When you vacuum an area,** use slow, even strokes and go back and forth several times, so that you work both with and against the grain of the carpet pile. Finish with strokes that all go in the same direction. In plush carpets with pile, this will give a smooth finish, rather than just-cut lawn stripes.

● **Move light furniture** into the centre of the room before you start. The ZAP cleaning method described in Chapter 1 (see page 64) has a full explanation of this.

Carpeting

- **If you have a rug,** occasionally turn it over and vacuum the underside to prevent a build-up of dust and other allergens.

- **If your vacuum cleaner** won't suck up cat hairs, threads or other fine items, use a lint roller or a piece of doubled-over tape to pick them up.

- **New carpeting** produces a lot of extra fluff. It's normal – there is nothing to worry about.

- **Professional steam cleaning** is the ideal way to remove ground-in dirt from your carpet, and hot water extraction, or steam cleaning, done by professionals using a truck-mounted unit is probably the best. However, a good compromise is to shampoo the carpet, using a water-extraction machine. You can hire these from DIY stores. Or you can buy your own machine.

- **To use a home-cleaning** carpet shampooer, first vacuum the carpet. (You're cleaning up grease and dirt with the shampoo. Wetting dust will only slow you down, so you need to remove it.) Move furniture out of the room, or to the sides. Follow the machine instructions on filling with shampoo and water. The best machines heat the water to the correct temperature. Make sure you keep a check on this: the water must be warm, not hot, for wool-based carpets, to avoid shrinkage.

  Start in the far corner of the room, and move very slowly up and down. Move too quickly, and your machine will still lay down the wet shampoo solution, but won't have the time to suck it up. Which means your carpet will stay wet for far longer than needed. Accept that you'll have to keep stopping to empty out the dirty water, and refill with shampoo and fresh water. When you've finished, open the windows to air the room. Wait until the carpet is quite dry until putting back furniture or walking on it in shoes; wet carpet is most vulnerable to damage.

Carpeting

- **The techniques for removing spots** on carpeting are as varied as the stains themselves, so if you want advice on how to clear up a particular problem, look up what you've spilled in the index. You'll find plenty of suitable suggestions in Chapter 1 (see Everyday stains, p.30; Stain specifics, p.40), and in Chapter 3. Your approach depends in part on how much you value your carpet. If your carpet is old and beaten up, you can afford to be daring. If it's brand-new, of high quality and you want it to last for many years to come, be more cautious.

  Using the Stain Removal Pyramid described opposite will help you choose the best spot-removing strategy for your carpet spill. The broad bottom section of the pyramid includes that most gentle and universal of cleaning substances – water. The higher you go on this pyramid, the more extreme the treatment and the less of the solution you should use.

- **Before we examine each step** in the pyramid, you need to remember a few basics: stain removal usually requires tenacious blotting. Be sure to blot, not rub. Before moving on from one step in the pyramid to the next, test the next solution on an inconspicuous area of carpet. Put a little of the treatment on the carpet, let it sit for about 10 minutes, then blot with a clean white rag. Inspect the rag for any dye from the carpet, and inspect the carpet for any damage from the cleaner. If either

SIMPLE solutions

If you're unlucky enough to spill some red wine on your new beige carpet, don't be tempted to reach for the salt. You may have heard that adding salt will minimise the spread of the spill. Although this trick is suitable for red-wine spills on worktops or machine-washable tablecloths it's not right for carpets. While it will stop the spill spreading, it can also leave a residue in the carpet that you will never be able to shift. So reach for the paper towels instead and get blotting.

Carpeting

occurs, the solution isn't really a solution; it's another problem. In the case of wool, if it doesn't respond to water and the mild soap solution, you should call a professional.

Here are the techniques to try, in order, as you ascend the Stain Removal Pyramid. Use these techniques only one at a time, and rinse well between steps.

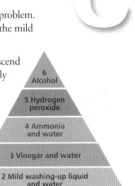

| Blot up liquid spills promptly, then dilute anything that remains with water and blot some more. You can also dilute spills with still or sparkling mineral water. The fizziness and salts it contains will sometimes help; it works better than tap water, and it's just about as safe.

2 Next, try a general-purpose spot cleaner. Mix 1 teaspoon mild washing-up liquid with 100ml warm water. Blot it on the spot. Be sure to rinse the carpet thoroughly with clean water to remove any remaining solution.

3 Mix 1 part white vinegar with 2 parts water for mildew stains and spills with a strong residual odour, such as urine.

4 Try a solution of 15ml ammonia and 50ml water on old spots, blood and chocolate.

5 Try full-strength, 3 per cent hydrogen peroxide (from chemists, sold as mouthwash) on tomato-based stains, red drinks, fruit juice, alcoholic drinks, grass stains, chocolate and coffee. Dab the solvent onto a cotton bud and press into the stain. Use a fresh bud to lift off the solvent and, you hope, the dissolved stain.

6 Use alcohol, in the form of full-strength methylated spirit, on oily stains, ballpoint-pen ink, candle-wax residue and grass stains. Use the cotton bud treatment as described in step 5.

Carpeting

- **Special situations may call** for special carpet-cleaning techniques. Your choice of method will depend on your spill.

- **For oily spills,** such as mayonnaise, salad dressing and butter, try saturating the spot with cornflour, a good absorbent. Allow it to dry, then vacuum up.

- **For candle wax dripped** onto your carpet, use a warm iron over a sheet of greaseproof paper to take up as much wax as possible. Then dab on methylated spirits. If there is still a stain, move on to the general-purpose spot cleaner described in step 2 of the Stain Removal Pyramid.

- **Pet accidents produce odours** as well as stains and the problem is compounded when urine is not detected immediately. The longer it stays, the worse it gets. First, flush the spot with water and blot with an old towel or rag. Then use the general-purpose spot treatment in step 2 of the pyramid. Rinse that with the vinegar mixture from step 4. Rinse again with water and blot. Finally, apply a 1cm thick layer of dry, clean white rags, towels, or paper towels, weight them with a heavy object, and allow them to sit for several hours. If they're still damp when you remove them, repeat with a fresh layer of absorbent materials until they come up dry. (This is also a good formula for treating spilled beer.) The odour will not come out as long as any urine remains. So you just have to keep repeating this, until you're sure you've hit success. Most commercial products sold to eliminate odour just mask the smell temporarily.

- **If a carpet has a musty smell,** bicarbonate of soda will help. If you've been removing spots from the carpet, let the carpet dry out completely first. Then sprinkle bicarbonate of soda over the entire carpet, let it sit for three to five hours, then vacuum it up.

Carpeting

- **Not all substances can be removed** from carpeting. Chlorine bleach, iodine, mustard, insecticides and plant fertilisers, to name a few, are likely to create permanent stains. Many foods, drinks, medicines and cosmetics contain dye, and their spots also may be permanent.

- **Sometimes a professional** restorer can fix a permanently damaged area by spot-dyeing, reweaving or retufting. Or a professional installer can replace a section of carpet using a scrap or a piece taken from an inconspicuous spot. As a last resort, use nail scissors to snip off the very worst of the stained pile. Then, leave a small ice cube to melt on the spot. The remaining fibres should swell a little to help plug the gap.

Carpet materials

How your carpeting responds to dirt and your efforts to eradicate it depends on the material – of both the carpet and of the dirt. Unfortunately, most people have little idea about the materials their carpets are made of, unless the carpet is wool. The majority of carpet sold in the UK is now synthetic, with polypropylene and acrylic as top choices.

- Polypropylene carpets are inexpensive and fairly stain-resistant. It is the only carpet material that sometimes accepts bleach. Its chief disadvantage is fibres that crush easily.

- Acrylic carpets are also relatively inexpensive. It is unsuitable for high-traffic areas, so bedroom carpets are often acrylic but stair and sitting room ones rarely are. And it is susceptible to pilling and fuzzing.

- Nylon carpets are tough and resistant to stains, but have a tendency to conduct static. If the carpet fibres get compressed by a heavy object they can be revived with steam.

- Blended carpets will have the characteristics of their components, but since these can react differently to stains, spot removal may be more difficult.

- Wool is durable and naturally resistant to stains and dirt. It also washes beautifully. However, wool carpets will be the most expensive.

- Sisal, hemp, jute and sea grass are all made from plants and they come in a wide variety of weaves. Plant-based materials are more likely to be found in area rugs than in wall-to-wall carpeting. These carpets will not stand up to shampooing or steam cleaning. Use as little liquid as possible when treating stains.

Cars

For most of us, cars are our second most expensive possession. We choose them to reflect our personalities and our dreams – yet, when it comes to cleaning, the rules are nearly all the same.

● **Over the metal-frame exterior** of your car is a layer of primer, then a single layer of waterborne acrylic paint with pigment, and then several layers of paint with no pigment, called clearcoat. While the clearcoat adds depth and brightness to the colour, it gives no additional protection, so total coverage is often no more than 5mm thick. That's not a lot between the metal and any corrosive elements. Or between a surface scratch taking out the entire colour.

So the idea is to boost your car's ability to cope with the elements and brush contact with other surfaces (such as prickly hedges) by regularly adding a solid protective layer of wax. Interior surfaces take a beating from the elements as well – just think how often you open the car doors when you drive on wet days – so they need regular care, too. The International Car Wash Association recommends washing your car every 10 days and waxing every 6 months. Beyond aesthetics, it's a way of protecting your investment and avoiding damage.

● **Choosing a car-washing site** is the first step. Don't wash your car under a tree, as debris, pollen, falling leaves or bird droppings will undo your good work. Direct sunlight is also an enemy. When intense heat dries the car very fast, you're more likely to be left with irritating water spots, as the heated metal of your car's bodywork dries soap into a film before you can rinse it away and your wax crusts into hard-to-wipe streaks.

Cars

- **Better choices are** a carport, a garage with good ventilation and drainage, or a shady area not directly under a tree. Another alternative is a coin-operated car-wash bay.

- **You need a good four hours** to devote to the process if you want to do a totally thorough job. Remove your watch and any belt buckle or jewellery that might scratch against the car.

- **Selecting the right cleaner** is important. Remember that washing-up liquid is strictly for dishes. Used on a car, it can do more harm than good. The detergent can thin the vehicle's protective layer of wax or, if the finish is worn, it can actually scratch or further break down the paint.

- **You'll find detergent-free car cleaners** at car-supplies shops such as Halfords. Avoid those that promise a shine, because they are likely to contain silicone, which can streak your paint and result in glare from shiny interior surfaces. Mix the cleaner according to the label instructions for the exterior and in a more dilute mix for interior surfaces (1 drop per litre).

SIMPLE solutions

When cleaning your car there are a few simple rules to follow to ensure success.
- Park the car in a shady spot – but not directly under a tree.
- Have everything ready before you start – you don't want to have to drive a soapy car to the shop because you've run out of something.
- Use a non-detergent car cleaner – washing-up liquid is for dishes.
- Use soft, clean 100 per cent cotton rags, free of any fabric softener or sizing.
- Resist the impulse to blast away dirt and grime. It's better to hose the car with a moderate stream and constant flow of water because this creates a sheeting action that gently washes away debris and cleanser without scratching.
- Don't leave the car to drip-dry as this leads to water spotting and leaves soap film. Work in sections, washing, rinsing and drying as you go.

Cars

- **Selecting cleaning rags** is a matter of personal choice, but a near-universal favourite is a piece of 100 per cent cotton towelling. Towelling is very absorbent and grows softer with use and age. It is especially good for drying. Be sure to use a really old towel; new towels contain unstable dyes and silicone for sizing, which could leave unwanted silicone streaks on your car.

- **All-cotton T-shirts** and rags are fine for interiors, but their weaves can be abrasive on your car's tender outside. And be careful when using sponges on the paint. Some, such as natural sea sponges, are notorious for hiding grit in their holes. Other options are disposable wash mitts filled with car soap, microfibre towels and chamois cloths. Chamois tends to cling, so use it only to push water across the car, not to dry. Never drag it flat across the finish – it will drag away wax.

  When you machine-wash your cleaning rags don't use fabric softener or put fabric-softener sheets in the tumble dryer. These products contain silicone, which causes streaking.

- **Using a garden hose for rinsing** makes life a lot easier. If you don't have a hose at home, you can use the wand in a coin-operated car wash. Spray in a steady, medium flow, not a high-pressure blast, which can grind dirt granules into the paint. With a continuous, moderate stream, the water flows across the car's outer surface in sheets, gently washing away sand, salt, pollen, dirt and other debris as well as soap. But the wheels are the exception – a strong blast works well to get hard-to-shift muck out of the tyres and alloys.

- **When rinsing the car,** spray in directions that water normally travels across or down the car, because that's the way it is designed to slough off water. Otherwise, you may shoot water into the vehicle's body vents and other design features where water isn't meant to go.

Car caddy
When you are ready to clean the car, you don't want to waste time looking for supplies, so it's a good idea to have all your cleaning materials to hand before you start. Keep all your car-cleaning products and cloths together in a sturdy caddy or a bucket. And remember to store all the materials in the same place when you're done.

Cars

- **Car polishes are made** with fine abrasives and are designed to lift light oxidation so you can see the true colour of the paint better. Read labels carefully. Find a polish that indicates that it is 'safe for modern car finishes'. And always apply polish onto a clean car with a cool surface.

- **Selecting a wax** is easy because a number of good brands are widely available. Liquid waxes are easiest to use. With a paste wax, it's easy to transfer grit into the original container – putting your finish at risk. Not only does wax give the paint its glossy sheen and sharpen the colour, but it also preserves the paint by helping it retain oils that reduce oxidation, the process that leads to rusting. It's also a layer between your paint and the world, a barrier to ultraviolet rays, pollutants, bird droppings, grime, insects, tar and tree sap. If you live near the coast, rust can be a particular enemy. So you may want to wax more often, possibly every three months. And if your car is red, black or white, consider waxing more often, since these colours are more susceptible to acid rain and UV rays.

  Be very careful with spray-on, wipe-off products that promise to help maintain that freshly waxed look between wax jobs. Many are alcohol-based, so they actually strip wax.

- **Clear the drain holes** early in the car-washing process. Many people are astonished to learn that cars have drain holes that need occasional attention – they are located under each bumper and at the bottom of each door panel. The rubber eyelets let out rainwater and melting snow that would otherwise leak down the outside of the bumpers, panels and windows. If the holes are plugged with any debris, moisture can get trapped inside the body and can cause your vehicle to rust from the inside. Clear the drain holes by running a cotton bud into and across the opening. When you rinse off the car, any build-up will drain out.

Cars

- **Start cleaning the car interior** by vacuuming the seats and seat crevices (use the vacuum cleaner's crevice attachment), then the floor mats and floor carpeting. If you don't have a driveway and are washing your car on the street or away from your house, you will need a cordless hand-held vacuum cleaner.

- **Cleaning the floor mats** is the next step after vacuuming. Take out the mats and, if they have carpet tops, simply vacuum. Hose down rubber mats, then fill a bucket with water and add two or three drops of all-purpose cleaner. Dip a stiff-bristled brush into the solution and scrub. After scrubbing, rinse the mats until the run-off is clear. Let them air-dry.

- **To clean the doorjambs,** open the door wide and thoroughly clean around the door opening and the edges with a soapy rag. Afterwards, take a dry exterior-use rag and wipe the inner door and sills dry. Dry all the painted surfaces, then polish and wax (see the information on waxing on page 133). By starting with the parts of the door you don't see when the doors are closed, you won't risk getting cleaner and wax on already-clean surfaces, such as your seats and carpet.

- **To clean the carpets,** scrub them with a stiff-bristled brush and use a carpet or upholstery cleaner. (You can use one intended for household cleaning here.) If you're using a wet/dry vacuum, don't be afraid to wet the carpet with a little water to loosen tough deposits of dirt before you scrub it. Then sweep up the water, loosened salt, soil and debris.

- **Unless you often have children** in your car, the seats will need only a quick once-over. With child passengers, you may want to turn to the Everyday stains and Stain specifics sections in Chapter 1 (see pages 30 and 40, respectively) to see how to remove food and drinks stains, and chewing gum.

Cars

- **Depending on the type of seats** in your car, you will be choosing between using upholstery cleaner and a soft-bristled brush (for fabric seats), vinyl cleaner and a clean rag (for vinyl-covered seats, or saddle soap and a dampened sponge (for leather interiors).

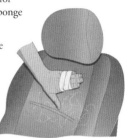

- **To remove pet hair from upholstery,** wrap wide masking or packing tape around your hand and dab over the seat with the tape.

- **For leather seats,** make sure your rag or sponge is barely damp, because too much water will damage the seats. After cleaning the leather, apply a thin, even coat of protective leather conditioner. Don't over-condition; leather needs to be able to absorb moisture from the air.

- **Cleaning door panels** is tricky because their surfaces have lots of crevices and, usually, electrical switches. After first wiping the panel with a soapy rag, dampen (don't get it sopping wet) an old toothbrush and a thin cloth, and use the toothbrush to clean out crevices. Wrap the cloth around a plastic picnic knife to clean the electrical switches, repositioning the cloth as needed to keep soft fabric over the knife edge. Remember that a just-damp cloth won't drip into switches and cause them to fail or short-circuit. You can also use the same method for dials and switches on the dashboard. Wipe dry.

- **To clean the window interiors** use a solution of 1 part white vinegar to 8 parts water, mixed in a spray bottle. Or use a non-ammonia glass cleaner. (Ammonia-based household glass cleaners and foam glass cleaners can dry out neighbouring plastic, rubber and vinyl.) You may hear hot water being recommended for cleaning glass, but when the air temperature is low, the hot liquid may cause cracking.

> **Car-window winter wonder**
> One of the worst things about winter is having to scrape a layer of ice from the windscreen when you're late for work. To wake up to a frost-free car windscreen, coat it the night before with a solution of 3 parts vinegar to 1 part water.

Cars

- **Newspaper is an old favourite** as a glass-cleaning wipe and is reputed to have a polishing effect. However, it may not be as effective as it used to be, since formulations used in printing newspapers have changed. Also, it's ridiculously messy, when a clean cloth does just as well. If you do use newspaper, be careful not to leave smudges on non-glass parts of the car. For no-streak drying, use a low-lint cloth such as an old pillowcase. Finally, roll door windows down and clean the tops, where dirt and film tend to be thickest.

- **Cleaning the dashboard,** steering column, centre console and other vinyl and plastic surfaces is the finishing touch for the interior. If they are dusty, first wipe them down with a household dusting cloth. A convenient new alternative are non-woven disposable dusting cloths. Use a small, dry natural-bristle pastry brush to dust hard-to-reach areas such as vents and dashboard corners.

- **Make up a mixture of 1 part** all-purpose household cleaner and 8 parts water in a spray bottle and spray the interior surfaces. Wipe with a clean cloth. Use a damp, cloth-covered plastic knife on dashboard dials and switches (see Cleaning door panels, page 129.) If there are any scratches on the clear plastic lenses on your dashboard, mask them by rubbing on baby oil or WD-40.

  Use a suitable silicone-free protectant to add a finishing shine to the dashboard and other non-upholstered, non-glass surfaces. This will also help to prevent your car's interior surfaces from cracking and fading.

- **Start cleaning the car's exterior** by checking the finish and trim for insects, bird droppings, asphalt and tar. Deal with these first. Use a soft dampened cloth and even a flattened finger to prise off what you can. See Chapter 1 for information on individual stain-shifter methods.

Drivetime music

If you have a cassette player in the car, swab the heads, tape guides, chrome pin and black rubber roller with some cotton buds soaked with methylated spirits. Wipe the chrome heads both vertically and horizontally. Keep cleaning until the final cotton swab comes away clean with no brown residue.

Cars

- **Washing wheels and tyres** is one activity where it's all right to blast the car with water, since it takes force to dislodge stubborn road grime. Fit a pressure-nozzle attachment to your hose, then wash out the inside of the wheel wells and give the tyres a cleaning blast. Mix detergent-free car cleaner with water in a bucket according to the packet directions. Then scrub the wheels with the solution, using a stiff-bristled brush or a rag. A soft-bristled toothbrush will let you get at places where the scrubbing brush won't fit.

- **Remember that once** you've used rags, brushes and car-wash solution on the wheels and tyres, you should not reuse these same dirty materials anywhere else on the car. They are ready for a hot machine wash – or just put them straight in the dustbin.

- **Start washing the bodywork** by using a hose to spray the car – working from the roof downwards. With the first rinse, water will flow through the newly unplugged drain holes and wash away any residue from inside the doors and body. Mix non-detergent car cleaner with water in a bucket. Apply the solution with a car-wash mitt or a soft rag. Go for a mitt that's all wool or a wool-polyester blend – 100 per cent polyester is too rough for your car's paint.

- **Never shampoo the entire car** and then rinse, because that will give the cleaner time to air-dry and leave a film. Work your way around, soaping, rinsing and drying the metal and trim in sections no larger than you can reach without moving your feet (about 1m by 60cm). Work from the roof down, making sure your rag stays free of stones, tar and debris. Don't use a mitt that has fallen on the ground.

Cars

- **Keep two buckets** of car-cleaner solution on the go at one time. Either designate one for 'rough' or especially dirt-prone surfaces and the other for smooth, less debris-laden ones or use one bucket for your first soaping (the 'dirty' bucket) and the other for a second soaping (the 'clean' bucket). Likewise, segregate your rags accordingly.

- **Wash and dry** the painted metal parts of your car very gently. There's no sense in thinning its protective wax layer or making it uneven by rubbing too hard. For gentle drying, hold a towel at both ends and drape it over the wet surface. Drag it across the surface towards you. That way, you don't apply any potentially wax-stripping pressure, as you might when rubbing with the rag in your hand. Do two rounds of drying as well, to make sure you've done a thorough job.

- **Cleaning the trim** is the next step. Spray any vinyl and plastic parts of the exterior with a solution of 1 part all-purpose household cleaner and 8 parts water. Alternatively, use a non-silicone vinyl cleaner with a matt finish and follow the instructions on the label. Clean chrome with a specialist chrome cleaner, according to label directions.

  Use fresh water to rinse completely under any mouldings and any recesses around door handles and other fixtures – hidden debris and dirt can collect there, creating a layer that can trap condensation. Trapped moisture in these areas will eventually lead to rust.

- **Cleaning window exteriors** is no different from cleaning their interiors. Just spray and wipe the glass with a vinegar solution or non-ammonia cleaner. (See Cleaning window interiors, page 129.) Use low-lint cloths for drying.

Cars

- **Once the car is clean,** unless it's brand-new or you're sure the wax layer is holding up (see the box, right), you may need to polish, wax and buff it.

- **Polishing removes surface paint** that has oxidised. Use a car polish if your paint finish appears bright, not hazy, and follow label instructions. A visible haze on the paint indicates more oxidation damage than a polish can fix and means your car could benefit from a professional re-wax.

- **Waxing can be done** with either a liquid or paste wax. Follow the label instructions to the letter. As noted earlier, it's easy to pick up grit with paste wax, so be careful how you handle the applicator. A favoured method for applying and removing wax is to use long, straight strokes that follow the same pattern that air takes as it moves around the car. This is because straight strokes don't leave behind the swirls in the finish that circular motions can. And if, by chance, you scratch the car, straight scratches are easier to remove. However, always read and follow label instructions for applying the product you're using. Again, work in sections. When your applicator or rag starts to drag as you pull it, flip it over or use a clean section. If the product instructions say to wait until the wax dries to a haze, do it – this gives the wax time to work and makes it easier to remove.

- **Keep wax away** from plastic mouldings and rubber seals and trim, from which it will be next to impossible to remove once it dries. There is no need to scrub as you apply or buff wax. The idea is to leave a good coat of wax behind. Even pressure, just using the weight of your arm, is all that's needed.

- **For buffing** use your softest rags. Do it in the same straight motions you used to wax. When your rag moves smoothly across the surface and the residue is gone, you've finished.

> ### To wax or not to wax?
> Use a bead test to find out whether you need to wax the car. Rinse the entire car with the hose and notice how the water droplets bead up on the surface of the car. Tight, rounded beads mean things are looking good. If they are more than 1cm across or if the water stays on the surface in sheets, it's time to wax.

CD players

When your CDs start skipping or the disc won't spin, there's a good chance the player's laser lens needs a quick shine. A clean machine will give a better sound, and regular maintenance will mean you won't miss a beat.

● **Cleaning the laser lens** is inexpensive and simple on top-loading players and portable units. Front-loading players and carousel units require removing the player's cover and finding the lens. Often there are too many mechanisms in the way, and extensive disassembling should be left to the professionals. In those cases, you can attempt to clean the lens with a cleaning disc, available at CD shops and on the internet.

This disc looks like a CD, but its shiny side has tiny brushes on it and as the disc spins it brushes the lens. However, the lens has to be able to 'see' before the disc can spin, so a really dusty laser lens often won't respond when a cleaning disc is inserted.

● **If your player's laser** is in plain view in a top-loading model, it's simple to clean. Before you begin, unplug the CD player from the mains, or if it's battery-powered, make sure it's off. Then do the following:

1 Locate the laser lens, which is a round glass bubble about 5mm in diameter. The slightest spec of dust can prevent the laser from 'reading' the CD.

2 Dip a cotton swab in methylated spirits and squeeze out the excess into a paper towel so it doesn't drip.

3 Using a circular motion, gently rub the lens for 5 to 10 seconds. The lens will move a little, but that's not a problem.

4 Leave it to dry; depending on how much alcohol was left on the lens, this should take 10 to 20 minutes. The CD player won't turn until it has sufficiently dried out.

Dust-free discs
To keep your CDs clean you can buy CD wipes. But if you prefer, you can use a CD cleaning cloth or just about any lint-free soft cloth, moistened with a little methylated spirits. Hold the outer edge of the CD in one hand then wipe it from the centre to the outer edge.

Ceilings

If you want to brighten up your room without redecorating, then consider cleaning the ceiling. Ceilings attract airborne dirt, cigarette smoke and grease. Cleaning them is a project that's tempting to put off, since ceilings are hard to reach and awkward to clean. Whenever possible, use long-handled tools rather than balancing on a stepladder or stool.

● **Dusting the ceiling** is sometimes all that's needed and, to do that, all you need is a long-handled duster. If you'd rather not take up storage space for an item you won't use that often, simply tie a duster onto the end of a broom. Or you can suck, rather than sweep up dust, using your vacuum cleaner with a brush attachment.

● **To clean a truly dirty ceiling** you'll have to use water. First, do a little preparation work. Lay down dust sheets or newspapers to protect furniture, electronic equipment and floors. Wear safety goggles or other eye protection, because you're likely to dislodge small particles that you can't really see from a distance. You should also wear rubber gloves, and wearing sweat bands designed for sport on your wrists will stop dirty water dripping up your arms as you work.

● **To wash the ceiling,** use a sponge mop with an extender handle (the one you use for the kitchen floor). Working upside

SIMPLE solutions

If you use liquid cleaners to clean your ceiling, there's a good chance that some of it will come dribbling down your arm onto your clothes or into your face. Wear rubber gloves and fold the ends up into cuffs, so anything that drips from your hands stays in the glove. Or if you really, really hate drips, wrap a child's thick sports' headband round your wrists twice, to catch all drips.

Ceilings

down from your usual floor cleaning isn't that natural a thing to do, so you'll have to be careful to apply even pressure and get an even distribution of the cleaning product so it won't streak.

Or you can use a dry foam sponge, and stand on a stepladder. Take care to follow basic safety rules, such as placing the ladder securely on a level surface to prevent tipping and never standing on the top step. Don't lean over too far; instead, divide the ceiling up into imaginary small squares and get off and move the stepladder each time you start on a new 'square'.

● **For painted ceilings,** whether they're covered with emulsion or gloss paint, a general-purpose cleaner, such as Flash, works well. Or use a concentrated one, like Zoflora. Mix both according to packet instructions. Dip your sponge in the solution, wring out the excess and wipe the dirty area. Rinsing is necessary only if the ceiling is heavily soiled, but whether or not you rinse, you'll need to wipe away the excess moisture with a dry towel to prevent bead marks.

● **Artex ceilings** and those that have a rough surface are best kept dry. So keep them dust free by regularly running over them with the vacuum cleaner and the soft brush attachment.

Ceramics

Handmade ceramics used only for display run the greatest risk of being damaged during handling. So use both hands when lifting and support the item from its base. Wearing a clean pair of cotton gloves makes this easier: also, the hand that is holding your object won't make it any greasier with natural dirt that is always present on hands. You should only have to dust a decorative ceramic item very occasionally.

Ceramics

- **Machine-made,** functional ceramic bowls and other pieces that do regular kitchen duty can be cleaned in the dishwasher.

- **Handmade ceramics** that are soiled should be cleaned by hand, using a soft cloth, mild washing-up liquid and water. Don't soak the item in water, which can lead to staining, especially if there are small cracks. Instead, dampen a cloth with soapy water, wipe away the dirt, rinse with a clean, damp cloth, and let the piece air-dry in a drainer to avoid the risk of it slipping through your fingers as you dry.

- **To protect decorative ceramics** on display in your home, use a dab of Blu-Tack under your item to hold it firmly, yet invisibly in place. If someone bumps into the table where it's displayed – or your pet brushes up against it – it won't go tumbling. The Blu-Tack can be easily removed, yet will hold firmly enough that you have to twist the object to remove it.

> **The light touch**
> Feather dusters are ideal for precious ceramics. They simply blow the dust off the object you're cleaning, allowing you to then vacuum or wipe the dust up – useful with delicate objects requiring minimal handling.

Ceramic tiles

Ceramic floor and wall tiles are durable and need little maintenance. An alcohol-and-water solution is usually all that's needed to keep ceramic tiles shining, assuming that they were properly sealed during installation.

- **If you're not sure** your tiles are adequately sealed, then play safe and use just a dampened sponge. Water and chemicals will easily penetrate unsealed areas. On all tiles, overly harsh cleaners will do more damage than anything else, because the wrong cleaners can strip away the sealant that protects them.

- **Clean ceramic tile floors** regularly so that tracked-in dirt isn't able to build up and scratch through the protective sealant. Begin by removing loose dirt with a vacuum cleaner, broom or

Ceramic tiles

oil-free dust mop. Then add an all-purpose floor cleaner; avoid products that contain natural waxes – you don't want to slip up later. Waxes can also penetrate the grout (the substance in the seams between the tiles) and cause it to discolour.

- **Rinse twice with clean water;** you need to remove any chemicals that could break down the sealant. When the water rinses clean, dry the floor with a clean, soft cloth.

- **Ceramic wall tiles** don't need to be cleaned as frequently as floor tiles, but it's a good idea to wipe them down once or twice a month using an all-purpose cleaner. In the bathroom, use the same cleaning product that you use on the sinks and bath. Areas such as the shower surround and the sink backsplash, which collect soap scum and spatters, may need more frequent attention, especially in a large household.

- **Cleaning the grout between tiles,** especially floor tiles, is occasionally necessary. Mix together 2 tablespoons vinegar with 3 litres water and scrub the grout with a toothbrush or nylon scrubbing pad. Don't use steel wool, because it can scratch the tile surface.

SIMPLE solutions

For really grimy grout, try a solution of chlorine bleach and water. Make sure the area you're working in is well ventilated and wear rubber gloves. Then mix together 40ml bleach and 2 litres water in a bucket. Using a toothbrush or nylon scrubbing brush, scrub the dirty areas, then let the solution soak for 10 to 20 minutes before rinsing with clean water. Rinse a second time with clean water and wipe the area dry with a fresh cloth. After the grout has dried thoroughly, apply a silicone sealer (available at DIY stores) to reduce future maintenance. Good care means your grout should look good for years, without constant renewal.

Chandeliers

It's only when they are sparkling clean that expensive, elegant chandeliers can be told apart from cheap imitations. You can buy the finest crystal in the world, but if it gets dirty, it's indistinguishable from cheap crystal. So if you are fortunate enough to have a fine example, clean it up and show it off to its full potential.

- **A chandelier should be cleaned** whenever it looks dusty, milky or cloudy. There are several methods to restore a chandelier's dazzle, depending on how dingy it has become. But if you maintain it regularly – say, a couple of times a year – you probably won't have to remove all the crystals and wash them by hand.

- **If a chandelier is not too dirty,** set up a stepladder in a spot where you can easily reach the chandelier without stretching and use one of these two methods to clean the crystals:

1 **Make sure the switch is off,** then lightly dampen a chamois cloth with a little water and wipe down each crystal while it is still attached to the chandelier frame. To clean the chandelier frame itself, wipe it with a dry cloth.

2 **The two-glove method** is also popular. Buy a pair of white cotton gloves, available in supermarkets and DIY stores, and dampen one glove with an ordinary glass cleaner. Spray the cleaner directly onto the glove – never onto the chandelier. Massage each crystal with the damp glove, then wipe it immediately with the dry glove.

- **If a chandelier is really dirty,** you'll have to take down the crystals and wash them by hand – there are no dishwasher shortcuts. Start by climbing your stepladder and removing the bulbs and setting them aside. Then carefully remove the

> **Crystal clear**
> Before you remove chandelier crystals for washing, make sure you know how to put the chandelier back together again. Either use the diagram that came with the chandelier or take a photo or do a drawing of the chandelier before taking it apart.

Chandeliers

crystals. Run warm water in a bowl until it's about a quarter full. Add 2 tablespoons white vinegar and 1 drop washing-up liquid. The combination will remove any grease or residue on the glass but will minimise the amount of suds created, which are hard to rinse off.

- **Place a folded towel** in the bottom of the sink – you don't want to break a crystal if it slips through your grasp. Wipe each crystal with your hands, then individually rinse each one under running water and dry with a soft cloth. If you don't dry them properly you'll end up with unsightly water spots.

- **Finally, wipe the light bulbs** with a damp sponge and dry them with a cloth. Only return them to their sockets once you are sure that they're completely dry – and enjoy the light show.

Chimneys

Where there's fire, there's smoke – and when it's in your fireplace, you'll eventually have a chimney that needs a clean sweep. Sooty chimneys can lead to chimney fires, which occur when creosote, a highly combustible residue created by burning wood, is ignited by rising sparks. The resulting flames burn many times hotter than the wood in your fireplace and could set your house on fire.

- **To prevent such disasters,** you should have your chimney cleaned regularly by a professional chimney sweep (find one using Yellow Pages or go to <www.yell.com>). Cleaning chimneys is difficult, dangerous work that requires special brushes and equipment tailored to fit the precise measurements of your fireplace flue. However, you can and should clean out the ashes in your fireplace when they start piling up.

Chimneys

- **Shovel the ashes** into a metal container with a tight lid – never use a paper bag – and store it away from any combustible materials (including a wooden deck) before final disposal. There's no need to shovel up every last ash, except when you're doing a clear-up after the last fire of winter. Get the very last ashes up by just damping your shovel, so that they stick onto it.

- **We would not recommend** that you ever try to inspect a chimney yourself. Being on the roof is best left to experts.

- **To cut down on creosote build-up,** burn wood that's been dried for six months to a year. Freshly cut wood has a higher moisture content than seasoned wood, which results in a smokier fire. Hardwoods such as oak, maple, elm and ash burn more slowly and with a steadier flame than softwoods such as spruce and pine, which cause faster creosote build-up.

China

The term 'fine china' evokes images of fragile delicacy, but most china manufactured today is made to be functional as well as elegant. So most china made in the past 25 years is dishwasher safe and says so explicitly on the bottom of the piece.

- **A notable exception** is fine china with a band made of a precious metal such as platinum or gold. Although you'll probably have few problems, one day the high heat of the dishwasher's drying cycle could cause the metal to soften and small pieces might become dislodged. Hand-washing is also necessary for antique or hand-painted china. The force and heat of the dishwasher is too much for fragile pieces.

China

- **Washing your best china** in the dishwasher does require a little extra care. Load the pieces into the machine carefully so they won't bump into each other and chip. Make sure aluminium utensils and lightweight foil containers that are also in the machine don't rub against dishes during the wash cycle, because that can create black or grey marks.

- **To hand-wash antique** or hand-painted china, start by lining the bottom of your sink with a rubber mat or folded towel. Half-fill the sink with warm water and stir in a few drops of mild washing-up liquid. To prevent china pieces knocking against each other and chipping, take care not to overload the sink. Remove any rings and jewellery to prevent scratching the china and, for the same reason, wash cutlery separately. Use a soft cloth or sponge for cleaning.

- **Wash or soak the items** as soon after dining as possible, to prevent the problem of dried-on food and staining. Acidic foods such as mayonnaise and eggs can damage the glaze if left to dry on the surface for long periods.

- **To remove dried food,** soak the china in a bowl of sudsy water, then scrub gently with a nylon scouring pad. Never use a metal pad, and avoid steel wool and gritty cleansers as well.

- **Be careful when placing the dishes** to dry to prevent scratches and chips. Using a drying rack means that two pieces don't have to touch each other.

- **Wash china figurines** and sculptures by hand using water with just a few drops of washing-up liquid. Hand-dry with a soft cloth. If the piece has a wooden base, don't let the wood get wet.

Water marks
Hard water can cause a film on china. To remove it, place a bowl filled with 150ml of chlorine bleach in the lower rack of the dishwasher. Load your china and run the washer up to the dry cycle, then turn it off. Empty and rinse the bowl, then add 300ml of white vinegar, and return it to the dishwasher. Turn the dishwasher back on and let it run through the rest of the cycle.

Christmas decorations

Good storage is the key here – 11 months is a long time for paper, plastics, metal and glass to sit in a box. If your storage room is damp, many won't survive. So when you put your decorations away each year, give careful thought to where everything is going to go. The attic is fine, if it's dry. Ideally, you should not put anything away dirty, but if you're pressed for time, concentrate on providing secure, safe storage.

- **To clean painted ornaments,** separate them so you can pick them up one at a time by their hangers. Lightly dust each ornament with a feather duster. Try not to handle the ornaments, since the oils in your hands can damage the paint. If you need to touch the ornament, wear rubber gloves (a must if your ornament is old and fragile).

- **To clean glass ornaments,** spray ordinary glass cleaner onto a soft cloth and wipe gently.

- **To clean porcelain or crystal ornaments,** use a feather duster, brushing across the surface in a downward motion. Don't handle crystal decorations unless you are wearing gloves. A buffing jewellery cloth is also fine for use on crystal. Simply wipe over the surface of the ornament with the cloth.

- **To clean resin and wood ornaments,** a soft cotton cloth works well. Again, just wipe across the surface of each piece.

- **Sterling-silver and gold-plated ornaments** will come clean when wiped with a jewellery polishing cloth. When you use the cloth, wipe in circular motions to remove dust, grime and fingerprints.

- **Cleaning glittery ornaments** is a tricky business. Try using a feather duster on one area. If a lot of glitter comes off, it may be best to leave the decoration alone.

Christmas decorations

- **To clean leaf garlands** use a hairdryer on a low setting to get dust out of wicker rings. They may fall apart if you try the more usual method of giving them a shake.

- **Storing your clean ornaments** properly will ensure they will be sparkling, dust-free and ready to hang the next year.

- **Store ornaments in a box** that is large enough to be useful, but not so big that it becomes too heavy to carry safely.

- **Place a thick layer** of scrunched-up tissue paper (use only acid-free paper) in the bottom of the box and wrap each ornament individually with one layer of tissue.

- **Put the more sturdy ornaments** on the bottom of the box and the delicate ones on top. Don't use more than two layers. Try to offset the top layer so that they don't sit directly on top of ornaments below. Don't pack the ornaments tightly, because they may break.

- **Lay a full layer of ornaments** on top of the scrunched-up tissue paper. Then lay one or two layers of flat tissue paper on top of the first layer of ornaments. Place a new layer of wrapped ornaments on top of the tissue paper over the previous layer.

Festive flags
If you have any decorative banners or bunting find out what fabric they are made of before cleaning. Nylon or polyester ones are usually safe to wash on a gentle cycle with a mild detergent; line-dry. Dry-clean cotton ones because their colours are likely to bleed if washed. Always dry-clean woollen banners or bunting.

Chrome

Chrome is usually plated onto another metal, so be gentle when you clean it or you can scrub it right off. And don't get abrasive with chrome. Cleaners with 'scratch' in them can indelibly spoil the surface.

- **When cleaning chrome** cookware remember never to wash items in greasy dish water. If you do, the next time the items get hot during cooking, the grease is likely to burn on. To begin with, use washing-up liquid in warm water, applied with an old toothbrush to work into cracks and crevices. Rinse with water and polish to a shine with a soft cloth.

If that doesn't do the trick, use bicarbonate of soda sprinkled onto a damp sponge or cloth. Let it sit on the chrome for an hour, then rinse with warm water. Then dry it off and buff to a shine with another cloth. Or rub down chrome with undiluted cider vinegar or white vinegar – no need to rinse. Ammonia can also be used – but rinse it off with water and dry completely.

- **Chrome oven rings** often get grimy. To shine them up, rub with a paste made from vinegar and cream of tartar.

- **Rub a chrome surface** with half a lemon dipped lightly in salt. Or use white vinegar and salt on a soft cloth. Rinse well with water and buff with a dry cloth or paper towel.

- **For chrome trim** on taps and kitchen appliances, apply baby oil with a soft cloth and polish to restore lustre. If hard water has left deposits on taps, use a product that removes limescale.

Clocks

The most important aspect of cleaning a mantelpiece, wall, grandfather or other mechanical clock is careful maintenance of the internal mechanism to prevent wear and tear.

- **It's best to entrust your clock** to an expert to have its inner workings cleaned and oiled. Clocks are too easy to damage if you do it yourself. Get the mechanism serviced every two to three years.

- **Cleaning and oiling** the interior of a clock is possible if you're careful. The first step is to wipe the inner workings with a dry, soft cloth to get rid of the worst of the dust and grime. Then apply special clock oil, which you can obtain

Clocks

at clock shops; it typically comes with a pen-like applicator. Don't be tempted to use WD-40 since it wears the mechanism out even faster, attracting dirt rather than repelling it. If you do clean and oil the clock yourself, use a clamp to hold down springs and other movable parts and don't put too much oil on the gears and the plate.

- **Clean the exterior of a wooden clock** with a furniture oil. To dust a clock case, use a dust remover, such as Lemon Pledge, sprayed onto a soft cloth, not on the clock itself.

- **Wipe whatever covers the face** with a clean, soft cloth. If this is glass, you can use a window cleaner sprayed onto a cloth – never spray it directly on the clock as excess liquid could get in.

Coffee grinders

When you clean out an electric coffee grinder, don't immerse it in water or this might ruin the workings.

- **Clean a coffee grinder** after every use. Unplug and then brush out with a pastry brush or old toothbrush. This doesn't have to be a big job – just make sure you leave the stainless steel inside the grinder shiny, so that tomorrow's batch of beans won't be sullied by stale grounds from yesterday's pot. Wash the plastic lid with a sponge in washing-up liquid and warm water; rinse and dry with a soft cloth.

- **Alternatively, dampen a paper towel** and use to swab the inside of the grinder clean.

- **You can also run** a spoonful of uncooked white rice through the grinder, especially if you use it for grinding anything other than coffee. Most coffee experts advise against grinding spices in your machine since the smells are nearly impossible to get out.

Coffee makers

The harder your local water, the more deposits it will form on the inside of your coffee maker. To keep your coffee maker in working order, clean it at least once a month – if you use the maker every day – to rid it of this whitish scale, or every two months if you brew a pot less often.

- **Failing to clean your coffee maker's** inner workings will lengthen heating and brewing time and will adversely affect the taste and aroma of your cup of coffee. Always check your owner's manual before embarking on any of the following cleaning methods. But in general, no electric coffee maker should be immersed in water.

- **To clean an electric drip coffee maker,** fill the water reservoir with half cold water and half white vinegar. Place a clean paper filter in the basket. Run the coffee maker through its entire cycle. Repeat the brewing cycle two more times, using plain water each time to flush out the remaining grains.

- **Alternatively, fill the reservoir** with hot water and add a denture-cleaning tablet. Run the machine through its complete brewing cycle, then run it once more using plain water.

Expert **ADVICE**

Coffee expert Chris Gimbl suggests making your own coffee-maker cleaner with lemon juice instead of white vinegar because the smell is more pleasant.
- Fill the reservoir half full with water, then to the top with pulp-free lemon juice. Use a ready-to-use juice, such as Jif Lemon, to save time.
- Run the coffee maker through its entire cycle. Discard the solution that collects in the coffee pot, then run the brew cycle two or three more times with plain water until you don't smell lemon anymore. Wash all removable parts of the machine in hot, sudsy water, then rinse and dry.

Coffee makers

- **Wash the coffee pot in hot water** with washing-up liquid and rinse with clean water. Then take out any other removable parts and do the same. You can wash these pieces in the top rack of the dishwasher, but their colours may fade. If you do wash them, buff with a soft, dry cloth.

- **Cleaning a home espresso machine** mainly involves keeping the steam wand and froth head clear. Get into the habit of turning off the machine, removing the froth head, then rinsing it under warm water every time you use your machine. Wipe the steam wand with a damp cloth. Turn the power back on and set the selector control to the steam position briefly. The shot of heat will clear any milk remaining in the steam wand. Every so often, run water through the unit with the filter in place, but with no coffee. If the filter holes do get blocked, use a nylon washing-up brush to dislodge tiny, stuck pieces of coffee.

Coffee spills
Resist scrubbing coffee stains with soap – this makes tannin stains harder to remove. For advice on cleaning up coffee spills look under Tannin stains in Chapter 1 (see page 35).

Combs

To clean a comb, first remove any hair still clinging to the teeth. Then disinfect it in a bowl of warm water with a generous dollop of medicated shampoo. Rinse in clear water. If you want something more potent, add one cup of Dettol or a similar disinfectant, to a basin of warm water.

- **Submerge the comb** in the liquid and leave it to soak for around 10 minutes. Using a small, stiff-bristled fingernail brush or old toothbrush, scrub the comb to loosen up hair oils and grime that might be clinging to the teeth. If you're still concerned, the best way to disinfect it is to rub the teeth with a cotton ball saturated in neat Dettol (wear gloves to do this). Air-dry, then rinse thoroughly before using.

Combs

- **To clean a baby's comb,** simply wash it in the baby's bath water. Alternatively, swish it in a solution of 1 teaspoon bicarbonate of soda dissolved in a basin of warm water. Rinse with fresh water and air-dry.

- **To clean a fine-toothed metal comb** used to rid a child's hair of lice and their nits or eggs, you need to take extra care.
  Soak the comb in a solution of 1 part chlorine bleach to 9 parts water for 15 minutes, rinse and air-dry. (If you don't dry it thoroughly, a metal comb will rust.) You can also soak combs in hot water (at least 60°C) for 5 minutes. Alternatively, seal combs in a plastic bag for two weeks.

Compact grills

Although the grills named after boxer George Foreman are the best known, there are several makes of compact grills – but the cleaning methods apply to all of them. Make sure the unit is unplugged before you start. The grilling surface needs the most thorough cleaning and it's easiest to do when still slightly warm, before food particles harden.

- **If the grilling surface** is not removable, don't immerse the unit in water. (Some compact grills have parts that can be safely cleaned in the dishwasher.) Use the plastic cleaning spatula that comes with your unit to scrape off charred food particles from the grilling surface and into the drip tray. Once you have dispensed with the larger bits of food, wipe the ribbed grilling surface with a paper towel to take off any major grease. You can then dispose of this in the rubbish bin. If you use a sponge, the grease is more likely to end up down the sink resulting in a possible blockage. Next, take a damp sponge or cloth – not a

Compact grills

wet one. To tackle especially sticky stuff, put a little washing-up liquid on the sponge. Rinse the sponge frequently, since it will get grimy quickly. Follow the sponging step with a few swipes of a damp cloth – again not a wet one – to get rid of as much moisture as possible. Then deal with the plastic drip tray. Again, remove any serious grease with paper towels, then use washing-up liquid and a wet sponge.

- **To clean the outside** of an electric grill, first remove the grilling surface (if you can) and leave it out while you clean the other surfaces. Wiping the exterior with a damp sponge takes care of most grease splatters. As an alternative, use a waterless hand cleaner such as Dettox. First, clean up surface dirt with dry paper towels, then apply a little hand cleaner to a clean paper towel, and rub the exterior in small circular motions.

- **Let the cleaned grill air-dry** or, if you need to accelerate the drying process, use a hair dryer on a low setting. Make sure the grill is perfectly dry before you plug it in again.

Computers

Computers are a magnet for all sorts of dirt and the keyboards can collect a wide range of detritus – tea splatters, biscuit crumbs and stray hairs.

- **A computer can be given a once-over** with a vacuum or dust cloth as part of your regular cleaning procedure. But it's a good idea to give it a more thorough cleaning occasionally. Once every three months is sufficient, although you should clean the screen every month or so. First, turn off and unplug.

- **To clean the screen** of a traditional tube monitor, dust it with a clean cloth or a facial tissue. To remove fingerprints,

Computers

wipe with a slightly damp cloth. Special wipes for cleaning PCs, sold at office supply stores, may be used on the screen, but they sometimes leave a soapy film. Try a glass cleaner instead, sprayed very, very lightly on a cloth and then wiped on the screen. Avoid ammonia-based cleaners, because they may leave unsightly streaks.

● **To clean a new flat screen monitor,** you need to use special care as the screen is less robust and can scratch easily. This also applies to the screen on a laptop. First unplug the power supply, then lightly dampen a clean, soft, lint-free cloth (no paper towels or facial tissues) with water. Wipe the screen gently with a back-and-forth motion, never in a circle. Wipe the display case gently with a non-abrasive, soft, dry cloth to pick up dust. And take these precautions to prolong the life of your flat screen – never tap or touch the screen with your pen, finger or other object. And don't put sticky notes on your screen.

● **To clean the keyboard,** which is a magnet for all sorts of dirt, first turn it upside down over a waste-paper basket and give it a good shake. Most crumbs and dust will fall right out. Then vacuum it with your brush attachment. To clean the keys, rub them and the surrounding plastic with a microfibre cloth. Or purchase a special keyboard cleaner-degreaser, sold at electronics stores.

● **Using a can of compressed air,** available at camera shops, blast away hair, crumbs and dust from between the keys. Rubbing keys with a fabric-softener sheet will also keep dust-attracting static at bay.

● **To clean the mouse,** unscrew the mouse-ball cover on the bottom and take out the ball. Wipe it down with methylated spirits, available at paint stores, on a soft cloth. Remove any

> **Computer care**
> If you have a new flat LCD monitor – or a laptop – never use products containing acetone, ethyl alcohol, ethyl acid, ammonia, toluene or methyl chloride to clean the screen. They can damage it.

Computers

dust or fluff inside the mouse-ball socket with your finger. Then, with a cotton bud dipped in methylated spirits, clean the three rollers the ball touches inside the socket.

● **To clean inside the computer,** you can also use compressed air. But be aware – opening up your computer could invalidate your warranty. Follow manufacturer's instructions to open it up and keep your fingers away from cards, cords and other parts. And be sure the compressed-air wand is at least 12cm from the machine. Blow air into the power supply box (that is where the power cord enters) and the fan at the back of the case. Then blast a little air into the CD and floppy disk drives.

● **To clean computer equipment exteriors,** simply wipe the outside surfaces with an all-purpose cleaner, sprayed on a soft cloth. Dust can collect in ports where you attach cables. Use the compressed-air wand to blow the ports clean. Or give them a wipe with one end of a cotton bud.

● **To clean the printer,** open the case and use compressed air to blow away any dust. If you spot a toner spill in a laser printer, don't use compressed air, because toner can be toxic. Instead, wipe it up carefully with paper towels. Avoid getting toner on your hands or clothes because it's hard to remove.

● **To clean the glass bed of your scanner,** use mild soap or an ordinary glass cleaner without ammonia. (Ammonia cleaners, unless they're completely wiped off, leave a film that could make scanned documents look oily or speckled.) Spray the glass cleaner onto a soft cloth, not on the glass itself. If there's a metal ruler scale along the edge of the glass, avoid getting it wet. Never use paper towels on your scanner – they can make fine scratches on optical surfaces. Use soft, lint-free cloths instead – an old T-shirt is perfect.

Old technology

If you still use a typewriter, then it's worth keeping it clean – it may be an antique some day! So dust it regularly using the upholstery attachment of your vacuum cleaner. Alternatively, use a can of compressed air to blow the dust out. You can also brush carefully between the keys using a small, dry paintbrush.

Concrete

Your first step is to work out what caused the stain and then act swiftly and appropriately. The longer an untreated stain stays on concrete, the more likely it is to seep in and become part of the whole. Methods for cleaning concrete vary, but cleaning up the garage floor, patio, walkway, driveway or other concrete is an essential part of regular home maintenance.

- **Clean concrete at least once a year.** Protect adjacent glass, metal, wood, plants or other decorative materials with a tarpaulin or large piece of old plastic. Test the method in an obscure spot to make sure it works. Never use a metallic brush on concrete, as metallic fibres can get trapped and rust.

- **If concrete is old and crumbly,** brush it lightly with a soft brush. If that doesn't work, move on to warm water and mild detergent, adding white vinegar to the water if soil and stains persist.

  Wet the concrete with the water and scrub with a soft, non-metallic brush. Wash off the concrete with a garden hose fitted with a high-pressure nozzle and let it dry.

- **If that doesn't work,** add a measure of non-biological washing powder to a bucket of warm water and scrub again.

- **Or add a measure of biological detergent** to a bucket of warm water and 20ml of ammonia, and apply it to the concrete with a stiff nylon brush.

- **Rent a pressure-washing machine** to squirt off dirt that's not ground into the concrete.

- **To remove fresh grease stains,** first sprinkle dry cement, cat litter or sand on the spot, letting it sit for an hour to absorb at least some of the grease. Then sweep it up with a broom and dustpan. For more difficult grease spots, use a commercial degreaser and follow label instructions.

Contact lenses

You should always follow your optician's advice on cleaning contact lenses. Most suggest that you don't casually switch between solutions, but stick to those recommended on your last appointment. If you wear disposables, you can skip this section of course – you will simply throw lenses out at night and reach for a new pair the next day. But if you wear soft fortnightly, monthly or longer-wear lenses, cleaning is crucial. Here are a few basic guidelines:

- **Clean and disinfect your lenses** once a day. Always use fresh solution to clean and store your lenses.

- **Always wash and rinse your hands** thoroughly before handling the lenses. This is especially important if you've been eating spicy foods with your fingers. Dry your hands with a clean, lint-free towel.

- **Don't use perfumed soaps** or scented moisturising cream on your hands before handling the lenses.

- **Put in the plug in your sink,** or at least cover the plughole with a flannel when putting them in. A dropped lens can easily slip down the plughole.

- **Never use water as a substitute** for the store-bought lens-care system that your eye-care expert recommends. Water can carry a micro-organism (*Acanthamoeba*) that can cause serious eye infections.

- **Clean your accessories** (lens case, cleaning/disinfecting containers, vials for enzymatic cleaners and the like) after each use, exactly as the directions advise. Typically, this involves cleaning, rinsing and air-drying.

- **Throw out your lenses once a month** or as often as is recommended, to reduce the chance of infection.

Contact lenses

- **Get into the habit** of always handling your right lens first to avoid confusion. Most modern solutions are now so streamlined that all you have to do is put your lenses in the case, pour in the solution, then open up the next day. So no rubbing or exact timing is required.

- **Soft lenses will pick up protein** deposits more readily than gas-permeable types do. If your lenses start to feel grainy or your vision becomes at all clouded, the chances are you will need to use an enzymatic cleaner daily or weekly, according to packet directions.

- **Some people have allergic reactions** to contact lens solutions. About 10 per cent of people are allergic to thimerosal, a preservative sometimes used in saline lens solutions. If you hit a problem with one solution, ask your optician to recommend another.

Cooler boxes

Ideally, you should clean your cooler box after each use. The method for cleaning depends a lot on what you've had in it. If you've just kept some canned drinks on ice in it, then simply rinse it out with water. But if you've had a full picnic, with meat and other foodstuffs, you're going to have to do a thorough clean.

- **To clean a large, rigid plastic cooler** pour a couple of drops of washing-up liquid onto a sponge, then clean thoroughly. Swish out with clean water, then turn the cooler upside down so that the water drains out quickly.

- **To disinfect a cooler box** – if you've been carrying raw meat in it, for example – mix 5ml bleach in a litre of water.

Cooler boxes

Apply the solution to the cooler with a sponge or rag or pour it into a spray bottle, squirt it on and wipe clean. Then rinse with fresh water. Once your cooler box is clean, let it air-dry with the lid open before you store it.

- **To remove stubborn food stains** left in your cooler box, first make a paste by mixing bicarbonate of soda and water in a bowl. Dip a clean rag or sponge into the paste and rub it on the spot you want to remove; rinse. If that doesn't work, apply a non-abrasive household cleaner and rub with a rag before rinsing. However, don't be tempted to use an abrasive cleaner. This type of product could scratch the interior surface of your cooler, giving dirt and bacteria a place to hide – and making your cleaning job harder.

- **To clean a soft-structure cooler box,** mix a little mild washing-up liquid into a bucket of water and wipe the cooler down inside and out with a clean rag or sponge. Rinse and air-dry. Don't put it in the washing machine and don't use bleach on this type of cooler.

SIMPLE solutions

Like cooler boxes, Thermos flasks need cleaning after each use, too. Use hot, soapy water and scrub them with a bottle brush, if possible. Rinse well and air-dry. Try not to get water between the outer casing and the inner insulating flask.

- For stubborn or hard-to-reach stains, fill the Thermos with hot water, drop in two denture-cleaning tablets and leave to stand overnight. In the morning, rinse the Thermos with clean water and leave to air-dry.

- If your Thermos has developed an unpleasant odour that regular washing will not overcome, pour in a few tablespoons of vinegar or bicarbonate of soda. Fill the Thermos the rest of the way with hot water and let it sit for half an hour. Then pour the solution out and rinse.

Copper

Although copper is harder than silver, it's still softer than either brass or bronze. For cleaning purposes, it comes in two varieties – lacquered and unlacquered. Lacquered copper – usually decorative items – has a finish baked on at the factory. Unlacquered copper – mostly cookware – tarnishes easily but will brighten with elbow grease and the right techniques.

- **To clean a copper item** with a lacquered finish, you only need to dust it as part of your regular cleaning process. If it's dirty, you might want to wipe it with a damp cloth. If cracks appear in the lacquered finish of a piece, it must be stripped of its coating with acetone or paint thinner, applied full strength with a cloth. Or boil the item in a large saucepan or preserving pan, using 4 litres water and 100ml soda crystals. The lacquer should peel off. Wash with dishwashing detergent, rinse with running water and dry with a soft cloth. If you want the piece lacquered again, get it done by a professional.

- **Never use any scratchy cleaning tool** on copper cookware. You run the risk of leaving marks. And bleach will seriously discolour copper if it stands for a few hours or more.

- **Sprinkle the piece with salt** and a little white vinegar and rub gently. Alternatively, cut a lemon in half, dip it in salt and rub. And if the piece can stand the heat, boil it in a large pan filled with water, 100ml white vinegar and 50g salt.

- **Whatever method you use,** always rinse with fresh water, dry well with a tea towel and buff with a soft cloth. If you want more shine, apply a commercial copper cleaner according to label directions.

- **Crevices can be tough to clean** and can be magnets for paste-polish build-up. Use a cotton bud or natural horsehair brush and methylated spirits to banish the grime.

Shiny isn't always best

While shiny copper saucepans look wonderful on display in your kitchen, there's a school of thought that says that it's the dull copper-bottomed pans that transfer heat more swiftly to the foods inside. So if you want a reason to skimp on the cleaning, this is it.

Cork

When cleaning a floor covered with cork tiles, be sparing with whatever liquid you use. Most cork floors are sealed with polyurethane to prevent them from soaking up spills and stains. But as the seal starts to wear away, excess water can find its way into the seams between the tiles, weakening the glue and causing the edges to lift.

- **When cleaning a cork floor,** keep it dry if you can, by sweeping up loose dirt with a broom and dustpan first. If it's still dirty, use a just-damp mop that has been dipped in a bowl of sudsy washing-up liquid and water, and then wrung out very thoroughly. Towel the floor dry – if it's easier, wrap a towel around your broom to do this. Every year, use a specialist liquid wax to maintain the cork floor's waterproof qualities. Heavily trafficked areas of floor – the hall and kitchen, for instance – should be coated with polyurethane every two to three years. It's best to get an expert to carry out this task and the cork floors must first be scrubbed over with a special pad to roughen up any old sealant.

- **To clean cork walls,** which usually aren't sealed, rub them with putty-style wallpaper cleaner or a dry foam-rubber sponge, available at hardware and paint stores. Any spots or stains on the cork may be carefully hand-sanded with fine-gauge (0000) sandpaper to remove them. Cork on walls is usually only 3mm thick, so be careful not to turn your cork into an unsightly patchwork by over-rubbing.

- **To clean a cork or cork-backed item,** such as a coaster, a trivet or a mat, wet it first with cold water, then scrub the surface with a pumice stone or pad. Rinse with water and air-dry in a cool, dry place.

Cork tips

You can use bread to clean up your cork. Tear off a hunk from a stale loaf of bread and then use it to scrub gently over stained cork. It will clean the cork without damaging it. An alternative is to wrap some light masking tape around your hand, sticky side out, then pat it on grimy spots to lift out dirt.

Crystal

Never put crystal in the dishwasher. Crystal is too fragile and soft for the dual action of dishwasher and detergent, which can etch and dull its surface. To preserve the special sparkle of crystal, always hand-wash it in sudsy washing-up water – unless it has silver or gold gilt, in which case you should use only plain, warm water.

- **To wash crystal,** line the bottom of the sink with a doubled-up towel and fill the sink with warm water – not hot – and add two or three drops of washing-up liquid. Wash one item at a time. Grasp glasses by the bowl, not the stem, and wash gently. Pump the glass up and down in warm water to rinse. Dry upside down on a lint-free cotton towel or plastic dish rack. Better yet, put clean thick gloves or cotton socks over your hands and dry the crystal immediately with an old linen towel. This way, you'll leave no fingerprints or watermarks.

- **To remove stains, first mix a paste** of lemon juice and baking powder and rub gently on the crystal with a sponge, then wash and dry. Baking powder is about as abrasive as you can get with crystal without risking damage: bicarbonate of soda, which is coarser, is too much.

- **You can use rice to clean** off tougher stains. Place 2 teaspoons of uncooked rice into the crystal piece, add water and swirl. Repeat, if need be.

- **For stubborn stains,** fill the crystal receptacle with warm water and drop in a denture-cleaning tablet. Leave for a few minutes, then wipe and rinse.

- **For extra shine,** add a few drops of white vinegar or lemon juice to the water you use for rinsing.

- **To clean the grooves of cut crystal,** dip a frayed toothbrush into vinegar, lemon juice or soapy water and rub.

Curlers

To wash curlers that are submersible in water – plain rollers, Velcro rollers and foam-coated wire sticks – fill your bathroom sink with warm water, mix in a couple of teaspoons of shampoo or facial cleanser to create suds and let them soak.

- **As a general rule,** if a cleaner is gentle enough for your face or hair, it is fine for your curlers. Use a wide-toothed comb to gently pull out any hair stuck in the curlers. Then wipe with a rag to remove caked-on film. Rinse with fresh water and either dry immediately with a clean towel or air-dry.

- **For stubborn stains,** add 1 tablespoon liquid fabric softener to around 50ml water. Use a soft brush – a nail brush is ideal – to scrub the curlers. Rinse with water and dry.

- **To clean electric curlers,** which are not submersible, use a rag or soft, nylon bristled brush and the fabric-softener solution described above. Rinse by wiping with a damp rag, then dry.

Curling irons & straighteners

Cleaning curling irons and straighteners can be difficult. You must remove the crust of singed hair and hair-styling product that builds up over time. But because they are electrical appliances, you can't soak them in water. And you should not use toxic chemical cleaners, since they can leave chemical residue in your hair.

- **Instead, use cotton buds** dipped in a solution of fabric softener (15ml fabric softener to 50ml water) to dissolve the gunge. Clearly, only do this when your appliance is switched off and has grown cold. Wipe clean with a damp rag, then with another dry one.

Curtains

Dust your curtains once a month or so as part of a regular household clean. Use the upholstery tool on the vacuum cleaner or a feather duster.

- **Clean your curtains** about once a year. First, look for the manufacturer's cleaning recommendations, which should be on a tag sewn inside the hem – or if they are homemade, make sure you keep the cleaning instructions that come with your fabric. Depending on the material, you will either machine-wash, hand-wash or dry-clean.

- **If curtains can be machine-washed,** use the delicate cycle. Curtains are continually exposed to the sun and this can break down the fibres in the fabric. Consequently, the minute you wash them, they may begin to deteriorate.

- **You must also be gentle** if drying curtains in a machine. Take them out very promptly to reduce wrinkling. An alternative to tumbling curtains until they are dry is to remove them from the dryer and hang them while they are still damp. This will reduce wrinkling and may help you avoid having to iron your curtains.

> **Dusty drapes**
> To keep your curtains free of dust, vacuum them where they hang, with the upholstery attachment. Start at the top and work down. To avoid sucking up the fabric into the nozzle, grasp the bottom of each curtain and hold it taut. Always clean matching pelmets at the same time.

Cushions

Dust mites, which can trigger allergies, often lurk inside scatter cushions or sofa cushions. By removing the dust regularly, you not only keep your cushions looking fresh (and keep the dust from staining them once it is ground in or moistened), but you also improve the quality of the air in your home.

- **To remove dust** clean cushions about once a month using a vacuum cleaner with the appropriate attachments, such as an upholstery brush and a crevice tool.

Cushions

- **To be more thorough** or to remove stains, wash your cushions. Unless you have machine-washable cushions, you should do this in situ, without taking out the pad. First, check any manufacturer's cleaning suggestions; these will tell you whether you should use a water-based shampoo, a dry-cleaning solvent or neither of the two. Next, pick an inconspicuous spot on the cushion and pre-test whatever cleaning technique is recommended. If there is shrinking or bleeding or running of colours, contact a professional cleaner. If not, proceed.

- **Even if you can use shampoo,** use as little moisture as possible. You do not want to wet the stuffing, because it dries very slowly and can make conditions even more suitable for dust mites. The trick is to clean using suds only.

- **You can use a foaming** carpet shampoo in an aerosol can. Follow the directions on the can, which typically tell you to allow the foam to stand until dry and then vacuum it off.

- **To make your own shampoo,** mix a squirt of washing-up liquid with a litre of warm water. Make suds by squeezing a sponge in the solution. Scoop the suds off and apply sparingly with a sponge to the cushion. Rub gently in the direction of the fabric's grain. Work on a small area at a time, lightly rinsing each area as you go with a clean, damp sponge. Again, avoid soaking the fabric. Be sure to remove all the suds, or the residue will cause the fabric to soil faster.

- **If the fabric is dry-clean only** and you only want to clean a stain, you can do it yourself, using a commercial dry-cleaning solvent. Moisten a clean white cloth with the solvent and use the cloth to draw the stain out. Blot repeatedly – never rub. Always use solvents sparingly and in a well-ventilated area. But if you need to clean the entire surface of a dry-clean-only cushion, have it professionally cleaned.

Cutlery

Rinse knives, forks and spoons under running water immediately after eating. You may not want to actually wash up if, say, you're entertaining, but rinsing will remove food that might cause pitting or staining.

- **Be especially diligent** about the remains of eggs, fruit juices, tomatoey foods, lemon, vinegar, salty foods (including butter), mustard and salad dressings. Silver is most vulnerable to damage, but stainless steel, despite its name, isn't completely immune to the threat of corrosion. It's fine to soak both totally stainless steel and silver in a sink full of warm water but don't soak hollow-handled utensils for long, lest it loosens the soldering that holds the handle in place.

- **Wash cutlery in the dishwasher** along with your dishes, taking care not to spill detergent directly on the pieces, because it could pit or spot them. For a beautiful polish, however, you will have to dry everything afterwards by hand using a soft dishcloth.

- **To brighten dull stainless-steel cutlery,** soak it in 4 litres hot water mixed with 1 teaspoon ammonia. Rinse with clear hot water and dry thoroughly with a clean cloth.

SIMPLE solutions

To keep your best silver in good condition, you need to store it in a clean, dry drawer. But you still have to look after it, even when it's not in daily use.
- Take it out of storage now and then. Frequent use and buffing will enhance the patina and will give pleasure to you and its other users.
- If you store your silver for a long time, use either velvet fabric cutlery rolls or a wooden, felt-lined chest to deter tarnish. You can also prevent tarnish by storing silver pieces in plastic cling film, making sure to remove as much air as possible.

Cutlery

- **Wash plate and sterling-silver cutlery** by hand. Use washing-up liquid in hot water. Rinse with clear hot water and dry immediately with a soft dishcloth. Don't use abrasive cleaners or scrubbers such as steel wool. They will dull the finish.

- **The sulphur in eggs and egg products** (such as mayonnaise) will cause silver to tarnish – instantly. So do pollutants in the air, but they work more slowly. Tarnish is not removed by regular washing and you will have to use a silver polish to remove it.

- **Clean pewter cutlery** with a drop of methylated spirits on a soft cloth. Then follow up with the hot, soapy water treatment.

Cutting boards

The most effective way to keep cutting boards completely hygienic is to have several, so that you never mix one used for raw meat with a board on which you chop up cheese or fruit salad. But however many you do have, it's essential not to skimp on the cleaning that is needed to kill the germs that could give you salmonella, *E.coli* and more.

- **To wash a plastic cutting board,** run it through a dishwasher, and the hot water and disinfecting ingredients found in dishwasher detergent will kill harmful bacteria. Wash your cutting board as soon as possible after each use, especially after preparing meat or poultry products.

- **To wash a wooden cutting board,** it's best not to use a dishwasher because the dishwashing process may warp or loosen the glue that holds together laminated wood. Use a scrubbing brush to scrub the board by hand with washing-up liquid in hot water each time you use it. To kill germs, the

Three boards

Top chefs advise having not two but three chopping boards: one for raw; one for cooked; and one for smelly foods (for example, garlic and onions). That way, strong or spicy flavours won't be transferred to blander ingredients as you prepare your meals.

Cutting boards

water must be too hot for your hands to bear. To do it right, you'll have to wear rubber gloves. When done thoroughly, hand-scrubbing is just as effective as machine-washing.

- **To disinfect a cutting board,** mix a teaspoon of bleach in a litre of water and apply it directly to the cutting surface with a scrubbing brush. Do not rinse. Instead, let the board air-dry to give the bleach a chance to work. If you need the board sooner than that, let it stand for at least one minute, then pat it dry with a clean paper towel.

- **To clean a butcher's block** don't ever use any household chemical cleaners. They could be harmful and, at the least, the residue may remain on food. To keep preparation surfaces hygienic mix up a solution of bleach and water, as above. Dip a small scrubbing brush in the solution and scrub in hand-sized circles, taking care not to saturate the wood. When wood absorbs water, it swells. Then, when it dries out, the wood will crack, making a convenient trap for food, grime and germs. So brush the butcher's block clean and quickly wipe away excess water with a hand towel.

- **As an alternative,** mix enough salt into a few drops of lemon juice to make a paste. Rub it, with a cleaning cloth or sponge, hard enough onto the wood to free stuck-on or wedged-in food particles. Then rinse out the cloth or sponge and wipe the block clean. The result won't be as germ-free as cleaning with bleach, but it's a good, fresh-smelling alternative.

- **If the surface is oily or sticky** even after a brisk scrub, you might need to get out the toolbox. Scrape up any build-up with a putty knife. Then gently attack the block with very fine glasspaper, graduating to finer grades, until you're satisfied. Then wipe clean with a damp cloth or sponge and season the block (see box, right).

Season liberally

To keep a butcher's block like new, season it before first use. Warm a little vegetable oil in a small saucepan on the stove, but don't let it get hot. Using a soft cloth dabbed into the oil, rub in the direction of the grain. Let the oil soak in for four or five hours, then wipe off any excess using a soft, dry cloth. Repeat this once a month.

Decanters

Start with the outside of your decanter, washing it by hand. Never put a decanter in a dishwasher; the heat and vibration can easily break its delicate glass neck. If the decanter is antique or made of fine crystal or cut glass, wash it in a plastic basin rather than in a hard sink to reduce the chances of breakage. Or line the bottom of your sink with a folded towel. Then just use a sponge or soft-bristled brush, warm water and mild washing-up liquid to wash the outer surface.

- **The simplest way to clean** inside a decanter is to fill it halfway with soapy, warm water, hold your hand over the top and shake gently. If it is still stained, swirl around a mixture of rock salt and vinegar; the salt will gently scour the surface while the vinegar helps remove stains, especially lime deposits. If it doesn't remove wine stains, try swishing around a mixture of warm water, bicarbonate of soda and rock salt.

- **Alternatively, put water in the decanter,** drop in a denture-cleaning tablet and let it stand overnight. No matter which method you use, rinse with clean, warm water.

- **Dry your decanter completely,** so that it does not fog up after you replace the stopper. The moisture could harbour dangerous micro-organisms. Instead of drying your decanter by inverting it in your dish rack, which increases the chance of breakage and takes for ever, try this trick.

  Drain most of the water out of the decanter by holding it upside down. Then wrap a paper towel around the handle of a long-handled wooden spoon so that the towel extends slightly beyond the end. Put the towel-wrapped spoon into the decanter and let it rest on the bottom overnight. By morning, the towel should have absorbed most of the condensation. Alternatively, gently blow warm air into the decanter with a hair dryer. Be careful, as too much heat can crack delicate glass.

Decking

Think of your deck as an outdoor room, one that is exposed to sun, wind, rain and ice. To keep your deck looking its best, you need to clean it – not as regularly or meticulously as you do your indoor rooms, but well enough to maintain it for the long term. Even decks made of weather-resistant or pressure-treated wood deteriorate unless they are cared for. And, contrary to popular belief, using a pressure washer is not the best way to clean wooden decking.

- **Sweep your decking regularly** to keep it free of leaves and twigs. This is the most basic step you can take. Otherwise, pollen and twig debris from trees will stain the wood surface and the piles of decomposing organic matter will hold moisture, leading to mildew and rot forming. Sweep your deck regularly with a heavy-duty broom, taking care to keep the gaps between boards clean. If leaves or twigs get stuck in between the gaps, scrape them out with a putty knife. The more often you sweep, the easier it will be on you and the deck, especially if the leaves are dry.

- **To remove dirt and mildew** and brighten the colour of your decking, periodically (once a year or so) give it a more thorough cleaning. Use a specialist decking cleaner and follow the manufacturer's instructions. Using a long-handled, stiff-bristled brush (a long handle is easier on your back and knees), scrub the deck with the decking cleaner. Rinse by washing down the deck with a hose.

- **If you have a covered** or partially covered deck that is not built to withstand rain, clean it as you would an indoor hardwood floor – with a barely damp mop or, on occasions, with a cleaner made especially for wood, such as Pledge Soapy Wood Cleaner. Do not completely soak the deck with water, or run the hose over it.

Decking

Time savers
Cut the time spent cleaning your decking by regularly pruning any trees and shrubs that overhang it. You'll also cut down on that greatest deck enemy of all: bird droppings. Grow plants in containers and remember to stand each pot on a saucer: otherwise, each time you water, you'll create a pool of damp that will rot your wood.

- **To remove stains and stubborn mildew,** use a solution of 40ml oxygen bleach and 5 litres warm water. Unlike chlorine bleach, which can break down the lignin that holds the wood together and harm plants, oxygen bleach is relatively gentle and non-toxic. Simply apply it with a mop or brush and wait 15 or 20 minutes for it to soak in – don't scrub – then hose down the deck to remove the solution. If you have used a wood sealer on your deck, you will need to reapply it after washing with oxygen bleach, which strips away wood sealers along with dirt and mildew.

- **Don't use a pressure washer,** as this will break up the wood fibres of your decking – exactly what you are trying to prevent – leaving the surface fuzzy, more susceptible to the weather and in poor condition for refinishing with stains and sealers. Only use them as a last resort and then be very careful. Use the lowest pressure setting available. Hold the nozzle at an angle at least 30cm away from the deck's surface.

Expert **ADVICE**

If you've got an area of decking in your garden, then you'll know that it's an ideal spot for lounging around on a sunny day. It's also the perfect place to string up a hammock. To make your hammock last longer, you need to keep it not only dirt-free but as dry as possible. And as ever, prevention is better than cure.
- Before use, spray your hammock with a fabric guard, following manufacturer's instructions. Renew treatment every three to five months.
- Don't leave the hammock out in the full sun, as the rays will fade synthetics and weaken the fibres of cotton.
- Don't sunbathe in your hammock. Sunscreens are very damaging to polyester and acrylic fibres and can prematurely age them. If you do spill sunscreen on a hammock, spot-clean it promptly with a teaspoon of dishwasher powder in 60ml of water. Scrub with a soft-bristled brush.

Dentures

As with real teeth, dentures should be kept free of food particles, plaque and stains so that your mouth can remain healthy and attractive. And removing plaque from dentures requires the same regular brushing that real teeth need. The difference, of course, is that with dentures, you take them out to brush them.

- **Brush your dentures twice a day.** Do this over a folded towel or a bowl of water; dentures are delicate and expensive, and they may break even if dropped a few centimetres. Go over them lightly with a recommended denture brush or a soft nylon toothbrush, using a cleanser your dentist recommends.

- **You can keep your dentures cleaner** by also lightly brushing your gums, tongue and the roof of your mouth.

- **Soak your dentures** for at least 30 minutes a day in a dentist-approved denture cleanser. Soaking will remove stains and kill germs, reducing mouth infections and odour. For convenience and privacy while you are without your teeth, soak your dentures overnight or while you're showering. Then rinse off the cleanser by lightly brushing the dentures with a soft-bristled brush under cold running water.

- **Never use a brush with stiff,** coarse bristles, which can damage the materials from which dentures are made. And don't use gritty powdered cleansers or toothpastes, which can also cause damage.

- **Don't clean dentures with bleach.** It can whiten the pink part of the dentures and corrode the metal framework on partial dentures.

- **Never rinse in hot water;** the heat could warp dentures. And never let them dry out; this could also warp your dentures or make them brittle.

Diamonds

As hard as they are brilliant, diamonds can cope with rigorous cleaning. Whenever you clean diamond rings or earrings, take time to check on how secure the setting is. Do any claws look out of line? If so, stop cleaning, put the item into a jewellery box and take it to be repaired. If you don't, you'll regret it if the diamond falls out.

- **Assuming all your settings look secure,** the simplest way to wash diamond jewellery is by soaking it in hot, sudsy water – washing-up liquid is fine. Do this in a teacup or a small bowl, never the sink. If a stone were to dislodge, you might be unable to find it and it could drain away with the water.

- **Use an old toothbrush** to scrub where the stone meets the setting and dirt can get ingrained. Rinse, shake dry and – if the stone is large enough – polish with a microfibre cloth.

Dish drainers

Since your dish drainer is meant to hold clean dishes, a dirty one will defeat the purpose.

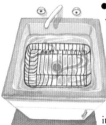

- **Wash your dish drainer** periodically in warm water with a little washing-up liquid, using a clean sponge. Do it separately, not while you're washing other dishes, since harmful bacteria can taint the things that you are trying to clean.

- **Use a scrubbing brush** to remove stuck-on food and mould. Air-dry upside down on a clean towel. Disinfect the dish drainer every few weeks by soaking it in a solution of 40ml bleach per 5 litres water.

Dishes

Washing dirty dishes can be a bit of a Herculean task; and every time you cook and eat a meal, you have to wash up all over again. It can seem like a never-ending chore. Here's the right way to wash up:

- **For everyday washing-up,** squirt a blob of washing-up liquid into the sink and fill with moderately hot water. Agitate the water to make soap suds. If the plates and pans that you are cleaning are particularly greasy, then add 2 tablespoons of white vinegar to the water.

- **Slide the dishes in edgewise** into the water, which allows the temperature of the dish to equalise gradually. If very hot water hits a fragile dish too quickly, cracks may occur.

- **Once the dishes are stacked carefully** in the sink, pour a little extra washing-up liquid onto a sponge or dishcloth. Then resist the urge to scrub. Instead, wash the dishes using small circular movements. It might take longer than a vigorous scrubbing, but it will protect your china.

- **Empty the water and fill again** with plain water for rinsing. If you have some glass items, put 1 tablespoon white vinegar into the final rinse. If you have a double sink, then you can simply fill this with clean water for rinsing the soapy dishes.

- **When using the dishwasher,** load dishes so that they are separated and face the centre of the machine. Put glasses and cups between prongs, not over them.

- **Don't position large dishes** (or pots or pans) in the dishwasher so that they block the spray arm, the spray tower, or the flow of water to the detergent dispenser.

- **Use only dishwasher detergent** in your machine – never soap, laundry detergent or washing-up liquid. Follow

Hands that do dishes
It's worth wearing rubber gloves when washing up; they can protect your hands from frequent exposure to detergent and enable you to work with the hottest water possible. For general household use, standard latex dishwashing gloves are fine. Replace them before they wear out and can't protect you.

Dishes

the label directions for the amount. Less is needed if your water is soft (or artificially softened), more if it's hard.

- **Use a rinse agent** to speed drying time if your water is hard, but skip it if you have soft water.

- **Don't pre-rinse** moderately soiled dishes under the tap. Just scrape off any bits of food that remain.

- **Use the hold-and-rinse cycle** when you haven't got enough dishes to use the machine right away – or when the noise of the dishwasher means you prefer to do it overnight or when you're out. A quick rinse stops odours building up.

The new dish test
If you have a set of dishes and you're not sure if they are dishwasher safe, try this test. Buy an extra cheap item in the range – like a saucer – and put it in the back of the dishwasher. Leave it for a month and use the machine normally. If, at the end of the month, there's no change in its appearance, you'll know the rest of the set can go in the machine.

Dishwashers

Each time you use the dishwasher, take the time to empty grunge from cutlery baskets, filters and check the spray arm. If you skip this task then you'll be washing the next load of dishes in the food residue from yesterday's load.

- **When rinsing out the cutlery bucket,** use the power of water and turn it upside down under a fast tap. This way, you'll propel dirt and food bits back out the way they came. Use a tooth pick to remove tiny particles of food that get trapped in the spray arm.

- **Every month, run the dishwasher** on empty – but with a full supply of dishwasher powder or tablets.

- **To keep the dishwasher smelling fresh** if you're not going to use it for a while, slosh in 100ml white vinegar.

Dolls

Whether it's a child's plastic fashion doll, an expensive collector's doll or an heirloom from your grandmother, all will benefit from careful cleaning and maintenance.

- **To wash a doll's clothing,** begin by stripping the doll. Then make sure its clothes can be washed – do a test on an inconspicuous spot on the clothing. Using an eyedropper or a small syringe, put a drop of detergent where it won't easily be seen, such as on a seam or a hem. If you can't see it after it dries, you should be safe. Place the doll's clothing in a lingerie bag (or use the tiny white mesh bags that come with laundry tablets) and put it in the washing machine on the delicate setting. Don't dry the clothes in the dryer as they may shrink. If the weather is good, hang them to dry on an outside clothesline for a fresh smell. In bad weather, lay the pieces on a towel to dry.

- **To clean the doll itself,** remember that a damp cloth will remove a lot of the grime a doll picks up in the attic, or just from being loved. If the doll needs a bath, fill a sink with warm water and mix in a large squirt of baby bubble bath. If the doll's body is all plastic or rubber, you can submerge it, much as you would a real baby. You might even invite your child to give the doll a scrub with a facecloth made soapy with a little bubble bath.

- **Saliva mixed with anything** – dirt, biscuits, sweets – can set like cement, so for the extra-tough dirt that comes with dolls your children have played with a good deal, a gentle scrub with a soft toothbrush may be necessary. If you need a little extra cleaning power, dip the toothbrush in a solution of 5ml hydrogen peroxide and 50ml water. Just make sure you rinse everything well before you return the doll to your child.

Dolls

- **To clean a collector's doll,** also begin by stripping the doll. Never use a damp cloth on a porcelain doll, because it might etch the paint. Instead, use a dry, soft cloth to remove surface dirt. For detailed areas, use a natural-bristle artist's paintbrush to remove trapped dirt and dust.

- **You can remove the musty smell** you sometimes get with old doll's clothes by hanging them out in fresh air. If the clothing is not fragile, you might want to wash it using the method described on page 173 – but be sure to do the eyedropper test first. For clothing stains you don't want to wash, a household spot remover might work. Or try a solution of a teaspoon of lemon juice mixed with 100ml water. Dip an absorbent cloth or a paper towel into the solution and dab – don't rub – at the stain. It should lighten up right away.

Doll care
To preserve a collector's doll, keep it in a dry place, away from tobacco smoke, fireplaces, airborne grease and food particles, the oil from human hands and direct sunlight.

Doormats

At some point, your doormat will have absorbed all the dirt it can take. Then it simply becomes the bridge over which dirt travels into your house.

- **First, go outside** and grab two corners of the mat. Shake hard; the loosest dirt will come off easily. Then, wearing glasses or goggles to protect your eyes, drape the mat over the clothesline and beat it with a stick or bat. After beating out all loose dirt, take a wire brush and dislodge the stubborn stuff.

- **To remove serious stains** on a mat made of rubber or rope, use an aerosol spot remover, such as Vanish. Alternatively, wash it in the washing machine on a gentle cycle.

- **If you have wooden doormats** that are badly stained, you may need to strip the coating, sand right down and revarnish.

Doors

Doors can collect dust and dirt just as much as walls do. So whatever cleaning method you use on painted walls is just right for painted doors, too. Treat wooden doors as you would furniture made from the same material. Few doors are as flat as walls, though, so you have to be equipped to attack beading and crevices to get them really clean.

- **To remove surface dirt,** dust down the door with a dry towel. Then tie a soft, old towel over the bristle end of a broom and brush into the angles and crevices where dust mounts up. If there's a lot of detailed moulding on the door, use a soft toothbrush to get into the tightest corners.

- **Wash the door** once you've cleaned off all the surface dust and dirt. If you have a stained wooden door, use soapy wood cleaner and mix it with water according to the directions on the label. For painted doors, an all-purpose cleaner is the quickest and cheapest option.

- **If you are feeling very particular,** sugar soap (available from DIY stores) is a more expensive but highly effective way of removing grease and surface dirt from paint. Use a sponge and wash from the bottom upward to avoid run marks. So, beginning at the bottom of the door, scrub with the sponge in small circular motions. Rinse the sponge often and thoroughly to avoid putting dirt back on the door. If you keep the solution clean, you won't have to rinse.

- **To clean door hardware** – the knobs, handles, knockers and letter boxes fixed to your door – place some light masking tape around the fitting to protect the surface of the door. Then use the cleaning solution that is appropriate to the material of your hardware, such as Brasso for brass handles. With glass or ceramic doorknobs, a few wipes with a rag dampened with methylated spirits should be sufficient.

Down

Most down jackets and sleeping bags are machine washable. The only thing that makes them any different from the rest of your wash is that you need to make sure that all the down is securely inside your item before you start. Otherwise, the tiniest little hole can leave your washing machine full of feathers. When you're sure all items are secure, put them into an empty washing machine and follow the care label for maximum temperature and spin (some may advise no spin).

- **You can dry a down item** in the dryer, but use the low temperature setting. Some people throw in a tennis ball, too; the action of a small, dense object rattling around the dryer stops your large, bulky item from getting tangled. Halfway through the cycle, take the down item out and give it a shake.

Prevent blocked drains
Pre-empt blocked drains by giving them an effective flush through once a month. Pour 50ml bicarbonate of soda down the kitchen sink and follow immediately with the same amount of white vinegar. The mixture will fizz and bubble (this is harmless). Wait 30 minutes. Then flush with cool water.

Drains

When a drain becomes slow moving, act fast. By tackling the problem right away you are more likely to avoid the whole episode ending with a plumber's bill.

- **If you have a slow-moving drain** it means sludge is building up in the pipe. When that happens, pour 100g salt into the drain, followed by 100g bicarbonate of soda. Then pour a full kettle of boiling water down the drain. The abrasive salt and bicarbonate of soda will break down the clog. If the problem is congealed grease, the clogging will loosen immediately. Don't turn on the tap for several hours, if possible. The longer you can go without diluting your work, the better.

- **If matted hair** in the pipes is the problem, you'll need a stronger solution. Dissolve 30ml soda crystals in a litre of water and pour it slowly down the drain. Let it work for 10 minutes; then run hot water until the drain seems clear.

Drains

- **If the waste-disposal unit drain** is slow, it is probably blocked with food particles. Pull out the drain trap (the basket-like object that sits in the drain hole at the bottom of the sink) and tap it into your bin to loosen the debris trapped inside. Replace, twisting the knob to closed, and fill the sink with warm water to a depth of 10cm. Add 100ml bicarbonate of soda. Turn on the waste-disposal unit and run it for a couple of seconds before you twist the drain-trap knob to open. The water pressure will push any remaining food particles through the drain trap. Turn on the tap for running water and let the disposer run until you get a free-spinning 'all clear' sound.

Drawers

We all have junk drawers – which act as receptacles for hundreds of objects that have no other obvious home. There are treasures in there we'll need one day so they deserve a regular cleaning.

- **Empty the drawer** onto a table top that you have first covered with old newspaper. Then sort through and throw away everything you no longer want.

- **Clean wood drawers** with a little soapy wood cleaner, mixed according to directions, or mix a litre of warm water with 2 tablespoons washing-up liquid in a large bowl. For laminated plastic, use 30ml white vinegar mixed in a litre of warm water. For metal drawers, put some bicarbonate of soda in a small bowl and add just enough water to make a paste.

- **Thoroughly soak a sponge** and squeeze well, then wipe away at the drawer, inside and out. You can let the drawer air-dry, but if you're in a hurry to put your bits away again – only the must-keep stuff – dry it with a paper towel.

Dust

More than 5,000 different materials, including skin flakes, pet hair, human hair, food bits, pollen grains, spores, insect parts, sawdust and clothing fibres combine to make the dust that settles on every surface in our homes.

● **Many methods of dusting** simply push dust around, which is why we try not to recommend them, unless for a specific task. Feather dusters are great, for instance, for cleaning blinds – as long as you make sure to shake the duster outside frequently. But basically, a dry dust cloth just moves the dust or suspends it. However, if you use a just-damp duster, the dust will cling to your cloth and disappear for ever when you wash it in the washing machine.

● **To dust a room** and cut down on the time dusting takes, vacuum everything first – furniture, walls, windowsills, upholstery, the coffee table. Vacuuming removes a lot of dust without creating a dust storm in the process. Follow up with a damp cloth and your room should be dust-free for awhile.

SIMPLE solutions

Here are some no-fuss tricks to try when you want to do some spot dusting:
● To clean woodwork (except for painted surfaces), put a tea bag in hot water and let it cool. Then dampen your cleaning rag or sponge with the cooled tea and run it over the woodwork.
● To clean blinds, wipe the slats with a cloth dampened with vinegar, which disinfects as it cleans. This is a good trick for chandeliers, too.
● To remove dust, lint or hair from fabric upholstery or an item of clothing, wrap masking tape or packing tape around your hand, then press your hand over the surface of the item. Unwanted fuzz, dust or lint will stick to the masking tape.
● To get rid of all the dust trapped in a pleated lampshade, use a small, medium-bristled paintbrush. This works for figurines, too.

Dust

- **Naturally, you want to truly remove** the dust rather than kicking it up into the air. Microfibre cloths are great at holding onto the dust, because they have so many extra fibres. Generally, a little water on your just-damp dust cloth is all it takes. But if you're up against a great deal of grease, for example, you'll move faster if you spray on a dot of all-purpose surface cleaner, provided that you just use it on the hard surfaces of your home that are listed as 'safe' on the cautions panel of your cleaner.

Dustbins

Being scrupulous about only putting rubbish inside your dustbin that is itself inside securely tied plastic bags, does a lot to lessen how often you'll need to clean your dustbin. If you don't use sturdy sacks – or if you get a split – you'll need to disinfect your bin each week, after it's been emptied by your council rubbish contractor.

- **Hosing out the bin** is the easiest option, but you can also use an old watering can, marked as not being suitable for watering flowers anymore. You can direct the flow of water needed more easily than pouring it from a bucket.

- **First, take your dustbin to an outside drain:** you won't want to tip foul-smelling water onto your drive or flowerbeds. Fill the watering can with a mix of 40ml bleach to 5 litres water and use this to rinse around the bottom and side of the bin. Empty down the drain and repeat.

- **Wash the lid with the same solution,** then invert both to dry. When you next need to put a sack out in the dustbin, you can put your clean bin back together again.

Duvets

Before you start any cleaning of your duvet, check the care label first. It's also worth weighing your duvet, too – try rolling it up tightly, tie it securely with a length of string and placing it on the bathroom scales. Many synthetic double duvets are washable, but they may weigh more than the capacity of your washing machine, which will mean a trip to the launderette.

Down and out
If you have a feather and down duvet, check the edges and stitched areas for holes before you take it to the dry-cleaner. A lot of the filling can come out of such holes, so stitch up any you find to ensure your duvet remains plump.

● **Single, synthetic duvets** shouldn't be a problem and can be simply machine-washed and tumbled dry.

● **Feather and down duvets** are best professionally cleaned. In truth, it's not the washing that is the big problem – your feather duvet may indeed be up to machine washing. But the drying can be near impossible. It is no exaggeration to say that it can take days to dry a quality feather duvet. For this reason, when accidents happen – a child wets the duvet, say, or you spill some coffee – it is best to restrict your washing to the stained section only.

● **Take the duvet to the bathroom** and, using a solution of hand-washing detergent and water in the sink or bath (whichever is more appropriate), immerse the soiled section only. Squeeze out and then rinse with fresh water. Put the duvet between two dry towels and blot off as much water as you can. Finish by spot drying with a hair dryer.

● **For pet urine** or other related accidents, first blot up as much of the mess as possible as soon as possible, using paper towels. Then wash the soiled area of the duvet, as described above, using cold water. Rinse with cold water, and continue rinsing until all traces of the accident have gone. Remember, pet-urine stains can leave a smell, which will cause the animal to return to the spot and repeat the accident.

DVD players

The more mechanical parts a DVD player has, the more likely it is to accumulate dirt and dust. Portable models are even more susceptible. Dirty discs or lenses lead to mistracking, skipping, irregular speed and poor reproduction quality. If your player displays any of these symptoms, give it a careful cleaning.

- **Keeping discs clean** is important, because they can carry dirt into the player's interior. Hold them by the edges and blast off dust with a shot of compressed air. Then wipe with a soft, dry cloth, starting at the centre of the disc and moving out to the edge. Don't use solvents or household cleaners. Always store a disc in its case to keep it dirt-free and keep discs out of direct sunlight and away from heat sources.

- **Cleaning the player's lens** is the next step. Don't open anything that requires a screwdriver. Most warranties become void if you open the casing. Instead, press the button to open the mechanical drawer where the DVD sits. Spray a gentle blast of compressed air inside to force out any dust or lint. It's not a bad idea to spray the disc tray, too. Don't hold the can any closer to the player than the distance recommended on the can – generally at least 10cm away. For less power, take your can further away from the player before you aim.

- **You can buy a special lens-cleaning disc;** simply place it in the drawer that holds the DVDs, close the tray and hit Play to clean. Some cleaning discs use an angular brush made of ultra-fine synthetic fibres containing copper that will also dissipate the static that attracts dust.

- **To clean a player's exterior,** wipe it with a soft, dry cloth. A cloth just dampened with a solution of washing-up liquid and water should be enough for dirtier cabinets; avoid solvents.

Elastic

Elastic is found in everything from underwear to high-fashion jeans and tops. Lycra – the trade name for spandex – doesn't need special care, in that the rest of the garment material will determine how you wash it. But there are a few precautions worth following:

● **Body oils on elastic** will cause it to break down in time. So it's important to wash items with elastic in them promptly. If the item ever needs bleaching, only use an oxygen bleach.

● **To maintain the life of elastic,** only ever tumble dry on a low setting and don't over-dry.

● **Wash a swimsuit after every wearing;** both chlorinated swimming-pool water and salty sea water can be damaging. You also need to get rid of the body oils, sweat, sun-protection creams, sprays and lotions that your suit absorbs. Always do up the straps on bikinis that tie with a metal fastener, otherwise this can snag on other garments that are in the washing machine.

Electric shavers

To keep your shaver in proper running order, brush it after each use to dislodge hair, dead skin and other stuff that's clogging the works and damaging the blades.

● **Many shavers have a removable head cover;** pop it off and brush the underside, avoiding the delicate screen. If you've lost the tiny brush that came with your shaver, use an old small toothbrush. Then gently brush the cutting mechanism itself. A blast from a can of compressed air (from camera shops) will also dislodge any embedded dirt that stands in the way of a smooth shave.

Electric shavers

- **If you use a shaving stick** – a compressed-powder product that dries up perspiration and facial oils to give a smoother shave – the powder can gum up electric-shaver blades. To cure this, dip a cotton bud in methylated spirits and wipe the blades.

- **If your shaver requires more cleaning,** go commercial. Some manufacturers of shaving goods sell an aerosol spray cleaner and lubricant for electric shavers. In general, you spray the shaver with the cleaner and run it for several seconds. Follow the packet directions.

- **To clean the exterior,** unplug your shaver and wipe the surfaces with a damp flannel. If anything clings to the outside, use a little methylated spirits to wipe it off.

Enamel

Enamel is a baked-on coating for metals that doesn't rust or react with acids or chemicals and is usually easy to clean. Enamelled steel or enamelled cast-iron cookware can be a little more of a challenge because of the heat-meets-food factor.

- **To clean enamelled surfaces,** such as appliance surfaces, dissolve 2 tablespoons bicarbonate of soda in 1 litre warm water. Wipe the surfaces with a cloth or sponge dipped in the solution and rinse with fresh water on a clean cloth or sponge.

- **To clean enamelled cookware,** let the pot cool first. Wash in hot water with washing-up liquid, rinse in running water and dry. Pots with metal or plastic handles may be washed in the dishwasher, but pots with wooden handles should not. Never use an abrasive cleaner or metal scouring pad. A plastic or nylon scourer is fine.

Burned-on food
If you burn food onto your enamel pan, cover it with bicarbonate of soda and leave for several minutes while the powder absorbs the acids and oils. Then wash as usual. If that doesn't work, add 1 litre water and 2 teaspoons bicarbonate of soda to the pan, simmer for 15 minutes and wash again.

Erasers

The simplest way to clean the felt erasers used on blackboards is to get two together, go outside and clap them together. Keep your arms outstretched – there will be a lot of dust.

- **Erasers used on white boards** will be full of washable pen. So wash these out in a bowl of sudsy water. Scrub under running water, then rinse and leave to air-dry.

- **To clean a pencil eraser,** simply rub an emery board or piece of glasspaper over it until the black part is gone – you're really just taking off the top, dirty surface. The newly exposed rubber will be clean and soft.

Extractor fans

Hold a tissue up to the grille where the air enters your fan. Turn on the switch. The tissue should stay tight against the grille. If it flutters, the fan isn't working effectively. Dirt is often the problem, particularly if it's been more than six months since you last did a clean.

- **Turn the switch off** and unplug the fan. Remove the grille and wash it in warm water and washing-up liquid; rinse and dry. Vacuum the housing and fan blades with the crevice attachment. Then wipe them off with a damp cloth. Clean the motor and other dusty parts with a stiff paintbrush. If you notice bad wiring or if the fan doesn't work, call an electrician. Don't attempt to fix it yourself.

- **Wash the filter in a cooker-hood** extractor fan every month or two. This filter, usually made of aluminium, is designed for catching cooking grease. Remove it and wash it in the dishwasher or in a mix of hot water and washing-up liquid.

Fans

Ceiling fans have propeller blades that need regular cleaning. Use a lamb's-wool duster and a stepladder and give the blades a quick dusting. Other types of fans have grilles that protect the blades. Clean the grilles and other housing regularly, using a vacuum cleaner with a small brush attachment.

● **Do a more thorough cleaning** every month or two during times of heavy use. First, disengage the circuit breaker for a ceiling fan and unplug others. Remove the grilles. Then get together the following: a solution of water with a little washing-up liquid and a sponge or brush. Dampen the sponge and wipe the blades. Rinse the sponge in clear water and wipe again. Then dry with a clean cloth. Be careful not to bend the blades, because that may upset their balance and make the fan wobble.

● **If the grilles have accumulated** a lot of grime, it may be simplest to take them outside and wash them under a hose. Use a stiff brush to clean off caked-on dirt and grime.

Filters

Anything designed to catch dirt – such as a filter – should be cleaned often. Dirty ones don't just not work very well; they also cost more money, because their motors will use more energy to pass air or water through dirty filters than clean ones.

● **Cleaning air filters** is usually simple. You throw out the old one and install a new one. So follow pack instructions and it's not a cleaning job at all. Air-conditioner filters, which may be disposable or washable, also need monthly attention. If the filter is washable, remove it and vacuum up as much dust as you can. Then rinse it under warm running water or swirl it

Filters

around in a solution of 1 tablespoon bicarbonate of soda and 1 litre water – don't use soap. Rinse and dry.

● **Home water-filtering systems** often use activated carbon filters that extract chemicals from the water. The activated carbon usually comes in cartridges that need to be replaced when they no longer work. The tricky part is figuring out when this has happened. Sometimes you can tell by the taste of the water – if the filter is designed to remove chlorine, say. But it's more reliable to simply mark on a calendar each time your three or six-monthly filter change is due.

Fireplaces

Ironically, fireplace cleaning is simpler during the fire-burning season and more of a task at that time of year when you don't have a fire. During the colder months, cleaning will usually be simply removing some of the ashes periodically.

● **Some fireplaces have an ash pit,** which is a receptacle underneath the area where you build a fire. If yours does, open it and push excess ashes into it. Or use an ash shovel to deposit the ashes in a metal bucket with a tight-fitting lid. Store the ashes outdoors in the tightly covered can for two days before final disposal, an important precaution because 'dead' ashes containing live embers have started many a fire.

● **During the months** when you don't have a fire, do a more thorough clean. Use a rubber eraser on any smoke streaks that have crept up the exterior of the fireplace. If your fireplace has warm-air circulators, clean the ducts thoroughly with a vacuum cleaner. And get the chimney professionally swept.

Fireplaces

- **You may also want to remove** the black layer of creosote, a highly combustible residue created by burning wood, on the inside of the firebox. (The firebox is where you build your fire.) Remove the screen, irons and grate and sweep up all the ashes. Then brush away the creosote with a wire-bristled brush.

- **If you want the firebox** to be cleaner, use 50ml soda crystals (from supermarkets) in 4 litres water and apply it with a sponge. Brush with a stiff-fibre brush and rinse with clear water. Wear rubber gloves, since washing soda is caustic.

Fireplace screens & tools

Fireplace screens and other tools can gather a lot of grime – especially if they are more than simply decorative and see regular daily use.

- **Clean the fireplace screen** with a vacuum cleaner as part of your regular cleaning routine in the room. A screen catches more than the sparks that want to go flying into the room. It also catches a lot of dust. Periodically, give it a more substantial cleaning with soap and water. Pick a sunny day and work outside. Make a sudsy solution of warm water

Expert **ADVICE**

The cleaning of fireplace doors is a subject that's rife with conflicting advice. Your best bet is to check your owner's manual for its recommendations. These doors are usually made of safety glass, making them harder to break, but some also have heatproof coatings that may be harmed by harsh cleaning materials.

Fireplace screens & tools

and a few squirts of washing-up liquid and scrub the screen
with a stiff-bristled brush dipped in the solution. Then rinse
it off with the garden hose. If you're working inside, rinse off
the solution with a sponge dipped in clean water. Allow the
screen to dry thoroughly. If it has any brass components, clean
them with a brass polish.

- **Clean fireplace tools** (shovels, pokers, tongs), as well as
irons and grates, with the same brush and soapy solution. Use
extra-fine (000) steel wool on rust or stubborn dirt. Dry the
tools with a soft cloth. Give them a light coat of vegetable oil
with a clean cloth; then wipe dry with another cloth.

- **If rust is a problem** on your screen or tools, you can renew
the finish with a coat of high-temperature black spray paint,
sold in hardware stores.

- **Clean glass fireplace doors** with a touch of caution (see
Expert Advice, page 187). But there is one certain guideline:
fireplace doors should be cleaned only when they're cool, never
when hot. Common glass cleaners, such as Windolene, don't
work very well on black creosote deposits.

- **A solution of ammonia and water** will clean up the black
creosote deposits, but this solution also may strip your doors
of their heatproof coating. Instead, try dipping a damp rag in
ashes from the fireplace and rubbing the glass with that. Then
wipe dry with a clean cloth. Or dip a cloth in white vinegar and
wash. Dry with newspaper.

- **If you're still** seeking perfection, try rubbing your glass doors
with white polishing compound, available from a car-supplies
shop. Or try using a speciality cleaner to shine up glass doors
or fireplace surrounds.

Fishponds

Too many fish can make a fishpond dirty: fish urine, like that of other animals, contains toxic ammonia. For a healthy pond, you need to clean it out occasionally.

- **Routine pond maintenance** consists mostly of removing debris such as dead leaves from the water. Use a long-handled swimming pool skimmer net. But don't expect your pond to be completely clear; the water should be a pale green. Environmental balance takes a long time to establish, so don't be too quick to upset it by emptying and refilling the pond.

- **A major pond cleaning** is called for when there is a lot of muck or too many fish in the water. The pond may have been overstocked, or the fish may have multiplied. In either case, you may have to find new homes for some of your fish. A rule of thumb is that each fish in a pond should have about a barrel of water. The best time – and many experts claim it should be the only time – to clean a pond is in early spring, when cool temperatures provide a less stressful environment for the fish and plants. Even so, always keep the fish and plants that you remove from the pond in the shade to avoid stressing them.

- **Begin by removing** the plants around the edge, and then take out the floating ones, pot and all. Put them in the shade.

- **Use a bucket to take off some water** from the top (the cleanest part) of the pond. Place a children's paddling pool, or other very large container, in a shady spot and fill it with this water, which will be the right pH level and the right temperature to hold the fish. Save as much of the rest of the pond water as you can in extra containers, unless it is really disgusting.

> **A cleaner home for your fish**
> To keep a pond cleaner, an aerator of some kind (any device, such as a fountain that mixes air into the water) will help as will freshwater snails, which will eat algae and unwanted plant growth.

Fishponds

- **When the pond has been half drained,** remove the fish with a net and transfer them to the paddling pool or container. Cover this with a mesh screen so the fish can't jump out.

- **Start removing the remaining water** in the pond with a pump or siphon. As the water level drops, remove submerged plants and put them in the paddling pool, too.

- **While there is still some water** at the bottom of the pond, clean the sides with a soft-bristled scrubbing brush. Continue to drain until the bottom layer of dirt is in sight. Then stop pumping and scoop out the bottom debris: you can put this in your compost bin.

- **Rinse the sides of the pool** with a hose and then remove the pump and rinse. Gently scrub the bottom.

- **Replace the plants** before you begin refilling. Use a water conditioner, available at pet or aquarium stores, to neutralise chlorine in the new water. Return the water that you have saved in the other containers to the pond and let the pond warm up slightly before returning the water and fish in the paddling pool to the pond.

cleaning out a **POND**

1 Remove the fish when the pond is half drained.

2 Siphon off the water that remains in the pond.

3 Scrub out the bottom of the pond.

Floors

Not all floors are the same – even among general categories such as wood, stone or tile, there are vast differences between specific examples. Maple isn't pine, marble isn't granite, and quarry tiles are not glazed.

- **All floors are subject to dirt and wear,** so some basic cleaning techniques apply universally. The Floor-Cleaning Pyramid on page 194 gives general floor-cleaning methods. When you've exhausted those, try the recommendations under the following headings for specific floor types.

- **To clean wood floors** you need to simply wipe with a damp mop or cloth. You can't swab water all over the floor – it must be used sparingly. But if damp wiping isn't enough to shift grease or serious dirt, you can try cleaning with 100ml cider vinegar mixed in 4 litres warm water.

  You could also try tea, brewed from 2 tea bags to 1 litre of water. Dip a soft cloth or sponge in the tea, wring it out and use it to wipe the floor. Finish by buffing with a soft, dry cloth.

- **Caring for wood floors** will save you having to re-sand them regularly, which can be time-consuming, costly and messy. And it also removes a layer of wood from your floor. Each time you sand, you're working your way towards the day when you'll need thin, worn-out wood flooring replaced.

SIMPLE solutions

High heels can leave stubborn black marks on your floors. To remove, try rubbing the marks with a pencil eraser. If that doesn't work, rub a hardwood floor with a rag dabbed in a little white spirit. On vinyl flooring, smear a drop of baby oil over the mark, wait a few minutes, then wipe the mark away with a rag.

Floors

- **If your floor was installed** or last re-finished before the mid-1960s, the finish is probably varnish or shellac. These rest on top of the wood, are often waxed and require a whole-floor sanding before a new finish can be applied. Later finishes such as polyurethane, which penetrates wood, should not be waxed and can be touched up by new urethane applied to worn places.

- **Scratch the surface** with a coin in an inconspicuous place. If the finish flakes, it is probably shellac or varnish. If the finish does not flake, it is probably urethane.

- **To check for wax,** put a couple of drops of water on the floor. Wait 10 minutes and check to see whether white spots have appeared under the water. White spots mean the floor has been waxed. If there are no white spots, it hasn't.

- **On varnished or shellacked floors** you can use a solvent-based liquid wax for wood. It removes dirt and most of the old wax, prevents wax build-up and leaves a thin coat of new wax. It's best applied on your hands and knees but you can also use an electric polisher, changing the pads frequently. In any case,

Expert **ADVICE**

Parts of your floor that don't get walked on very often can get a build-up of wax. Removing it requires harsher cleaning than usual and should be done only when necessary and no more often than once a year. You can use either 200ml ammonia and 400ml detergent in 4 litres warm water, or 100ml soda crystals in 4 litres warm water as wax strippers. Apply either solution and scrub with a stiff brush, electric scrubber or extra-fine (000) steel wool to loosen the old wax. Work on a small area at a time and mop up the solution after the wax has been softened. Repeat until the entire floor is stripped of wax. Rinse thoroughly with a solution of 4 litres water and 250ml vinegar. When completely dry, apply new wax.

Floors

you must buff the floor afterwards with a clean cloth. Never use water-based self-polishing wax on wood floors.

- **On urethane-finished floors,** rub with a cloth containing a little furniture oil to give them more shine. (Read the label to make sure it doesn't contain any wax.) Be sure to use very little; too much makes the floor slippery.

- **To clean stone flooring,** try sprinkling damp sawdust over the floor, scrub with a stiff brush and sweep up the sawdust with a broom and dustpan. Follow up with a vacuum.

- **Many kinds of stone flooring,** especially marble, need a neutral pH cleaner (sold by businesses that sell and install stone flooring). A mild washing-up liquid mixed with water will also work nicely. Consult the dealer who sold you the stone for recommendations for specific cleaners if more power is needed.

- **To clean ceramic tile floors,** a quick once-over with a damp mop is often all that is needed.

- **If damp mopping** isn't enough, mix a cap of methylated spirits in 4 litres of water. Apply the solution with a mop or an electric cleaner-polisher. Rinse well with clear water. A commercial floor cleaner for ceramic tiles has the added benefit of containing an anti-mould ingredient, which is handy if your floor is prone to dampness.

- **If the grout needs special attention,** mix 50ml vinegar with 4 litres water and scrub with a toothbrush or nylon scrubbing pad. For heavy-duty treatment, scrub with a mixture of 100ml chlorine bleach in 2 litres water (wear rubber gloves). Let the solution stand for 20 minutes, mop twice with clean water to rinse thoroughly; wipe dry.

Keep it simple
Marble floors can be damaged easily; acids (such as vinegar) will etch the surface, and strong alkaline solutions (such as soda crystals) will break down the marble and leave it rough. It's best to simply sweep and clean marble floors regularly, and then mild products will be all you'll need.

Floors

- **To clean vinyl flooring** that's not too dirty, use a damp mop. If you need something stronger than water, mix 250ml white vinegar with 4 litres water and apply a small amount with your mop. Rinse thoroughly by mopping with plain water.

- **To add shine,** apply a thin coat of wax to a dry, clean floor. The one-step-wax-and-clean products don't work as well as a regular wax. A self-polishing wax is easy to apply, but it will build up over time. A solvent-based paste wax is more work and must be buffed but provides superior results.

- **No-wax vinyl** has a polyurethane finish, intended to keep a shine without waxing. This works for a long time if it is kept clean, but eventually the finish will dull. Follow manufacturer's directions as to how to use a polish or sealer to renew the shine.

- **Laminate flooring,** like wood, should not be mopped by slopping lots of water around on the floor. (Laminate is the man-made flooring that comes in tongue-and-groove planks that often simulate wood.) Don't use ammonia, solvents, abrasives, general-purpose cleaners, polishes or waxes on laminate. Despite these restrictions, laminate is very easy to clean.

- **Some manufacturers recommend** their own special cleaner, which is usually fairly expensive. However, any cleaner for wood floors will be fine.

- **If your laminate gets scratched,** you may be able to buy a touch-up stick from the manufacturer.

The Floor-Cleaning Pyramid
At the broad bottom of the pyramid are those cleaning methods that apply to all types of floors and that should be used most frequently. Frequency of use declines as you go up the pyramid. At the top are specialised cleaners for different flooring materials.

Specialised cleaners

Damp mopping

Using a dry mop or duster

Regular sweeping or vacuuming

Flowerpots

A beautiful plant is wasted in a dirty pot. However, you don't clean flowerpots solely for aesthetic reasons. Plants and their soil may contain viruses, bacteria, fungi or pests, which can be passed along unknowingly to the next pot occupant.

- **Clean your flowerpots** using the same method, whether they're made of plastic, glazed or unglazed clay, ceramic or other materials. Wash with washing-up liquid and water, as you would dishes. Scour with a stiff brush to remove algae and mineral deposits. Wash again with a solution of 1 part chlorine bleach to 10 parts water. Rinse with fresh water and let dry in the sunshine – a great natural steriliser.

- **If you'd prefer to avoid scrubbing,** soak the pots for about an hour in a solution of 2 parts water to 1 part white vinegar. The minerals and algae should wash right off.

- **To avoid a crusty white build-up** of mineral deposits around the top inner edge of the pot, take a candle and rub it around the rim. That will seal the surface, making mineral build-up less likely.

- **To keep soil from spattering out** of the pot when it rains or when you water the plant, put a layer of decorative pebbles on top of the soil around the plant.

Foam rubber

The nice thing about foam rubber – whether it's the latex rubber used from the 1940s to the 1960s or polyurethane, the preferred material since the 1970s – is that it's porous. That means all you have to do to keep the foam that's in your cushions, pillows or mattresses fresh is to vacuum them. Spills are another story and will require a little more elbow grease.

Foam rubber

- **To clean spills or marks** on foam, first remove any covering (clean it separately); then use a rag dampened with washing-up liquid and water and rub the surface. Never put soap and water directly on foam, because it will absorb the liquid. Let the foam air-dry thoroughly before you put the cover back on.

- **Heavy spills** that have seeped inside the foam require special attention. Run water – only water – through the foam, then squeeze out as much water as you can. If you use soap or other cleaning agents, you'll have to rinse those out, too, or you risk creating a breeding ground for bacteria.

- **To clean a deep stain** from a small cushion or pillow, place the foam in the bath or sink and run water over it. For larger cushions, use a shower nozzle or garden hose. Don't try to do this on a mattress, which can only be surface cleaned.

- **Even if you're dealing with a major stain,** keep water to a minimum, because it will take 24 to 48 hours for the foam to dry. There's nothing you can do to speed the process, either. Above all, don't ever rest foam near a radiator or heat source or even try to put small pieces in a dryer – it's highly flammable.

SIMPLE solutions

To quickly and thoroughly clean a foam-rubber pillow or cushion, all you need is a plastic bag and a vacuum cleaner:
- Remove any attachment from the end of the vacuum cleaner's hose. Put the pillow in a plastic bag; then put the end of the vacuum hose in the bag, twist the top of the bag closed and hold it in place. Then turn on the vacuum cleaner. The foam will become condensed as the vacuum cleaner sucks the air and dirt out of the foam.
- When you turn the vacuum cleaner off, the foam will return to its original shape. This technique cleans both sides of the pillow at the same time.

Food

Clean food – and food that's safe to eat – starts with clean hands. The most important thing you can do to keep yourself healthy and prevent the spread of illness is to wash your hands frequently and thoroughly with soap and water. Once your hands are squeaky clean, you're ready to prepare food.

- **To clean fruits and vegetables,** you don't need anything special. Washing with plain water will do. Just be sure you wash all your fruits and vegetables – even the organic ones. You are not just washing off chemical residue, but also germs that may have got onto your produce as it has been handled and stored. So while organic items may not have residual chemicals on them, they may have the same amount of dirt, dust and mould spores as non-organic produce.

- **For vegetables and fruits with a firm surface,** such as potatoes, celery and apples, use a vegetable brush to scrub the skin under running water.

- **For leafy vegetables and fruits with a soft skin,** such as cabbage or peaches, strawberries and raspberries, rinse under running water only.

- **Rinse mushrooms** by holding them under running water or dunking them in a bowl of water.

- **To dry vegetables and fruits,** use a clean tea towel or paper towel. A lettuce spinner is a good idea for drying leafy greens. If you're preparing vegetables to cook, you don't necessarily need to dry them.

- **Cut away any bruised or damaged areas** from fruits and vegetables with a sharp knife. Immediately refrigerate any fresh-cut items.

Food

- **Rinse fish quickly** in cold water to remove ice, slime and any loose small scales that you can't see.

- **Don't use a brush** on soft-skinned vegetables or fruits. The bristles will damage them.

- **Don't use detergents or soap.** The produce could absorb the residues, which you could ingest.

- **Don't wash raw** poultry, beef, pork, lamb or veal before using. You may think you're helping to make the meat safe, but you're not; you could be spreading germs. Cooking the meat at hot temperatures will destroy bacteria.

- **Keep raw meat,** fish and poultry in covered containers. Never place them directly on counters or the refrigerator shelves. Never let the juices of raw meat drip onto other foods and never use the same utensils on cooked foods that you have used for handling raw meat.

- **Don't wash eggs** before storing or using them. They will have been washed during commercial egg processing. Washing will remove more of the 'bloom', the natural coating on just-laid eggs that helps to prevent bacteria from permeating the shell.

SIMPLE solutions

Rinsing is not enough to get the grit out of lettuce or spinach leaves. These leafy greens need a good bath:
- Fill a clean kitchen sink with enough cold water to cover the greens, and submerge them for 30 to 45 seconds. Swish the leaves around with your hand and then empty the water in the sink.
- Clean the sink to remove the grit. Repeat the process. Keep washing, draining and washing until you see no more dirt in the sink when you let the water out.

Food graters

The kitchen grater is a difficult tool to clean because some foods get trapped in the grates or leave a residue.

- **To clean a grater,** soak it in warm to hot, soapy water. Then hold it upside down and brush with a bottom-to-top stroke. You can put a grater in a dishwasher, as long as it isn't made of tin, which can quickly rust when it's not dried thoroughly.

- **To dry your grater,** place it on a dish rack or a lint-free tea towel. If you're worried about a tin grater not drying enough and possibly rusting, let it dry for 15 minutes in a low oven.

Food grinders

Because a food grinder is often used to process meat, poultry and seafood, proper cleaning is critical to prevent transmission of harmful bacteria.

- **To clean the grinding plates,** first soak the parts in a soapy solution of hot water and washing-up liquid to dislodge most of the food. You can finish the job in a dishwasher (always consult the manufacturer's instructions first), set on a hot cycle.

- **Soak the parts** in 1 tablespoon of salt dissolved in 2 litres cold water for about 10 minutes to dislodge food. Then scrub the plates and blade with a brush in hot, soapy water.

- **Lay the parts on a cloth towel** and let them air-dry. Or place the parts in the oven at 65°C for 10 to 15 minutes. If you put aluminium alloy blades in the dishwasher, they'll start to rust when they sit and dry. Once the blades are dry, rub vegetable oil lightly over them to protect them from rusting.

- **To clean a grinder's motor unit,** never immerse it in water. Wipe with an anti-bacterial kitchen cleaner and then wipe dry.

Food processors

For general cleaning, use water pressure from having the tap on at full blast to remove stuck on food from your food processor's discs and blades.

● **If your recipe doesn't require** the use of the feed tube on top of your food processor, cover the bowl with a strong piece of cling film before locking on the lid. This will prevent splattering on the lid and minimise cleaning.

● **To clean the power unit** of your food processor, turn it off and unplug the unit. Wipe it with a damp cloth. Wipe off the safety motor-drive cover and reinstall it on the unit, if necessary. Never use coarse or caustic cleaning products on the power unit or immerse it in water.

● **To clean the attachments,** put them in the dishwasher – all except the blades. Since items can shift in the dishwasher, the blades could bend, be dulled or be burned if they touch a heating element. Wash the blades in hot, soapy water, dry with a cloth and store for future use. Some food can be particularly hard to clean off, especially when it's dried. For tough jobs, take the blades outside and give them a squirt with the hose.

● **Some experts prefer to hand-wash** the plastic bowl of a food processor in hot, soapy water. This protects the bowl from the harsher dishwasher detergent, which can make the plastic brittle and prone to breakage. On some models, the plastic bowl has a safety spring located where the bowl attaches to the food processor. It's difficult to get this spring thoroughly dry, so after you've given the plastic bowl a quick wipe down, let it air-dry before re-assembling the processor. Otherwise, the spring may rust.

Fountain pens

All fountain pens – whether they have a metal or gold nib – should be cleaned after they have been filled four or five times or you have used four or five cartridges.

- **To clean your fountain pen,** flush the nib section by running it under plain tap water at room temperature. For ink deposits that may have stood in the pen for a long time, make one of the following three solutions: 1 drop of washing-up liquid in 1 cup of water at room temperature; a couple of squirts of all-purpose household cleaner, such as Flash, in 1 cup of water; or a few squirts (about a teaspoon) of an oxygen bleach cleaner in 150ml of water.

- **To clean self-filling pens,** the kind you dip into ink, place your cleaning solution (see above) in a glass and draw it into the pen, just as you would to fill the pen with ink. Then place the nib in the water and let it all soak for two hours to two days, depending on how long the ink has been in the pen. To rinse, draw fresh water into the pen and empty it a couple of times.

- **To clean a pen** that's not heavily caked with ink, fill it with one of the above solutions and empty it two or three times.

- **With ink-cartridge pens** there's no device on the pen to force the cleaning solution through the very fine internal channels of the nib. Squeeze an empty ink cartridge to force the air out, dip it into one of the cleaning solutions mentioned above and release it, drawing the solution into the cartridge. Attach the cartridge to the nib section as if it were full of ink and squeeze the cleaning solution out of the cartridge and through the nib. Repeat the procedure a couple of times.

- **Dry each section of your pen** before putting it back together. You can use a cotton bud for this task.

Fountains

Washing your fountain periodically with a solution of 1 part bleach to 10 parts water will help inhibit algal growth. To prevent mineral deposits from forming on bowls, the motor shaft or other parts of the pump (which could cause it to fail), always use distilled water, rainwater or dehumidified water in the fountain. If your fountain is so big that using distilled water is not practical, treat the water with a mineral deposit inhibitor recommended by your supplier or garden centre.

● **Removing mineral deposits** – should they develop despite your best efforts – will depend on the material your fountain bowl is made of. Some materials, such as resins and copper, are soft and should be cleaned with a cotton rag.

Slate can be cleaned with a soft-bristled brush – but don't use soap. Slate can be porous; if it absorbs soap, your fountain could turn into a bubble bath.

Other fountain-bowl materials can be cleaned with an abrasive sponge and white vinegar or a mineral deposit cleaner, available at hardware stores and home-improvement stores.

● **If your preventive maintenance** is working, you may need to clean your fountain parts only once a year. If you're getting mineral deposits or you're not using a water-treatment product, you'll have to clean them more frequently. In general, you should sterilise your fountain after you clean it and before you reassemble it by dipping all parts, including the pump, in the mild bleach solution mentioned above (1 part bleach to 10 parts water).

● **Most moulded fountainheads** are cast from a polyester resin mixed with fillers such as powdered marble. These materials are strong but scratch easily, so the best way to clean

Fountains

them is with warm, soapy water and a soft sponge. Before using tile cleaners or other acids on a cast-resin fountainhead, check it by putting a few drops of the cleaner on the bottom of the fountainhead and scrubbing it for a bit with a toothbrush.

- **When cleaning concrete** or natural stone, never use an acid cleaner. Washing-up liquid or bleach mixed with water, plus a scrubbing brush, will work fine.

- **Clean slate** as for removing mineral deposits (see page 202).

- **To clean a fountain pump,** first check to see how well it's working. Most pumps have some sort of inlet strainers or screens to ensure that small pebbles and other debris don't get into the pump and jam or damage it. Watch the water flow in your fountain. If you notice it's slowing down, clean the pump before it clogs entirely, overheats and burns out.

- **With indoor pumps** and simple outdoor pumps, follow the manufacturer's instructions to take them apart and reassemble. If your pump has an adjustable flow, note the setting when you remove the pump for cleaning, in case you inadvertently change it. Once you have taken the pump apart, clean it with warm water, washing-up liquid and an old toothbrush. Dip the parts in a bleach solution and reassemble it.

- **The more complex, industrial-type fountains** are trickier to clean and should be entrusted to a professional.

SIMPLE solutions

To combat slime and algae in a fountain, preventive maintenance will go a long way. A water-treatment product will keep algae at bay and yet is safe for birds, pets, and plants (not for fish, though). You typically add a few drops to the fountain each week. Treatment products are available at fountain and garden stores.

Fridges & freezers

Keeping your fridge and freezer clean is not only important to the appearance (and smell) of your home, it's also crucial to the hygiene of your food and your family's health. There are three major aspects of keeping refrigerators and freezers clean: removing dirt, killing germs and deodorising the interior.

- **Cleaning the fridge** is only a half-hour job, so there's no need to fret about keeping food cold. Instead, empty one shelf at a time, so food on the other shelves can stay chilled. Remove the first shelf and spray it liberally with a disinfecting all-purpose cleaner. Alternatively, a squirt of white vinegar in a spray bottle will cut though grease. Use paper towels to wipe the shelf dry, then re-insert it in the refrigerator. Repeat the procedure with each shelf.

- **To clean the drawers,** pull them out one at a time, place them in the sink and fill them with warm water and a squirt of washing-up liquid. Let the water sit for 10 minutes. Then pour this out, rinse with fresh water and wipe dry with a towel.

- **Meat and poultry juices dripping** on refrigerator surfaces are not only unsightly; they are potentially harmful vehicles for the spread of salmonella and *E. coli*. Even though a refrigerator's temperature is low, it doesn't stop the growth of all bacteria. And it doesn't kill bacteria that is already present.

SIMPLE solutions

To deodorise your refrigerator or freezer, open a box of baking soda, leave it inside, and change it every few months. This tried-and-trusted method will absorb most of the odours you don't want emanating from your fridge, but it may not go far enough to suit you. Leaving an egg cup of dried coffee also absorbs odours and brings a faint aroma of your favourite drink to the fridge, that you may prefer.

Fridges & freezers

- **So as you remove each shelf,** spray the inside of the refrigerator with a disinfecting all-purpose cleaner. Just because it looks clean doesn't mean that it is clean.

- **Cleaning the freezer is simple** if you have a self-defrosting model. Just put the food in the sink. Piling frozen items on top of each other will keep them cold. Soak a sponge in warm water and squeeze out enough water that you won't create trickles that will add to your work. Wipe each rack in the freezer, top and bottom. If you have a thick, frozen spill, scrape it first with a stiff plastic spatula that has a thin edge (don't use metal) and then spot clean it with a soapy sponge.

- **Defrost the freezer regularly,** before there's a tremendous ice build-up. If you don't, you're effectively reducing the size of your freezer.

  Store food in a cooler box; pack it tightly, with items that thaw fastest, such as ice cream, in the centre. Switch the freezer off at the plug and leave the door open. Put a thick towel tight up against the freezer in front of the door. Stand a tray under the drip edge at the base of the freezer (a pull-out slot that catches thawing ice). Do nothing while the ice melts.

  Using more towels, mop up the water. When this is complete, turn on the freezer, put back the food, and avoid opening the doors at all for as many hours as you can. This will help to bring the temperature down faster.

- **Regularly cleaning seals and door handles** is perhaps the most important aspect of fridge cleaning. When you're preparing food and handling raw meat it's easy to forget to wash your hands before touching door handles, potentially transferring germs to anyone else who opens the fridge. The solution is to keep some all-purpose wipes near the fridge and make it a habit to wipe off the handle frequently.

Furniture

Working out what type of finish your furniture has should be the first order of business. If your furniture has an oiled finish, you should only dust and re-oil it. If it has one of the more common hard finishes – such as varnish or lacquer – you have more cleaning options.

● **Oil finish or a hard finish?** Here's how to tell the difference. Put a few drops of boiled linseed oil on the wood and rub it in with your finger. If the wood absorbs the oil, you have an oil finish. If the boiled linseed oil beads up, you have a hard-varnished or lacquered finish.

● **To clean oiled furniture,** dust it with a dry cloth. Don't use a dust-attracting product on the cloth and make sure the cloth is soft and free of buttons, zips and anything else that might scratch the wood. Then apply oil to the wood (boiled linseed oil, teak oil or an oil recommended by the furniture's manufacturer). Rub the oil in with a clean cloth. Do this an average of once a month. If you've been neglectful, re-oil your furniture every two weeks for a couple of months to allow it to catch up on missing oil.

● **To protect oiled furniture,** never put cloth items or water on it. Cloth items will absorb the moisture from the oil and dry out your furniture. Unfortunately, oil offers the least protection of any finish – get any water on it and it's spoiled – yet it requires the highest maintenance.

● **To clean varnished** or lacquered furniture, dust it off first with a soft rag or a feather duster. It's all right to add a little dust-attracting product, such as Pledge, to the rag or duster but don't apply it straight onto the furniture. Let the product dry on the cloth before you dust. If necessary, you can clean hard-finished furniture with a damp cloth and washing-up liquid. Now you're ready to polish.

Furniture

- **To polish a hard finish,** apply an aerosol furniture polish. First, mist the surface of the furniture and use one area of a rag to spread the polish, wiping in a circular motion. Turn the rag over to expose a clean and dry area of cloth, and wipe off the excess polish. Avoid polishes that consist mostly of silicone and paraffin wax, because these tend to build up and eventually soften or ruin a finish.

- **To clean varnished** or lacquered kitchen furniture, you'll need to take a different approach, because it is exposed to grease and cooking oils. Use a cloth that has been barely dampened with washing-up liquid and water to remove the oily substances. Follow up with a cloth dampened with plain water and then polish. Every three months, clean it using the white-spirit method described in the next paragraph.

- **To give a hard finish** a thorough cleaning and to remove built-up wax, you'll need a few very soft rags. Soak one rag with white spirit. Wipe your furniture thoroughly, flipping the rag frequently. Thoroughly go over all areas several times with the rag. Now dry the surface completely with another soft, dry rag. Repeat this wiping and drying process at least three times using a fresh rag each time.

- **Once the furniture is clean,** you can polish. Spray the polish on the wood and rub it in with a rag, going in a circular motion. Now use another clean, soft rag – or flip the polishing rag to a dry spot – and wipe with the grain of the wood to remove excess polish. Carved wood should be cleaned in the same way, regularly with polish and once a year with white spirit. The only difference is that you'll need a soft toothbrush to get into the intricate details.

Furniture

- **If a finish has become sticky,** this usually means it has failed – the result of too much polish build-up, exposure to oils over the years, or the finish having degraded over time. Use white spirit and super-fine (0000) steel wool to remove the old finish, rubbing along the grain of the wood. Wipe three or four times with a rag and fresh white spirit. When you're done, the furniture will have to be refinished. Talk to a professional or follow the packet directions on the finishing product you choose. Don't do this to a valuable antique piece of furniture; take it to an expert.

- **To clean painted wood furniture,** dust it with a water-dampened cloth. If necessary, use a mild, non-abrasive detergent (such as washing-up liquid) and warm water. Dip a rag into the cleaning solution and wring it nearly dry. Work on a small section of wood at a time. Rinse with clear water. Dry the surface with a clean cloth quickly before continuing.

- **Waxes and polishes** are usually not needed on painted furniture, but if you do use a wax on a light-coloured painted piece, make sure you use a white, creamy type polish to avoid discolouration. Never use oil, oil polishes or oil-treated cloths on painted furniture.

- **An antique piece with its original finish** should usually not be repainted or refinished, because you run the risk of ruining the item's value.

- **To make your own furniture cleaner** for removing old polish and dirt, put 1 litre water in a saucepan on the stove, add 2 tea bags and bring to a boil. Cool the solution to room temperature. Dip a soft cloth in the tea and wring the cloth until it's damp. Wipe the furniture, buff it dry with a soft cloth and decide whether you should polish it.

Furniture

- **To make your own furniture polish,** follow either of these formulas: mix 50ml white vinegar with 150ml olive oil, or mix 3 drops lemon extract with 200ml vegetable oil. You can substitute baby oil for the olive or vegetable oil. Rub the polish into the surface with a clean rag, using circular motions.

- **Removing candle wax** from furniture is risky because you can cause further damage. Use ice directly on the wax to get it as cold as possible and immediately wipe up excess water. Once the wax is very cold, try carefully inserting a butter knife under the wax to see whether it will pop off. If this method doesn't work, don't attempt anything else; consult a professional.

- **If you get fresh emulsion paint** on your furniture, remove it with water; remove gloss paint with white spirit. To shift a dry stain, saturate the spot in boiled linseed oil. After the paint softens, lift it off carefully with a putty knife. Alternatively, wipe with a cloth dampened in the boiled linseed oil.

- **If paper is stuck to your wood furniture,** dampen the paper thoroughly with salad cream, wait five minutes, and rub along the grain with super-fine (0000) steel wool. Wipe dry.

SIMPLE solutions

If glue spills on your furniture start by scraping up whatever you can, using a butter knife. If the glue is white school glue, treat it as you would a protein-based stain, which means no hot water – the hot water can cook the proteins in the stain. Instead, spray the spot with cold water, then blot it with a clean cloth, repeating the process until clean. If it is model-making glue, blot it with a cloth dampened with dry-cleaning solvent or methylated spirits.

Garden furniture

Wooden chairs and tables need to be sealed when you first get them out to use each year. Use teak oil or, if you want to change the colour, a wood stain, to do this. Metal furniture that has been poorly stored in the winter may have developed rust spots. Use very fine grade glasspaper to get these off, then apply a coat of clear varnish to protect.

Clean shade
When you get out your patio umbrella for the first time, open it up and brush off any dust and cobwebs that may have accumulated over winter. Wash off any stubborn marks with a brush dipped in a solution of warm water and washing-up liquid. Rinse by spraying with the hose, then leave to dry.

● **Plastic resin furniture** tends to need just a good clean. Avoid bleach-based spray cleaners as they will pit the surface and – on greens particularly – you may suffer instant colour fade. Instead, make do with sudsy water from washing-up liquid. Use a large sponge or bundled rags to wipe down, then dry or leave out in the sun.

● **During the fine weather** keep on top of the cleaning by keeping a pack of multi surface wipes in the area where you store your tables and chairs. These are an effective and hygienic way to clean off the bird-droppings. You'll minimise clean-ups by taking the extra minute each evening to tip chairs up against the table, so that the seats are protected from rain and dirt.

Garden ornaments

To clean or not to clean – that is the question when it comes to garden ornaments. Just as some experts believe that antiques should not have their original finishes removed by cleaning, some people feel that a little algae, plus a bird dropping or two, give an ivy-clad concrete cherub a more natural look. The

Garden ornaments

decision on whether to clean your garden ornament is up to you. But if you want to clean, here's what you can do.

- **To clean garden ornaments,** remember that much of what you'll be cleaning is actually alive. Organic matter, such as algae, moss, mould and mildew, all make damp stone their host – in fact, they'll go anywhere there is moisture and warmth. Add to that dust and dirt, dead organic matter and bird droppings and you end up with quite a mess (or a lovely patina, if that's your view).

- **You can get rid of the organic matter** and remove the rest with a simple, inexpensive solution of 100ml bleach to 4 litres water, with a squirt or two of washing-up liquid thrown in and worked into suds. Wear gloves to apply it with a long-handled brush and gently scrub until clean. Rinse with the garden hose. This works for most materials used for garden ornaments and statues, including concrete, stone and polyester resins.

- **Because bleach can damage** the plants in your garden – and most noticeably the lawn – move the ornaments to the driveway or a path for cleaning. For anything too large to move, use the cleaning agent sparingly and rinse with a sponge and bucket of clean water instead of the hose. Don't ever use chlorine to clean a pond that contains fish. If you clean a birdbath, be sure to flush out the cleaning solution completely.

- **To clean mirror balls,** use a window-cleaning solution. Mix 100ml white vinegar in 4 litres warm water and add a squirt of washing-up liquid. Apply it with a spray bottle or a clean cloth. Gently scrub until clean and either rinse with a hose or dry with a dry towel or newspaper. If the mirror ball is stainless steel, wax it with car wax once a year to renew its shine and give it a protective coating. And wipe out scratches with a car scratch remover.

Garden trellises

Trellises make attractive
additions to a lawn or
garden, but all those cracks
and crevices provide a
wealth of places for dirt
and grime to hide.

**Pruning plants
out of the way**
To clean trellises
that are supporting
plants, wash them
in the early spring.
Prune climbing
plants back to
about 15mm –
most climbers can
easily take it – and
remove the rest of
the plant material
from the trellis.

- **To clean trellises** with
no plants attached, use
a hose with a nozzle that
sends the water out in a tightly focused stream. Apply with
a stiff-bristled nylon or fibre brush to scrub dirty spots. If the
trellises are wood, use the brush sparingly; you can use a freer
hand on trellises made of plastic, glass fibre or metal. You could
also use a power washer, available at tool-hire shops.

- **To attack the green** mouldy-mossy stuff that grows in shady
spots, mix a solution of 4 litres water and 300ml chlorine bleach
in a bucket. Apply the solution to the trellis with a brush and
scrub. Rinse with plain water.

Gemstones

Don't assume that all gemstones are like diamonds. Some are
so soft that brushing – and certainly cleaning in soapy water –
is enough to dull and damage them for ever.

- **The softest gemstones,** such as amber, opals and coral,
should be merely wiped with a silk cloth. This should be
enough to restore their shine and lustre.

- **Harder stones** – such as rubies, emeralds and topaz – can
be immersed in warm, soapy water, before being carefully
rinsed and air-dried.

Gemstones

- **The heavyweights of the gemstone world** – sapphire, cubic zirconium and diamond – are up to hot washing in soapy water and, if needed, you can scrub around the facets of the stone with a toothbrush to get out any ingrained dirt.

Glasses & sunglasses

For general cleaning of spectacles, wet cleaning is better than dry cleaning. Most of us have grabbed a tissue or pulled a handkerchief out of a pocket to wipe our glasses, but that can smear dirt around and scratch the lenses. Dirt particles are hard, whereas lenses are soft and getting softer – almost all lenses today are plastic and are especially susceptible to scratching.

- **For daily cleaning,** pass the glasses under running water and dry them with a tissue or a clean microfibre cleaning cloth made especially for glasses. Get them from your optician or at chemists. Packaged single-use towelettes made for glasses are also good cleaners and are convenient when you're on the move.

- **To remove oily smears** from your glasses, pick up a specially formulated lens cleaner at a chemist or supermarket and follow the packet instructions. Using water alone will not

SIMPLE solutions

Next to dirty lenses, the most annoying problem with glasses is having a screw loose in the hinge – which then allows the lens to fall out of the frame.

There are special repair kits with tiny screwdrivers that can tighten the screw. But if it comes loose repeatedly, you need something more than a screwdriver. Try welding it together with a drop of clear nail polish: just put a drop on the screw, then turn it as usual. Once the nail polish hardens, it will have extra strength.

Glasses & sunglasses

remove oils. Even mild washing-up liquid can damage coatings over time and harsher cleaners (including anything with ammonia) can damage them immediately. So though lens cleaners may seem like an unnecessary expense, they will help to keep your lenses from getting cloudy and scratched and prolong the life of your glasses. The best lens cleaners even leave behind a thin film, a kind of instant coating, which further brightens the lenses. There's one exception; if you have an anti-reflective coating on your glasses, you'll need to get a specialist cleaner from your optician.

- **To clean the frames of your glasses,** mix a few drops of washing-up liquid in a bowl of water. Dip a clean, soft toothbrush into the solution and gently scrub around the frame, the nosepiece and the earpieces, avoiding the lenses as much as possible. Rinse the frames under running water and dry with a clean cloth.

Glass furniture

You do need to clean glass furniture very regularly to make sure it looks its best. Clean it as you would a horizontal mirror.

- **Apply your cleaning solution** – 1 part white vinegar to 4 parts water – from a spray bottle directly onto your cloth, then rub into the glass. Take care not to hold onto the table as you clean, in order to avoid fingermarks.

- **When you come to move** glass furniture, say when you want to clean the carpet, take care to avoid breakage. Glass is amazingly heavy, so this may turn out to be a two-person job. Clearly, because you'll need to touch it to lift it, you should clean glass furniture as the final stage of your room clean.

Glass safety
Whenever you're cleaning something made of glass you need to take special care; broken glass can give you a serious cut. Place a rubber pad or folded towel in your sink (or use a plastic bowl) whenever you wash small glass items. In a double sink, also put a folded towel over the ridge. Handle glasses by the bowl, not the stem, and wash items individually. And when washing large items, such as glass furniture or windows, don't press down too hard as you clean.

Glassware

Anyone can clean a glass. Just use hot water and washing-up liquid. But to get rid of streaks, spots and unappetising rim stains – and make your glassware really sparkle – you have to know how to dry them properly.

- **Clean glassware first** when you're washing dishes by hand, since glasses are usually less dirty than pots, pans, plates and utensils. (If you don't clean the glasses first, then change the dish water before you get to them. Otherwise, the glasses will end up dirtier than they were when you started.)

- **Use washing-up liquid** mixed with hot water. Wash with a soft, clean sponge or dishcloth. Don't use an abrasive pot scrubber as it may scratch glass. Rinse with even hotter water – as hot as you can safely stand. Hot water not only helps cut grease, but it also beads up and steams off (the first step towards good drying is to dry fast). Avoid excessive suds, which make glasses harder to rinse and slippery to handle, which will increase the chances of their breaking or chipping.

- **No matter how well** you've cleaned glassware, if there is slow-drying water left, chances are it will leave streaks or spots. Fogging causes some of the worst spotting. To avoid the 'greenhouse effect' – when glasses placed upside down on their rims fog up inside – dry glasses upside down on a drying rack. If you don't have a rack, put them upright on a towel and make sure air can circulate inside the glass for rapid drying.

- **To remove the lime build-up** on glassware that occurs when it is washed in the dishwasher, use a commercial rinse agent during the washing cycles. This helps water stream off while the glass is drying inside the foggy dishwasher. Or fill a large plastic bowl with white vinegar and give each glass a 15-minute bath afterwards. Then rinse the glass with running water and allow to air-dry.

Glassware

- **To remove food-colouring stains** left in glassware by the dyes in powdered soft-drink mixes and other beverages, fill the glass with a solution of 2 tablespoons household ammonia in 1 litre hot water. Let it stand for 30 minutes and then rinse with clean, cool water.

- **Hand-washing is best** for fine glassware, even if you'd prefer to use the dishwasher. To avoid scratching the glasses, remove rings, watches and bracelets, especially those with diamonds. Move the tap head out of the way, so there will be no chance that you will accidentally smack any precious items against it.

- **Using both hands,** clean one piece at a time in hot, soapy water. Gently wash with a soft cotton cloth or clean sponge. For stubborn dirt, scrub gently with a soft toothbrush. Rinse twice, first in a sink full of tepid water with a capful of vinegar mixed in and finally under running tepid tap water.

SIMPLE solutions

If you're having a party and someone breaks a piece of glassware, then it's important to clear it up straight away to avoid anyone getting hurt:

- First of all, leave someone near the spot to warn others, then go and get a small cardboard box, a pair of work gloves, and a broom and dustpan (for hard floors) or a vacuum cleaner (for carpets).
- Wearing gloves, pick up the big pieces of broken glass and put them in the box. On a hard floor, inspect a wide circle around the crash site for pieces that may have spread. Check your guests' ankles, too – on top of shoes, trapped on trousers – for splinters of glass.
- Next, sweep or vacuum. Vacuum the carpet several times to make sure you have removed all tiny shards. Empty the vacuum bag when finished or tip a cylinder vacuum straight into your cardboard box. Seal the box with sticky tape and put it in the rubbish bin. The box will protect your hands and those of the rubbish collector.

Glassware

- **To clean really fine decorative glass,** wear gloves and mix up a solution of equal parts of methylated spirit and water, then add a few drops of ammonia. The water and the ammonia do the cleaning, while the spirit helps the glass to dry up very quickly. Apply the solution with cotton wool. Don't use this technique on glass with decorative gilt, as it could lift it off.

Gloves

Cleaning gloves can be tricky for a couple of reasons. First, in addition to stains and soil on the outside of gloves, you have to remove the dirt and oils left by your own skin on the inside of gloves. Second, gloves are complicated, full of cracks and crevices caused by the shape of our hands. There is a trick, though, that makes cleaning gloves simple and it's to wear them as you wash.

- **This way you can position each glove** exactly as you'd like it, while scrubbing with the other hand. Mix up a mild, sudsy solution of warm water and a drop of washing-up liquid. When you've finished washing, remove the gloves and rinse them in a sink full of clean water, emptying the sink and repeating until there is no more soap residue.

- **To dry gloves,** roll them up in a dry towel. After unrolling them, blow into them to bring them back into shape, then lay them out flat on the towel at room temperature. Never squeeze or wring gloves and don't dry them using a heat source, such as a radiator or hair dryer. If you need to iron them, lay them between the folds of a clean towel and pass the hot iron over the top layer of the towel.

Gold jewellery

While gold does not tarnish like silver, it will, over time, develop a dingy, oily film from lotions, powders, soaps and the oils secreted by your skin. And gold that has been alloyed with other metals – copper, silver or nickel – can tarnish and smudge. To revive your gold's lustre, clean it regularly.

- **The mildest way to clean gold** is to soak it briefly in a bowl of warm water mixed with a little washing-up liquid. Then gently scrub crevices and design details using a soft toothbrush or eyebrow brush. Place the jewellery in a wire strainer and rinse under warm running water. Pat dry with a chamois cloth or any clean, white, soft cotton cloth.

- **For a stronger cleaning solution,** mix equal parts of cold water and ammonia (cheaper than a commercial jewellery cleaner). Soak the jewellery in the solution for 30 minutes. Gently scrub with a toothbrush or eyebrow brush. Rinse with water and dry on a soft towel.

- **Having gold professionally cleaned** is the safest and most effective method. Ask a jeweller if they can put it through their ultrasonic cleaning machine. Jewellery is dipped into a container of liquid and when high-frequency vibrations are sent through the liquid, the dirt and grime drop off.

Expert **ADVICE**

Although gold is hard wearing, there are things you can do that might damage it:
- Chlorine can cause gold to deteriorate over time. Wedding rings are solid enough to be safe from its effects. But if you swim a lot, you might want to remove fine chains and delicate earrings.
- Don't clean gold with toothpaste; some toothpastes contain harsh abrasives, such as silica (found in quartz), which can dull a glossy gold finish.

Gore-Tex fabric

This brand-name membrane, found in rain jackets and other outerwear, is renowned for its ability to be both waterproof and breathable. Gore-Tex is both washable and dry-cleanable.

- **To clean a Gore-Tex garment** follow the instructions on the label. Typically, the instructions will be to put the garment in a washing machine with warm water and a standard detergent, but no fabric softener or bleach, then tumble in a dryer. If the garment calls for dry-cleaning, tell the cleaner you want a clear, distilled solvent rinse.

- **To preserve a garment's water resistance,** you need to reapply a water-resistant coating occasionally, because multiple washings (or a single trip to the dry-cleaner) will remove the fine water-resistant layer. (You've lost the water resistance when water no longer beads up on your garment's outer shell, but sinks into the fabric.) The actual Gore-Tex layer will be safe, but the outer shell will need a new application of its coating, called durable water repellent (DWR). Gore-Tex sells an easy-to-use spray-on durable water repellent called ReviveX.

Granite

Some worktops and other architectural stone sold as granite may have only the appearance of granite. So, when it comes to cleaning, knowing whether the material is genuine granite or not is important, because some cleaners considered safe for granite may react negatively with other types of stone.

- **There are also different types** of surface finishes to consider, from raw stone to highly polished stone to chemically sealed stone. This may all sound fairly complicated, but

Granite

cleaning the stone should not be. The best approach to cleaning granite is usually the simplest one.

- **To clean granite floors,** walls and other flat surfaces, use either a vacuum cleaner or a dry dust mop.

- **Dust granite worktops** regularly with a clean, dry rag and wipe up spills immediately to avoid staining. Wipe down surfaces with warm water and a soft cloth or sponge. Let caked-on food soak for a while before wiping. If that doesn't work, then add a little washing-up liquid to the water. Rinse well with plenty of clean water. Too much soap can leave a film or cause streaking. Avoid stronger cleaning products, such as bath and tile cleaners or scouring powders, which can stain or scratch.

- **Most stains on granite** consist of solid residue that has jammed in between the crystals of the stone after the liquid that carried it has evaporated. The trick is to put the solid back into a solution so it can be removed. First, determine whether your stain is water-based (for example, from spilled fruit juice) or oil-based (such as salad dressing).

- **If the stain is water-based,** pour hot tap water on it and let it stand for a few minutes. Wipe away excess water, then stack 1cm of paper towels on the stain and saturate with hot water. Cover with a piece of plastic (cling film will do) and a flat, heavy weight, such as a book. Let it stand overnight, or for about 10 hours. Remove the paper towels and let the spot dry. If some of the stain is still present, repeat the treatment.

- **If the stain is oil-based,** follow the same procedure, only instead of water use acetone (but do not heat). After the 10 hours is up, remove the paper towels and rinse the spot with clean water. If necessary, repeat. Acetone can be found in chemists, sold as nail-polish remover.

Keep it off the floor

Dirt and grit that you bring onto a granite floor via the soles of your shoes and boots can scratch the surface of the stone and wear it down. Ideally, you should remove outdoor footwear before you walk across a granite floor, but if this is impossible, try to clean up gritty dirt every day.

Greenhouses

The cleaner your greenhouse is, the healthier the plants housed there will be. Dust, debris and clutter are magnets for insects, diseases and harmful micro-organisms. Dirty windows also block the sun, so can mean your plants will grow less well.

- **Dust your plants** to remove fungal spores (such as grey mould and powdery mildews) and mites (such as the omnivorous spider mite). Most people hose off their plants, which is fine but tends to unsettle and spread the dust. An easier – and more effective – method is to vacuum them. Use an extension lead and your ordinary vacuum cleaner with a dusting attachment. This works best on sturdy leaves that you can hold in your hand while you quickly whisk the brush over the surface. Once a year is enough to halt the growth of the plant predators mentioned above.

- **Cut down on clutter** in your greenhouse. Piles of dead plants, stacks of dirty pots and sacks spilling over with potting soil can all be places for insects and micro-organisms to spend the winter. Remove all of these things – and any other clutter – regularly. Try not to pile them right next to the greenhouse. Either get rid of them or store them in a shed, garage or basement. Dead plant material is the worst offender. Purge dead plants and pick up dead leaves.

- **Keep your greenhouse weed-free** to get rid of yet another source of food for insects and bacteria. Weeds also boost a greenhouse's humidity level, which will make conditions even riper for disease and pestilence. Keep a sack of hydrated lime on hand (but don't clutter up the greenhouse with it). Sprinkle it under benches and in corners to deter weed growth. It lasts for a long time and is non-toxic to humans. You can buy hydrated lime at your hardware store. Never use herbicides in your greenhouse.

Greenhouses

- **Wash the greenhouse windows** at least once a year to keep them as clear as possible and kill any harmful microbial growth on the inner surface. Do it when you have the least amount of living plant material in your greenhouse – for most people, this is during autumn. Use a mild washing-up liquid; it not only loosens dirt, it also has ingredients that break up proteins and fats – and rupture the membranes of bacteria and fungi. Depending on the size of your greenhouse, either put the washing-up liquid in a hose-end sprayer or mix it with water in a clean spray bottle. Rinse by spraying with the garden hose.

Gutters & drainpipes

Make your own gutter scoop
Take a large plastic milk bottle and cut the bottom off – angle your cut so that the side with the handle is shorter than the opposite side. Keep the lid on. You now have a handy tool that is just right for scooping out rubbish from gutters and can be recycled in the usual way after use.

Water is your home's worst enemy and guttering and drainpipes are an important line of defence. You need to keep them clean so that they can work properly. A blocked gutter will force water down the side of your house, where it can cause serious damage.

- **Clean out gutters** any time they are blocked, but particularly in autumn. Wear heavy gloves, as thorns and roof nails can end up in gutters. Use a ladder tall enough to reach gutters safely and make sure someone else is holding the bottom. Each time you move it to a new section, check that you have anchored the ladder securely and safely and the rungs are square-on with the house before you begin your climb.

- **To clean the outside** of gutters, mix a solution of 100ml trisodium phosphate and 4 litres water and, wearing gloves, use a rag to wipe over the guttering. This is purely cosmetic; your guttering won't last any longer, but it will look shinier.

Hair & make-up brushes

Most of us don't clean our hairbrushes often enough. When we finally get around to it, we often spend more time untangling the balls of hair than we do on the cleaning job itself. Clean your brush more often using the following tips and you'll save time in the long run.

- **To clean a hairbrush,** first pull out any loose hair from the bristles. Then make your own economical and effective cleaning solution by mixing 2 teaspoons shampoo and 60ml vinegar in a sink filled with warm water. Soak the brush in the solution for several minutes. Pull a clean, wide-toothed comb down each row of bristles to remove any remaining hair.

- **By now, the soaking solution** should have loosened any build-up of oil, dirt, gel and hairspray on the brush. Scrub the brush clean with a nailbrush (hold it down in the sink to contain the splatter) and rinse with warm running water. Let the brush air-dry.

- **To clean a make-up brush,** avoid using commercial make-up brush cleaners, which often contain harsh chemicals. The chemicals aren't good for the sensitive skin of your face and can dry out a make-up brush, which can be quite expensive – especially the ones made of real animal hair.

    For a safe, non-drying alternative, mix 2 parts water with 1 part a gentle fabric wash, such as Woolite. Dip the tip of the brush into the solution. Don't dip the wooden or metal handle, because getting this wet can cause the bristles to fall out. Rinse the brush in clean water. Repeat the process until the brush is completely clean (no make-up colour is visible) and free of the wash solution. Dry the brush gently with a towel, being sure to move the towel 'with the grain', or direction of the brush's hair.

Hair dryers

Modern dryers require minimal upkeep, but some maintenance is essential. A dryer with a debris-choked filter can overheat. It will perform poorly, possibly even damaging your hair. To keep it blowing properly, plan to clear the filter every three months if you use the hair dryer daily.

- **Dryers work by fanning** the surrounding air, directing it through the appliance's heating mechanism, and blowing it out of the nozzle as a stream of hot air. But the dryer pulls in dust and lint along with the air, and these particles lodge in a screen that filters the air before it hits the heating coils. Enough debris can accumulate in the filter to block air from flowing through. That's when the dryer may start to overheat. You may detect a warning odour like that of burning hair.

- **When a dryer overheats,** its thermostat attempts to cool things down by tripping the heating coils off and on. You feel alternating hot and cold air blowing out, which won't provide the styling effects of consistently warm air. Extreme blockage may trigger the dryer's non-resettable shutdown device and ruin the hair dryer completely.

- **To clean your dryer filter,** first unplug the hair dryer. Top-quality dryers have a filter cover that lifts off, giving easy access for cleaning. Scrub the filter with a dry, soft-bristled brush or toothbrush to get out the lint, dust and hair. Or use your vacuum with a crevice attachment. Pull out any stubborn bits with tweezers. If your dryer doesn't have a filter cover, you'll need to brush, vacuum or tweeze the filter from the outside.

- **To clean the dryer body** and accessories, just wipe with a damp rag (not a wet one, which could drip water into the heating element). Even the stickiest hair products are generally water soluble, so a damp cloth should remove them.

Handbags

Most handbags are home to a host of essential items as well as attracting all sorts of dust and clutter. All will last longer and look better if they are cleaned properly.

- **Before cleaning any handbag,** first empty the bag of its contents. Brush away loose dirt – inside and out – with a soft white cloth, or vacuum it using an upholstery attachment.

- **If your bag is so deep** that you can't see what is inside, secure a piece of nylon mesh (from a pair of old tights) over the end of the suction tube of your vacuum (don't use any attachments). Dust and dirt will go through, but not jewellery and coins dropped in the bottom of your bag.

  Next (with the exception of suede bags), wet a soft cloth in a cleaning solution appropriate for your bag's construction material (see below and page 226). Wring out the cloth until it's nearly dry and rub the bag inside and out, taking care not to dampen it any more than it takes to clean it. As well as any visible dirt, you will wipe away skin oils, hand lotion, make-up and perspiration. The handle, clasp and straps are typically high-grime spots on the exterior. Inside, wipe the lining – especially the bottom – and interior hardware, such as zips and metal name tags.

- **To clean a leather bag,** use saddle soap or a cream leather cleaner/conditioner, available at shoe-repair shops. Follow the label instructions. Always follow an application of saddle soap with a solvent-free leather conditioner, to avoid drying out the leather. Then buff up with a soft cloth.

- **To clean a fabric bag,** use half a teaspoon a gentle fabric wash, such as Woolite, in 60ml lukewarm water for all-over cleaning of sturdy fabrics. Use the fabric wash full strength for stubborn spots. For bags made of delicate fabrics, use barely damp baby wipes for a gentler cleaning.

> **Dye-hard duo**
> Never stack a leather handbag on top of or directly under a plastic one. The dye from the leather bag will leach and be absorbed by the plastic of the bag above or below.

Handbags

- **To clean patent leather,** use a cream cleaner/conditioner if it's real patent leather. Be gentle – patent leather scratches easily. On imitation patent leather, use washing-up liquid or a car interior vinyl and plastic cleaner, such as Turtle Wax, available at car-supplies shops.

- **To clean plastic, vinyl or polyurethane,** try a plastic cleaner. Wipe softer synthetics with a solution of washing-up liquid or a gentle fabric wash and water. Alternatively, use baby wipes or a car interior vinyl and plastic cleaner. To restore shiny plastics, spray with silicone wax spray after cleaning, then buff.

- **To clean a straw bag,** use a solution of 1 part liquid hand soap to 3 parts water.

- **To clean a suede bag,** brush the nap with a natural-bristle shoe brush to remove dirt on the surface. Otherwise, have the bag professionally dry-cleaned. Use protectant sprays sparingly, since some solutions can attract dirt.

Hats

To keep a fur, felt or velour hat clean, regularly brush the dust and dirt from the surface with a nylon or horsehair brush. It's important for a hat to be dust-free because once the hat gets wet, the dust becomes much harder to eliminate.

- **With fur and felt hats,** always brush with the nap (in the direction of the pile) and use separate brushes for light and dark hats. To deal with more extensive stains or soiling, take your hat to a professional for cleaning and shaping. It's a job specific to the hat and is based on fabric and the type of soiling that has occurred that only a professional is equipped to handle.

Hats

- **Avoid the temptation** to use stain-removal products on your hat. There's a good chance the solution will damage your hat further and create stain rings.

- **If you spill something on your hat,** blot it immediately with a soft, absorbent cloth to prevent it from seeping into the hat. If your hat gets spotted with mud, let it dry first. Then lightly brush it off with a nylon or horsehair brush.

- **To remove dust and loose dirt** from a straw hat, brush it with a dry cloth or brush. Beyond that, these hats are not really cleanable, even by a professional. With time, most straw hats naturally turn yellow and there's nothing you can do about it.

- **To clean a wool hat,** use a sticky fabric roller designed to remove hairs and lint from clothing, or a new paintbrush. Firmer and older brushes are too rough to use on wool hats.

- **If a hat has faded** in spots and you're ready to hang it up for good, here's how to get a little more life out of it.
  For a white hat, apply talcum powder using a dry sponge – a make-up sponge works well. For coloured hats, grind down a crayon that matches the colour of the hat, mix with the talcum powder and apply.

Expert **ADVICE**

If the satin lining of your hat is removable, you can take it out and wash it:
- Fill a sink with cold water and add a couple of drops of washing-up liquid. Place the satin lining in the water and rub it with a stiff scrubbing brush.
- To rinse the lining, hold it under cold running water until the soap is gone. Let it air-dry. If you want to remove creases, expose it to the steam from your steam iron – without actually touching the iron to the lining.

Hearing aids

Hearing aids need daily attention to remain in top working order. Wax and moisture are common causes of hearing-aid malfunctions – wax on hearing aids that fit inside the ear, and moisture from perspiration on hearing aids worn outside the ear.

Aid protection
If you wear a behind-the-ear hearing aid, apply hairspray *before* you put it on. The spray could damage the microphone. And don't wear your hearing aid when you're working in the garden. Perspiration, hose water, soil and grass clippings could damage it.

● **To clean an in-the-ear hearing aid,** first wash your hands to avoid contaminating the device. Then, using a brush (either the one supplied or a clean toothbrush), remove any wax on the exterior of the hearing aid. Alternatively, wipe the surface with a dry cotton cloth or a cloth lightly dampened with alcohol. If you use alcohol, wipe only the shell of the unit, not over the microphone or receiver, which can be damaged by moisture.

● **Cleaning a behind-the-ear hearing aid** is a two-part operation. To clean the ear mould that fits inside the ear, use water and ordinary hand soap, or a germicidal soap such as Carex. Put the soap on a cotton cloth dampened with lukewarm water. Wipe the ear mould clean, giving it a good rub. Rinse with lukewarm water and dry with a towel. To clean the hearing aid itself, use just a brush: a toothbrush is fine.

● **Every three months,** take the hearing aid to a specialist for a thorough clean. He or she should have the appropriate tools for cleaning more deeply into the interior of your hearing aid.

● **In-the-ear hearing aids** have wax guards or wax sceptres that protect the receiver from getting clogged with wax; clean these with a brush. Behind-the-ear hearing aids can be fitted with a sleeve jacket that covers the component behind the ear, protecting it from moisture; wipe this clean with a cloth.

● **A hearing aid has an electronic chip** in it so watch the amount of liquid you use when cleaning. Keep your hearing aid in a dry place when you're not using it – for example, in the bedroom while you're in the shower, instead of in the bathroom.

Hoses

Hoses require little cleaning other than the removal of dirt by spraying water from the hose onto itself.

- **Always start cleaning garden hoses** with the least abrasive method and work your way up. If you need some extra cleaning power, dampen a rag in warm water and add to it some biodegradable soap (available at camping stores). Rub it over the hose and use clean water from the hose to rinse. If you still have some dirt stuck on the hose, use a vinyl cleaner on vinyl hoses or rubber hoses that are coated with vinyl. Follow the manufacturer's instructions on the packet.

- **If your hose is blocked up** but there are no kinks in it, you may have a build-up of calcium deposits from minerals in the water. Bend the hose back and forth along the entire length to break up the build-up. If there's a nozzle on the business end of the hose, remove it and then turn on the water. This will help to flush out the loosened deposits.

> ### Longer lasting hosepipes
> To increase the life of your hose, don't leave it out in strong sunlight or extreme cold. While not in use, store it on a reel to prevent kinks or knots forming. In winter, drain the hose and store indoors. And never walk on or drive over a hose; it isn't designed to withstand that much pressure.

Hot tubs

If you're lucky enough to have a hot tub you will need to clean it. But how often you clean will depend on how often it's used.

- **If two people use the tub** up to three nights a week, clean it thoroughly and drain every three months. If you have a lot of children and the family uses it up to six nights a week, clean it every two months. If your hot tub is an occasional luxury, clean it as needed. You should still test chemical levels weekly.

- **If you aren't keeping track** of your use, then don't keep the water in longer than three months – six months maximum.

Hot tubs

- **A dirty, worn-out hot-tub filter** will fail to trap spa contaminants and will put undue strain on your tub's pump motor and heater. Rinse the filter weekly with water to get rid of coarse dirt and debris. Take a garden hose, apply the stream  at a 45 degree angle, and give it a pressure wash inside and out. Allow the filter to dry. Next, remove any fine particles of dirt carefully with a brush or by applying a stream of compressed air (from an air compressor or from an aerosol can, available at camera shops) to the filter's outer surface.

  - **If algae, suntan oil or body oils** still leave a coating, soak the filter overnight in a degreaser solution from the hot-tub dealer. If it's still clogged, check the water chemistry and adjust, drain and clean the tub, or buy a new filter cartridge. Replace the filter annually.

- **Every three months,** drain the water and clean the acrylic shell inside and out with a non-soap-based cleaner – most bathroom cleaners are detergent based, so use one designed for an acrylic bath. Spray it on, leave for a minute and then wipe off any scum or stains. Refill the tub right away – or wax it after cleaning with an aerosol wax. Be sure not to spray the cleaning solution and wax into the jets.

- **If you're still getting cloudy water,** your jets aren't working properly, or gunk is appearing on the water, you may have clogged pipes and you'll have to use a spa-cleaning agent, available from your hot-tub supplier.

- **To clean hot-tub covers,** use a cover-cleaning product or a general vinyl cleaner, sold in car-supplies stores to clean soft-top cars. Applying a paste wax to your hot-tub cover is a good idea, because it creates a barrier between the cover and the sun.

Houseplants

Your houseplants need more than regular watering. To maintain their ability to grow, they do need cleaning and you can remove dust and dirt by giving them a shower. It is important to keep plants clean, because grime prevents photosynthesis, the process by which leaves absorb sunlight and carbon dioxide to make food for the plant. The shower will also help remove unwelcome insects.

- **First, prepare the plant's pot.** Put the pot in a plastic bag and tie the bag tightly around the base of the plant without damaging it. You want to be sure the plant's growing medium doesn't become waterlogged in the shower. If your plant has multiple stems growing out of the soil, lay extra plastic bags between the stems. Put the plant in the shower and set the water temperature to tepid – neither hot nor cold. Let the shower sprinkle the plant for a few minutes.

- **Sometimes minerals in the shower water** will build up on the plant's leaves, making them look dull. To clean the minerals off hard-surfaced (not hairy) leaves, wipe with a dry, clean rag. Support each leaf with your free hand as you wipe. Or gently scrape the minerals off with your thumb.

- **Cleaning plants with hairy leaves** is a little trickier. First give them a gentle dusting with a feather duster, then put the plant in the shower, as above.

- **After the plants have had their shower,** allow them to dry thoroughly in the shower stall or set them on paper towels or old newspapers until they're not dripping any more. If you return them to direct sunlight while they're still wet, the light may burn the leaves.

- **Now check your plant's surroundings.** Make sure the window where it sits is clean so that the plant will get

Bloom time

To enjoy cut flowers for longer, try these simple techniques:
- Cut off any leaves below water level.
- Wash the vase and change the water daily.
- Try a preservative in the water, such as 2 tablespoons white vinegar and 2 teaspoons sugar to 1 litre water. Or use 1 part tonic water to 2 parts water. A dissolved aspirin also works.

Houseplants

maximum sunlight. Check the surface of the soil and the inner rim of the pot for any white mineral deposits that may have accumulated: these can be toxic to your plants. If you have an extreme case of mineral build-up, put the pot in a sink where it can drain freely and run a lot of water through the soil to remove the minerals. (Don't do this during times of low light or dormancy, however. Plants should be actively growing; otherwise, they may develop root rot.)

- **Cleaning a cactus** requires a gentle touch – not only to prevent spiking yourself, but also to protect the waxy coating that helps the plant to conserve moisture in desert climates. Stick to misting your cactus with a spray bottle filled with water and even then only clean the areas of the plant that are showing dirt or dust. Make the cleaning quick and gentle and let the cactus dry before putting it back into direct sunlight. Or use long tweezers to carefully pick off any dust particles.

- **To clean succulents** with fuzzy leaves, use only a soft paintbrush or a feather duster to remove dust. The fuzziness protects the plant in arid conditions and washing with water can be hazardous to the leaves.

---

how to clean **artificial plants**

- If you have artificial plants or flowers then they will need occasional dusting. Use a feather duster or a hair dryer on its lowest, coolest setting to blow off the dust on sturdy blooms. Use canned air to squirt air on any especially fragile flowers.
- For a more thorough cleaning fill the sink (or bath, if necessary) with enough water so that the plants or flowers can be submerged. Add a squirt of washing-up liquid and slosh it around to make suds. Then put the plants or flowers in the water, holding them down until they are covered. Gently raise and lower them a couple of times. Drain the water and then rinse under a slow-running tap or under the shower in the bathroom. Leave to air-dry thoroughly.

Iron

Wrought iron, as defined metallurgically and by the process used in working the metal, is not produced any more except for restorations. (Real wrought iron is worked white hot, hammered and twisted into shape.) Today, the term is often used, incorrectly, to include decorative iron, 'mild steel' or cast iron.

- **Indoor iron pieces** – such as bed frames, lamps and chandeliers – are dust magnets. If your item has a black-satin finish, you might as well be focusing a spotlight on the dust – everyone will see it.

- **The easiest and quickest way** to clean indoor pieces is with compressed air (buy it in cans from camera shops). It simply blows the dust away and is especially good for all the edges, corners and crevices of detailed iron, which defy the reach of a conventional cleaning rag. Or try carefully dusting intricate ornamentation with a new, soft-bristled paintbrush.

- **To clean a smooth piece of wrought iron,** wipe first with a soft cotton rag, to remove dust, then wipe with furniture polish sprayed onto a clean section of the rag. If there's dirt stuck to the wrought iron, the furniture polish may help lubricate and remove it. Water isn't recommended. It will collect in areas that can't be reached by a drying cloth, leading to rust. Furniture polish, on the other hand, provides a protective coating that repels water and resists dust.

  - **Outdoor furniture** that isn't supposed to rust needs to be cleaned only when it looks dirty or has mud or grime caked on it. Remove dirt by spraying with a garden hose. Periodically check the piece for rust, which may start around areas such as bolts. If you see minor oxidation, gently use a dry wire brush to remove the rust. Wipe off any dust particles you create.

Iron

Before applying touch-up paint to the surface, wipe the area clean with acetone or paint thinner on a cotton cloth. This will make the paint adhere better by removing oils that have transferred to the iron from your hands. It also will dissolve any remaining paint in the rusty area. Let the paint thinner dry before painting. Wear gloves and goggles, as acetone and paint thinner can be quite harsh to the skin and eyes. If your wrought iron becomes very rusty, you may have to take it to a professional to be sandblasted.

● **To clean outdoor furniture** that has a rusty finish or patina, let your item reach the desired rusty brown before you clean. Wipe off loose rust, dust or dirt with a rag. Then coat the piece with a clear lacquer paint (available at hardware stores) to protect it from the elements and to prevent further rusting.

● **To clean cast iron** use the same cleaning methods as used for wrought iron. Cast-iron items typically include doorknobs, railings and fences. Hose down the item and then inspect it for rust. If you find any, clean it off with a wire brush. Wipe away any dust that your cleaning has produced, before putting on a rust-preventive paint. Spray and paint-on versions are available.

● **To clean well-seasoned iron cookware,** all that's usually required is a little boiling water, a light scraping with a wooden spoon and a quick wipe with a clean cloth. Dry thoroughly and lightly oil again. For badly burned-on food, use a copper-wool scouring pad. For extreme cases of burned-on food and grease, use any common oven cleaner following the packet directions; rinse well. Then, unfortunately, you'll have to season the item as if it were new (see the box left).

● **To remove rust on iron cookware** a wire brush is best. If the rust is hard to shift you may have to use glasspaper or a commercial rust remover.

Seasoning new cast-iron pots

First wash your new pot, then fill it about two-thirds full with water. Add 80ml white vinegar per 4 litres water and boil for one hour. Let it cool and then discard the liquid. Wash the pot with plain water, then apply a light coat of vegetable oil or lard on the inside and outside. Heat in a moderate oven for an hour. Turn off the oven and leave the pot to cool inside. Wipe off any excess oil; the seasoning process is complete.

Irons

Generally speaking, irons tend to need cleaning when you've had a minor mishap – for example, you've tried to press a synthetic fabric on too high a heat and some of the fibre has stuck to the soleplate of the iron.

- **To remove stuck-on fibres,** heat the iron until the fibres liquefy. Then, on nonstick and aluminium or chrome soleplates, use a wooden spatula or flat stick (for instance, a clean ice-lolly stick) to scrape off the fibres. Never scrape the soleplate of an iron with plastic, metal or anything abrasive. Run the iron over some towelling or other rough material that the remaining fibres will be able to stick to.

- **If you don't know** what it is that's got stuck on your soleplate and if the mark doesn't liquefy when you heat the iron, use any hot-iron cleaner, available at haberdashers and most hardware stores.

- **If the stain still remains** on an aluminium or chrome soleplate, your next option is to make a paste of bicarbonate of soda and water with the consistency of toothpaste. Rub it on a cool iron with a soft cloth, then wipe it off with another damp cloth. Don't use this method on nonstick soleplates.

- **On Teflon or metallic-coated,** nonstick surfaces, a damp cloth should wipe off any water marks and a wooden spatula should remove any fibre stains. Should any marks still remain, rub a nylon scouring pad on the iron's soleplate when it's cool.

- **Specific substances** require specific cleaning techniques. To clean a waxy stain (from a crayon or the residue of a dripping candle, for instance), heat your iron as hot as possible, then run it over a dry newspaper until the wax is completely gone. Rest assured that the print won't come off on your iron.

Irons

- **To clean sticky, oil-based residue** from an aluminium or chrome soleplate, use an all-purpose cleaner on a cold iron. Spray the cleaner onto the soleplate and rub with a soft cloth. Remove the cleaner by rubbing with a wet cloth. (Never immerse the electrical appliance in water or rinse under running water.) Before using the iron again, heat it first and rub the soleplate on an old towel to remove any traces of the cleaner and residue.

- **To clean acetate or nylon** that has melted and then hardened on the soleplate, use acetone on a cloth and rub the affected area of the cold soleplate until the melted residue is gone. Don't get the acetone on the plastic outer shell of the iron, because the acetone will melt it.

- **To remove small bits of burned lint** that have gathered, use your iron's 'burst of steam' feature as directed.

- **To prevent stains from forming** on the soleplate in the first place (so you can avoid having to clean), use a pressing cloth during ironing to act as a barrier between the hot iron and your clothing or linens. A pressing cloth – and this should be a piece of lightweight pure cotton, such as a bit of old, white cotton sheeting – will prevent synthetic fibres or starch from attaching to the iron.

- **To clean the iron's steam chamber,** check the manufacturer's guidelines about whether to use distilled or tap water. Generally, newer models use tap water – the minerals actually help in the steaming process. With the cord unplugged, fill the iron with water. Then plug in the iron and, depending on your model, either turn it to its cleaning mode function (most manufacturers recommend using the self-cleaning feature once a year) or to the steaming feature.

Irons

- **Hold the steaming iron over a sink,** with the soleplate face down, until the steam stops. Unplug the iron and leave it in the sink for about half an hour to fully dry.

- **Or place the iron face down** on a heatproof cooking rack while it steams. The steam will remove lint, dirt, dust and mineral deposits that have built up in the steam vents. Finish by wiping with a dry cloth.

- **If you haven't steam-pressed** clothes or linens with your iron for a while, you may find that when you do the water or steam looks rusty. This is actually burned lint, which can stain your clothes. So it's important to clean your steam chamber and vents every couple of months.

- **If the steam-cleaning technique** described above doesn't remove the mineral deposits from the steam chamber, try using vinegar if your manufacturer's instructions allow it. Pour white vinegar into the steam chamber and steam it through the vents. Rinse out the vinegar and refill the chamber with water. Let the water steam through the iron to remove all the vinegar. If you're not careful about removing the vinegar, it may stain your clothes the next time you use the iron. The acidic nature of the vinegar may also etch and damage the interior of the iron if left inside the steam chamber for too long.

- **If the steam vents on the soleplate** become clogged, unbend a paperclip and push it into the holes to reopen the vents before steaming the iron.

- **Cleaning the outer plastic shell of your iron** is simple. Just clean it with a damp rag, then wipe dry.

- **Always leave your iron** until completely cool and dry before putting it away. Store it in an upright position.

Ivory & bone

Treat ivory and bone with care. Whether you're cleaning a figurine or a beaded necklace, the condition and fragility of the item will determine your approach.

● **True ivory comes from the tusk** of an elephant or mammoth. Today, the tusks of other mammals, such as walruses and certain whales, and some synthetics are considered ivory as well. Ivory is chemically similar to bone and antler, but ivory has no blood vessels whereas bone does. Bone, therefore, is fragile and porous, but ivory is dense. Ivory and bone are both sensitive to heat, light and moisture.

● **If your ivory item is fragile,** take it to an expert to be cleaned. Because ivory readily absorbs oils and stains, wear white cotton gloves while working with ivory, or, at the very least, wash your hands thoroughly with soap and water to remove oils and dirt.

● **If your ivory or bone is sturdy and stable,** clean off the surface dust or dirt with a barely damp cotton cloth or cotton bud. To dampen, use a solution of mild washing-up liquid and water or use just water. Too much moisture may cause surface fractures to appear on the ivory. Wipe the surface of

Expert **ADVICE**

Experts in the care of bone and ivory advise that you avoid keeping precious pieces in the following situations:
● Display areas exposed to sunlight or a spotlight.
● A closed display case with light bulbs inside, heating the interior.
● Nearby ventilation or heating ducts, the tops of electrical appliances or other sources of heat or cold.
● Anywhere near rubber-based storage materials, adhesives and paint.

Ivory & bone

your item with a dry cloth, and apply a second cloth or cotton bud dampened with white spirit to remove any soap residue. Wipe with a dry cloth.

- **Never rub the surface of ivory and bone.** You may inadvertently remove the original surface coats, any original pigments or patina that have built up over time.

- **To remove wax or oil from ivory,** use a cloth or cotton bud barely dampened with white spirit. If your ivory or bone has scrimshaw (engravings or decorations) on it, test an inconspicuous part of the scrimshaw to see whether it will withstand the cleaning technique. If it doesn't react well to the test, don't try to clean the scrimshaw yourself.

- **If your ivory or bone is stained** in any way (a yellow stain is typical), you will have to call in an expert. These stains are usually due to the oxidation that comes with age or may be caused by the oils on your hands. Sometimes, placing the ivory or bone in sunlight bleaches it and helps it to regain its warm off-white colour. Keeping ivory or bone in the dark accelerates the yellowing associated with ageing. But do not expose ivory or bone to long periods of intense sunlight or heat, because that will dry it out and cause it to crack.

- **Store ivory and bone** in a carefully controlled environment, ideally 45 per cent to 55 per cent relative humidity and about 20°C, in low light. Conditions should be kept constant. The most severe damage to ivory and bone is caused by fluctuations in relative humidity and temperature. Low humidity will cause ivory to dry out, causing shrinkage and cracking. High humidity and changes in temperature can cause your ivory to expand and contract.

Kennels

If your pet has a kennel outside, you don't have to change the bedding as often as you change your own sheets. But at least once a month isn't too often to keep fleas and mites and other kinds of pests at bay and make it a clean and comfortable haven for your dog to sleep in.

● **Start cleaning a kennel** by treating it like you would a teenager's bedroom. First get everything out. If you use straw as your pet's bedding, throw it away. If your dog has blankets in the kennel, then put them in the washing machine and select the hottest water possible for the fabric of the blankets.

● **Hose down the kennel,** both inside and out. Then leave for a few minutes to let the water drain away; you might need to lift one end to get all the water out. Then get ready to scrub.

● **When washing a kennel,** don't use anything that you wouldn't want your pet to lick up. Chemical household cleaners will make a home sparkle, but dogs aren't as particular about the way their home looks as they are about the way it smells. A pine-scented house might smell wonderfully clean to you, but your dog might disagree and a strong, new smell might put your pet off their home. Instead, use a plastic-bristled brush to apply an organic cleaner or use a homemade solution of 100ml vinegar with 300ml water, or a solution of 4 tablespoons lemon extract or lemon juice with 4 litres water.

● **Replacing the bedding** is the last step. If your dog likes to lie on straw, put in some fresh straw and sprinkle it with bicarbonate of soda – this will absorb odours and make the freshness last longer. If your pet prefers blankets, let the washed blankets dry in the sun for extra freshness, then sprinkle on a little bicarbonate of soda. Brush this into the blankets and put them back in the kennel.

Kitchen units

To routinely clean kitchen-cabinet exteriors, dust with a clean cloth regularly and wipe with a damp cloth periodically. (In terms of frequency, the meaning of regularly and periodically will depend on your specific cabinets and frequency of use of the cabinets.) Never use abrasive cleaners or scourers on kitchen cabinets. Also avoid using your dishcloth, because it may contain grease or detergents that can add streaks and smears.

● **The stains around handles** will probably be the most troublesome, being a mixture of skin oils, food smears and softened finish, so you'll need to use a heavy-duty cleaner. On cabinets made of plastic laminate, metal or glass, try a strong all-purpose household cleaner. Spray it onto a cloth or sponge and apply to the dirty areas. Let the cleaner sit for a few minutes, then wipe it off with a rinsed-out cloth or sponge. Wipe again with a dry cloth.

● **To clean wood cabinets,** first try a little washing-up liquid applied directly to a cloth or sponge. Rub into the dirty areas around the handles. Then wash the entire cabinet with an oil-soap solution; use 4 tablespoons of a product such as Pledge Soapy Cleaner to 4 litres water. Apply with a cloth dipped in the solution and wrung out. Then go over the cabinets with a cloth dampened in plain water, followed by a dry cloth.

● **To clean cabinets that have windows,** wash the glass with a cloth or paper towel sprayed with a little glass cleaner. Don't spray cleaner, or even plain water, directly onto the glass – it can drip down and damage the surrounding wood.

● **To clean the shelves,** use the same methods as for the exterior surfaces. Shelves should need thorough cleaning only once or twice a year – assuming you clean up any spills as soon as they happen. To remove an old spill, sprinkle with bicarbonate of soda and wipe with a damp cloth.

Kitchen sponges
Kitchen-cleaning sponges can be a breeding ground for bacteria so disinfecting them regularly is important. First, rinse the sponges thoroughly, then either put them into the top rack of the dishwasher, put them in a microwave oven for 30 seconds, or fill the kitchen sink about one-third full of water, add 150ml chlorine bleach and soak the sponges for 10 minutes.

Knick-knacks

If you clean away the dust from your ornaments or curios frequently, it won't have a chance to turn to greasy grime that will require a more intrusive cleaning job.

- **To dust a whole display of knick-knacks,** you can blow away the dust every couple of days by using a hair dryer or a feather duster, but take care that you don't knock over anything fragile. Or wipe the ornaments, one at a time, with a clean microfibre cloth once a week. Either way, you'll probably rarely need to wash them.

- **To wash your knick-knacks,** mix a little washing-up liquid in warm water in a plastic bowl and immerse the objects, assuming they're made of china, glass, plastic or metal. Use a clean, thick cotton sock, worn over your hand, as a cleaning mitt. That will get into most crevices. Use an old toothbrush on places that your hand can't get to. Rinse the items well with fresh water and dry with a clean cloth.

- **To clean ornaments made of cloth** or with cloth parts, try the vacuum cleaner first, using the brush or crevice attachment. If that isn't enough, put the ornaments in a paper bag, add 2 tablespoons bicarbonate of soda, shake and then shake some more. Remove the items from the bag and brush or vacuum off any bicarbonate of soda that remains.

Care for curios
Don't use soap and water – and especially not the dishwasher – to clean hand-painted or antique knick-knacks. If a prized ornament needs cleaning, as opposed to just dusting, wipe it lightly with a damp cloth. The same gentle touch applies for wooden knick-knacks.

Knives

Do you want a bright and shiny knife at all times? Then choose stainless steel. The problem with stainless is that when it loses its edge, it doesn't take well to sharpening. Or do you prefer a really sharp knife, one that you can easily sharpen? Choose carbon steel. The downside is that it's difficult to keep bright and shiny.

- **Wash knives immediately after use** in a little washing-up liquid and hot water with a cloth or sponge. Rinse with hot water and wipe with a dry cloth.

- **To remove stains from a carbon-steel blade,** try a paste made of salt and vinegar. Rub it on the blade with a cloth. Or dip a slice of lemon into salt and rub that on the blade. Some stains will respond to a nylon scrubber or steel wool. After cleaning, you can shine the blade by using a silver polish.

- **To protect the edges of knives,** store them in a rack or, if in a drawer, cover the blades with cardboard sleeves. You can make a sleeve by cutting a piece of cardboard (from a cereal box, for example) the length of the blade and twice as wide. Fold the cardboard in half lengthwise. Use tape to seal the side and one end. Insert the knife in the open end.

- **To clean a penknife,** open all the blades – and in a Swiss Army-type knife, all the other accessories as well. Wash them in hot, soapy water. Remove dirt from the little slots with a toothbrush. Rinse in hot water, dry with a clean cloth and leave the knife open for a while to allow the slots to dry thoroughly. Lubricate the hinges periodically with a little sewing machine oil, available at sewing-machine suppliers or haberdashers.

- **To clean a hunting knife,** use the same method as for a penknife. After using your knife in the field, rinse it off in a stream, or wipe it clean with leaves or grass.

A keen edge

To sharpen a knife, hold the steel in your left hand (or your right if you're left-handed) and place the blade against the steel at a 20 to 25-degree angle. Draw the knife across, heel to tip, so that the entire blade passes over the top of the steel. Repeat with the other side of the knife on the bottom of the steel. Continue for about a dozen strokes.

Lace

Lace is usually an extremely delicate material, made up of fine threads. It's no surprise, therefore, that there is a long list of cautions to observe when you are trying to clean it.

● **Don't use the washing machine,** tumble dryer or your usual detergents to wash lace. And you mustn't use soaps, chlorine bleach, lemon juice or salt. Don't send lace to a dry-cleaner, except for recently made lace that specifies dry-cleaning on the care label.

Don't clean lace that is fragile, old or valuable, yourself. Give it to a professional conservator. You should wash only sturdy lace of no great value.

● **To clean lace,** place a clean white towel in the bottom of the sink or bathtub and lay the lace on it. Mix 1 teaspoon of Orvus WA Paste with 4.5 litres warm water. (Orvus, a pH neutral detergent used as an animal shampoo, is available via the internet.) Pour on enough solution to cover the cloth. Soak for 15 minutes, then agitate by gently lifting and lowering the towel – don't try to lift the lace itself. It's important not to rub at the lace while you're washing it; even the most gentle friction can pull apart the different threads that make up the fabric and ruin the look of a piece.

● **To rinse, use room-temperature** distilled water. Keep changing the water until it is totally clear. Drain off the last of the water, then use the towel as a sling to lift the lace. Don't pick up the lace by itself while it's wet; the weight of the water will pull it out of shape.

● **To dry, first blot up as much water** as possible with dry towels, and then lay the lace out flat on a clean, dry towel. Use stainless-steel pins (others may rust) to hold the lace flat if necessary. Leave until completely dry.

Lacquer

Lacquer is eye-catching because of its mirror-like finish. Keep your lacquer at its shining best with these cleaning tips.

- **To dust a lacquered surface,** use a large, folded piece of cheesecloth slightly moistened with water. Don't wipe in a circular motion – that could leave 'whirlpools' on the finish. Wipe in only one direction, the one in which the piece was originally polished, if you can determine that.

- **To clean lacquer when dusting isn't enough,** mix a little washing-up liquid in tepid water, dip in a soft cloth and wring it out. Wipe the surface down. Wipe again with a rinsed-out damp cloth, then again with a dry cloth.

- **To polish a dulled surface,** use a non-silicone paste wax – silicone will cause problems if the piece ever needs to be refinished. Apply the wax with a soft cloth in one direction, then buff to a shine in the same direction.

> **Lacquer don'ts**
> To avoid scratching, nicking or dulling a lacquer finish, don't place objects on the bare surface of your furniture. During use, dining tables should be protected with a tablecloth or place mats.

Lamps

Cleaning your lamps doesn't make them just look good, they will work more effectively, too: any dust on a light makes it shine less brightly.

- **To remove dust from a lamp,** use a microfibre cloth regularly. The vacuum cleaner with its brush attachment may work better on some materials, such as unglazed pottery or wood. The more often you dust, the less often you'll have to do more intensive cleaning.

- **Include the light bulb in your routine** – that's where the money-saving comes in. Dust build-up reduces bulb efficiency, wastes energy and raises your electricity bill.

Lamps

- **To remove dirt,** first unplug the lamp and remove the shade and the bulb. Start with a clean cloth or sponge dampened with plain water. Wipe all parts of the lamp, starting with the base and working up. Don't wet the socket or the plug.

- **To avoid dulling the finish,** buff the lamp immediately with a clean, dry cloth. To attack more stubborn dirt, try about ½ teaspoon washing-up liquid applied directly to a cloth or sponge. Wipe the dirty areas, scrubbing gently if necessary. Rinse the cloth or sponge in clear water and go over the surface to remove the detergent. Follow with the dry cloth. Polish the lamp occasionally with a polish suitable for the material from which it is made.

- **To wash glass globes or chimneys,** clean with a cloth or sponge and a solution of hot water and a little washing-up liquid. It's safe to immerse those parts as long as they don't have electrical connectors. Rinse with a solution of hot water and a dash of ammonia, then wipe dry with a clean cloth.

Lamp shades

A lamp shade can set the mood in a room by directing and softening light. It does this most effectively when it's clean.

- **Remove dust before it turns to grime** and go over the surface of the lamp shade – both inside and out – regularly. Use a vacuum cleaner with the small brush attachment for sturdy cloth shades. Or a microfibre cloth for glass, plastic, paper or metal shades. Regular dusting will help you avoid higher-impact cleaning later. This can be messy for you and dangerous for your lamp shade. Water, for example, can dissolve the glue that holds the shade together, causing it to fall apart.

Lamp shades

- **To remove serious dirt,** the safest cleaning method after dusting is to use a special sponge that's intended to be used dry. Ask for a dry-cleaning sponge at a hardware or DIY store. Use it like an eraser to rub away dirt. Try it on any shade, but be sure to use it instead of water on paper shades and any that are held together with glue.

- **To clean fabric shades that are stitched,** rather than glued, wash them in the bath. And while you're going to the trouble of doing one, it makes sense to do all your shades that need it. Metal and plastic shades can also be cleaned in the bath at the same time. To wash the shades, begin by running about 6cm tepid water into the bath. Add 1 tablespoon washing-up liquid and swish it around. Lay the shade on its side in the bath and gently roll it in the water. Metal and plastic shades can stand a little more vigorous cleaning, with a cloth or sponge. Change the water when it becomes dirty and wash again.

- **To rinse, drain the wash water** and run some clear water into the bath. Again, roll the shade in the water and change the water when it turns grey. Metal and plastic shades can be rinsed under running water and wiped dry with a cloth.

- **To dry a cloth shade,** use a towel to press out as much of the water as you can. Finish with a hair dryer, tipping the lamp shade upside down frequently so that no water settles in the bottom of the shade, where it could leave a water stain. Drying it quickly is important, because the metal parts of the shade can rust and stain the fabric.

- **To clean a glass shade,** fill a sink with warm water and add 1 to 2 teaspoons ammonia. Immerse the shade in the water and wash it with a cloth. Use a toothbrush to get into crevices. Rinse and dry with a clean cloth.

> **Dusting tip**
> If you've got a fabric lamp shade where the material is folded or pleated around the base frame, then try using a clean, soft paintbrush when you do your regular dusting. The bristles can be gently worked in between the folds in the fabric to remove any dust or dirt.

Lawnmowers

Take good care of your power mower and it will take good care of your lawn. Good care means keeping the lawnmower clean and maintaining it regularly.

- **To clean the underside,** make sure the engine is off and can't start accidentally. Remove the spark-plug wire (or in the case of an electric mower, make sure it is unplugged). Prop up one side of the mower on a block – don't turn it completely over. Use a garden hose to wash off loose grass and dirt. Then remove the remainder with a putty knife, followed by a stiff-bristled brush.

- **Keep the engine** free of dead grass, leaves and grease (which is a fire hazard). To keep the mower running well, brush off the air-intake screen and the cooling fins on the engine with a stiff brush to keep them free of debris.

- **Attend to a petrol mower's air filter** after every 25 hours of use. Replace a disposable paper filter (available where mowers are sold). A foam-type filter has a removable sponge that should be soaked in warm water and then dried. Follow by putting a few drops of clean engine oil into the sponge and squeezing it to distribute the oil. Then reinstall the sponge.

- **Consider an annual professional** tune-up for your lawnmower; it could save you a lot of trouble.

SIMPLE solutions

To prevent grass and dirt accumulating on the underside of your lawnmower, use some spray-on vegetable cooking oil. Ideally, you should squirt it underneath your machine when the mower is still new. If it's too late for that, clean the underside and then apply the oil on the metal after it dries. This will make it easy to clean the mower after each subsequent use.

Leaded glass & stained glass

The lead in leaded glass does not refer to the glass or to lead crystal. It refers to the cames or the grooved metal rods that hold the panes of glass together. Today, the metal is usually copper or zinc, but it's still referred to as leaded glass.

Although stained glass is associated mainly with churches, many Victorian and Edwardian properties still retain elaborate glass in their doors and upper window panes.

- **To clean leaded or stained glass,** wash each pane individually with a clean cloth dampened in plain, warm water. Wipe dry with a clean, soft cloth or chamois cloth. Never apply any force; you might bend the metal rods. Use only the damp cloth for cleaning the rods.

- **For more cleaning power,** use 1 teaspoon methylated spirits in 1 litre warm water and follow the procedure above.

> **Careful cleaning**
> When cleaning leaded glass, never use common household glass cleaners or homemade solutions containing vinegar, lemon, or ammonia. Never use any kind of abrasive cleaner. And if the glass has painting on it, don't clean it at all. Even water might damage or remove fragile paint.

Leather

There are two main categories of leather – natural and coated – and these require different cleaning techniques.

- **Natural leather** is not dyed with pigments, has little surface protection and is susceptible to staining. Even water or treatments suited to other kinds of leather may mar its surface.

- **Coated leather** is recognisable by its pigment-dyed surface treated with a polyurethane coating. Most – but not all – leather garments, upholstery, purses and shoes are coated.

- **For both types,** you should always follow manufacturer's cleaning guidelines. Always test any cleaning method on an inconspicuous area first. Avoid harsh cleaners and excessive

Leather

water, which can leave stains and remove dye and lubricants. Never dry wet leather near a heat source. For a valuable leather article or serious cleaning problem, consult a professional, such as a dry-cleaner who specialises in cleaning leather.

● **Keep natural leather clean** with frequent dusting using a soft cloth. You could try removing dirt with a new artist's rubber, but even that might leave a smudge.

● **To clean coated leathers,** dust regularly, occasionally with a dampened cloth. Every six months or so, remove loose dirt with a stiff brush or damp cloth. Rub a damp cloth on saddle soap and work up a lather. Rub this on the leather using a circular motion; wipe away the excess with another damp cloth. Allow to air-dry, then buff with a clean, soft cloth. Finish with a protective leather cream.

● **Apply unscented talcum powder** to greasy spots on coated leather and let it absorb the grease. Wipe off with a cloth.

● **Rub dirty spots** with a cotton swab dipped in surgical spirit. Alternatively, make a paste of equal parts lemon juice and cream of tartar, work it into the spot (including scuff marks) with a cloth, let it sit for an hour or so and wipe clean.

Light fixtures

Insects and spiders seem to get trapped in light fixtures with annoying regularity. Now and then you will want to remove their dried-out little bodies – and clean the fixture too.

● **To clean a wall or ceiling fixture,** first turn it off. Then remove any grilles, shades, light bulbs or light tubes. You may have to use a stepladder to do this.

Light fixtures

- **Wash the removable parts** in a sink filled with hot water and a little washing-up liquid. Lay a towel or rubber mat on the bottom of the sink to help prevent damage. Immerse the pieces – except for the light bulbs or tubes – and clean with a soft cloth or sponge. Rinse and dry well with a soft cloth. Wipe the light bulbs or light tubes with a damp cloth, avoiding the ends that go into the sockets.

- **To wash the fixed parts,** use a cloth or sponge dipped into the same cleaning solution and squeezed until it's barely damp. Wipe the fixture, being careful not to get any moisture in the socket or on the wiring. Rinse the sponge or cloth in clean water and wipe the fixture with it again. Wipe everything dry with another cloth and reassemble the fixture.

Litter trays

How, and how often, you clean your cat's litter tray depends on the kind of litter and the tray – and, of course, on your cat.

- **To clean a litter tray,** remove solids daily – and don't forget, or your fastidious cat may find another spot.

- **With clumping litter,** remove the faeces and urine clumps with a slotted scoop available at pet and discount stores. Clumping litter should be dumped and the tray washed about every two weeks – sooner if your nose or eyes say it's time.

- **For non-clumping litter,** remove the solids daily with a scoop and change the litter and wash the tray at least once a week or more often if needed.

- **With self-cleaning trays,** which can include motors and other moving parts, follow the manufacturer's directions.

> **Love that litter**
> Avoid using a deodorising powder in your pet's litter tray. Cats are extremely sensitive and if they don't like the smell of their tray, they may start going somewhere else. If your cat starts doing this – and you haven't used any scented products – try a different litter and see if that helps.

Litter trays

- **To wash the tray,** use a little washing-up liquid and water and scrub with a stiff brush. Avoid using any cleaner with a strong smell, such as scented detergents or ammonia, which could put your cat off using the tray. But do disinfect with a solution of 1 part chlorine bleach to 10 parts water. Rinse thoroughly with plain water – again, to remove smells – and if possible dry in the sunshine. Or wipe dry with a clean cloth or paper towels before adding fresh litter.

- **To stop any footprints** emanating from the tray area, put a piece of carpet or a rubber mat at the spot where your cat leaves the box.

Fixing a hard-to-turn lock
To loosen a dead bolt that resists turning, insert graphite shavings into the keyhole. The graphite comes in a tube and is available at hardware stores.

Locks

When turning the key in a lock becomes difficult or impossible, dirt may be the problem and it's time to clean.

- **To clean the lock exterior,** wipe with a damp cloth. You can also use a little washing-up liquid applied to the cloth. Rinse the cloth before rinsing the lock. Wipe dry with a clean cloth and buff. For more shine, apply an appropriate polish.

- **Clean the inside of a door lock** with WD-40. Fit the thin tube that comes with the lubricant over the spray nozzle. Poke the other end into the keyhole and spray for 10 seconds while holding a piece of paper towel underneath to catch excess lubricant. This will flush out any grime. Don't use conventional oil inside a lock, as dust will stick to it and clog the mechanism.

- **To clean a lock that no longer works,** first take it apart. Wash the inside parts with a degreaser, following the directions of the cleaner's manufacturer. Then lubricate the parts with a multipurpose lubricant.

Louvres

Louvre doors can be real magnets for dust, but frequent dusting will postpone the day you have to tackle a build-up of dirt.

- **To dust louvres** you have several options. You can use a vacuum cleaner with a brush attachment or you can run a clean, soft paintbrush along the louvres. You could also use a lamb's-wool duster. Another option is to wrap a clean cloth around a ruler or other flat object and use this.

- **Dust louvres from top to bottom,** using a wiping action, not a flicking one that will send dust back into the air. If you use a duster, shake it outside, not in the house.

- **To clean dirt from painted** or varnished louvres, wipe with a damp cloth. For any grime you can't remove that way, rub with a little washing-up liquid applied directly to the cloth. Rinse the cloth in plain water and wipe again.

- **Dampen a cotton glove in water,** squirt some washing-up liquid on it, put the glove on and slide each finger between a different slat. Rinse with another damp glove or a damp cloth.

- **To clean wood louvres** with an oil finish, wipe with a cloth dampened with boiled linseed oil, mineral spirits or turpentine.

---

cleaning **glass louvres**

Louvred windows attract a lot of dirt, both inside and out. Clean them with a solution of 200ml vinegar mixed with 3 litres water:
- Open the window to its fullest extent so that the louvred slats are perpendicular to the window frame.
- Take a thick white cotton sock and dip it into the solution; wring.
- Put the sock over your hand like a mitten and clean the slats on both sides, one at a time, starting at the top.
- Using a clean, dry sock, dry the slats in the same manner.

Luggage

The materials used in today's luggage make everything from flight bags to briefcases more durable and easier to clean.

- **To clean soft-sided luggage,** mix 1 part all-purpose cleaner to 7 parts water and use a brush, cleaning cloth or sponge to scrub dirt or spots with a circular motion, working your way outwards. Most can be easily cleaned.

- **To clean hard-sided luggage,** dip a sponge or cloth into water mixed with a little washing-up liquid, wring it out and wipe the luggage. Then rinse and dry.

- **To clean leather luggage and briefcases,** determine whether the leather is natural or coated and follow the directions under Leather, on pages 249–250.

- **To clean aluminium cases,** wash with a cloth dipped in the washing-up liquid solution described above. Never use ammonia-based cleaners, as they will darken the metal. For a good shine and protection, use a multipurpose metal polish.

- **Cleaning a hiking backpack** is easy; simply use a vacuum cleaner to remove dirt from the zips and seams. Applying water

SIMPLE solutions

If you travel infrequently and your luggage hasn't been used for a while, you may find it has a musty, mildewy smell when you next get it out:
- To eliminate this, wipe it out with a solution of 200ml white vinegar in 1 litre water. Wipe with a cloth dampened in water, then leave open to air-dry.
- To avoid such smells in the future, store luggage where it won't be subject to extremes of temperature or humidity and air it out periodically.
- And if you've been carrying luggage when it was raining, remember to wait until it's completely dry before putting it away. Mildew can destroy fabric so leave it out in the sun or near a radiator until all the moisture has evaporated.

Luggage

will work, too, but it's messier. The important thing is not to let the grit build up, because it will damage the zips and weaken the seams. Always tend to the backpack soon after a hike. Remove the items inside. If there is a food spill or crusted mud, wipe it off with a damp sponge dipped in a bowl of warm water with a little washing-up liquid. Remove stubborn stains with spot remover made for clothing.

Lunch boxes

Food can be a potent source of germs and disease. Make sure you clean your lunch box thoroughly so any remains from yesterday's meal aren't allowed to fester.

- **To clean metal or hard-plastic lunch boxes,** wash with a clean sponge or cloth in hot water and a little washing-up liquid. Rinse and dry. Always do this after each use.

- **To clean soft-sided lunch boxes and bags,** wipe the inside with a damp sponge or cloth. For spills, use a sponge dampened in hot, soapy water. Allow to air-dry thoroughly.

- **To clean a grimy old metal lunch box,** begin by removing any loose dust or dirt with the brush attachment of your vacuum cleaner. Wash the box using hot water with a little washing-up liquid. Mix it in a separate container – not in the lunch box itself. Wash with a sponge or soft cloth, never with anything abrasive, and rinse the sponge under running water frequently. Scrub tough grime gently with a toothbrush, which is also useful for cleaning the handles. Rinse in clear, warm water and dry with a soft cloth. Leave the box open for an hour to let it dry thoroughly. Any wet areas will be susceptible to rust.

Marble

Although marble is a heavy stone that may seem indestructible, it is actually extremely porous, prone to staining and far from impervious to harsh treatment.

● **Clean marble** with a gentle liquid soap that does not have a grease remover. The safest course is to take it easy. Mix about 4 tablespoons mild liquid soap with 4.5 litres water. Using a soft sponge, or a sponge mop if you're cleaning a marble floor, wipe the marble clean. Follow with two to three water rinses, depending on how soapy the cleaning mixture is. Then dry with a soft cloth.

● **Clean marble floors regularly,** before dirt and grit have a chance to scratch the surface. Wipe up spills immediately. As with a wood surface, avoid putting drinks glasses directly on marble, which can cause water rings. Water should bead on the marble. If the surface appears to be absorbing liquid, it's not sealed properly.

Gently does it
Never use lemon, vinegar or any other acidic ingredient on marble. Acids will eat through the protective finish and damage the stone. Avoid ammonia as well. Abrasive powders should not be used either, since the grit can scratch and dull the marble finish.

● **Re-seal your marble floor** at least once a year. Buy a stone sealer from a DIY store and, using a sponge, sponge mop or rag, cover the entire marble surface, including corners. There's no need to strip the floor before you seal.

● **To clean surface stains,** use a marble-polishing powder, such as tin oxide, which is available at DIY stores. Follow the product's directions to the letter. If the marble item you're cleaning is stained but not of great value, you can try removing stains with a thick paste made of baking soda and water; apply the paste to the stain. Cover the paste with a sheet of plastic to keep it damp and let it sit for 10 to 15 minutes before wiping it off. Rinse with warm water and dry. Repeat the procedure if the first application of paste doesn't fully remove the stain. If stains still remain, you will have to call on the expertise of a professional marble restorer.

Mattresses & box springs

Dust mites, tiny organisms that feed on the microscopic flakes of dead skin we all shed, make their homes in our beds and they can cause allergic reactions in some people, particularly those with asthma. Keeping your mattress clean will help keep dust mites under control.

- **Every six months,** rotate your mattress end to end and vacuum the exposed surface. Run the brush attachment over the entire mattress, including the sides. This will remove not only dust mites, but also mould spores. Empty the vacuum cleaner bag or cylinder outdoors after cleaning or, if the bag is disposable, throw it away.

- **Once a year,** flip the mattress over and vacuum it again. Remove the mattress and vacuum the box springs with the brush attachment. If you have the type of box springs with exposed springs, use a bottle brush to lift away dust.

- **Removing stains** from your mattress can be tricky, because moisture can be very harmful. Clean with upholstery shampoo, following the package directions. Or you can lift the stains out using dry suds, which are made by whipping a grease-cutting washing-up liquid or clothes detergent in water. Keep mixing until you have lots of suds.

SIMPLE solutions

If bed-wetting is a problem, use a waterproof mattress cover. But never totally enclose your mattress in plastic; mattress covers allow the mattress to breathe because the sides are made of cloth and the bottom part stays uncovered. Urine smells and stains are difficult to remove from a saturated mattress. Sprinkle dry borax power directly onto the wet spot and rub it in. Let it dry, then brush or vacuum away.

Mattresses & box springs

Using a clean cloth, soft brush or sponge dampened with warm water, apply the suds in a circular motion to the stain. Then draw out the moisture with a clean, dry towel. Repeat if necessary, then wipe the area with a clean cloth dampened with clear water. Again, press with a dry towel to draw out the moisture. The key is to leave as little water on the mattress as possible, because moisture can lead to mildew and mould growth.

● **To speed up the drying process,** blow an electric fan towards the mattress or take the mattress outside and let the sun do the job. If you've cleaned the entire mattress (one small section at a time), you may want to use a dehumidifier in the bedroom to draw out even more moisture.

Medicine cabinets

Experts recommend an annual review of the contents of medicine cabinets and urge consumers to get rid of expired prescriptions, leftover antibiotics, cough syrup that has separated and sterile gauze in broken packages.

Expert **ADVICE**

Many of us have our medicine cabinets in the bathroom, but a steamy room may not be the best place to store your remedies. Most medicines are best kept in a cool, dry place, since heat and humidity can affect their potency. Store medicines at the back of high shelves in cupboards, out of the sight and reach of children, rather than in bathroom medicine cabinets.

Medicine cabinets

- **Start by throwing out** medicine that is past its expiry date. Pour expired liquids down the drain and throw expired pills straight into the bin to keep them out of the mouths of children and pets. If you can't find an expiry date, then throw it away. At the least, expired medicines are ineffective; at worst, formulations that have degraded over time can create new problems when ingested. So when in doubt, throw it out.

- **Cleaning the medicine cabinet** itself is simple. Use a sponge and mixture of mild washing-up liquid in warm water to clean the interior and shelves. Or remove the shelves and put them in the top rack of your dishwasher.

Microwave ovens

Compared to conventional gas or electric ovens, microwave ovens are very easy to clean.

- **Wipe up fresh-food splatters** in the microwave with a sponge or paper towel dipped in a mixture of washing-up liquid and water. Follow with a clean water rinse. Use the same method for washing removable trays or turntables in the sink.

- **To remove dried-on food,** heat a bowl of water inside the microwave for three to five minutes on High power before cleaning. The resulting steam will soften the dried food. Then wipe down the interior with a sponge or soft cloth.

- **To get rid of odours,** combine 200ml water with 100ml lemon juice in a jug and heat on High power for 3 to 5 minutes. Let it stand in the microwave for 5 to 10 minutes before removing. Alternatively, make up a solution of 200ml warm water and 1 tablespoon baking soda and use

Microwave ovens

this on a soft cloth or sponge to wipe down the interior of the microwave. Rinse with warm water.

● **To remove stains** from the microwave's ceramic floor or turntable, make a paste of baking soda and water and apply it to the stain. Let it sit until the stain disappears, then wipe it off and rinse with a wet sponge or cloth. Clean the microwave door with paper towels and glass cleaner.

Mirrors

A variety of low-cost cleaning methods will produce sparkling mirrors that reflect a clear streak-free image.

● **When using glass cleaner on a mirror,** make sure you spray the glass cleaner on a lint-free cotton cloth or rag rather than directly on the mirror's surface. Not only do you use less cleaner, but you also prevent excess cleaner from running down the mirror's edges, where it can cause the mirror's silver backing to oxidise, turn black and brittle, and eventually flake.

● **Don't clean mirrors** with abrasive or acidic cleaners. Abrasive cleaners can scratch the glass and acidic ones might corrode the reflective layers of tin, silver and copper that back a mirror.

● **Old newspapers** can do a good job of cleaning glass. Wear rubber gloves if you choose this method, to keep the printer's ink off your hands.

Begin by mixing equal amounts of vinegar and water in a bowl or bucket. Crumple up the newspaper into a ball and dip it into the solution. Use this to thoroughly wipe the mirror. Then rub with a dry newspaper to eliminate streaking. For extra shine wipe the dry mirror with a clean blackboard rubber.

Motorcycles & motor scooters

It's not hard to make your motorbike look its best, so get out the garden hose and get ready to add some shine.

- **To keep water out of cables and controls,** cover the handlebars with plastic before washing the bike. Put a piece of plastic tape over the ignition keyhole to keep water out.

- **Spray the bike** with a garden hose before washing. If it's badly caked with mud and road grease, you'll probably need to use high-pressure water. But take care to not let the pressurised water hit the instruments, ignition keyhole, carburettor or brakes. They could be damaged if water were to get inside. Motorcycle shops sell a variety of wash sprays that remove oil and road grime. Use such a spray on the engine and wheels, wipe with a clean cloth and rinse immediately.

- **Next wash the bike's painted areas.** You can use a car-wash cleaner, but don't use laundry or dishwasher detergents – they're much too harsh. Rinse the bike well with fresh hose water before any cleaner-coated areas have time to dry.

- **Dry the bike to prevent** water spots. Cotton towels will work, but a synthetic chamois is best because it sheds less. Ride the bike within an hour of washing, to get rid of any water that has collected in the engine, handlebars and controls. This also dries the brakes, which can be damaged by corrosion.

- **If your bike's finish** starts to look dull, give the painted surfaces a coat of wax, applying it with a dampened sponge. Cleaner waxes and polishes are fine for older bikes. But on newer bikes, use Carnauba Wax, a natural wax that doesn't contain cleaners. Cleaners can literally take off the top layer of paint on a bike that is less than six months old.

Bike basics
Wait about an hour after riding before cleaning a bike: never clean a hot engine, because the exhaust pipes can burn your skin if they haven't had time to cool. Make sure you clean the bike on level ground; otherwise the stand could slip and cause the bike to fall on you. And remove all rings and bracelets that could scratch the bike before you begin to clean.

N

Needlework

Cleaning needlework isn't as simple as it may sound. Techniques will vary according to the age of the item and the fabric on which it's embroidered. If you are unsure of a piece's age or fabric, consult a professional, particularly if the item is a family heirloom with sentimental value.

- **To clean needlework** that's less than 15 years old and that's embroidered on cotton or wool, first take it carefully apart. If the piece has cut edges that might unravel, zigzag the edges on a sewing machine before cleaning. Measure the piece so you'll be able to return it to its original size.

- **Fill a clean sink** with slightly warm water and a squirt of washing-up liquid that doesn't have a grease-cutting formula. (If you're unsure whether the threads are colourfast, use cold water. Red threads in particular are notorious for bleeding when warm water is used.)

  Gently work the soapy water through the fabric, squeezing and agitating the piece. For stains, use a spot remover made for cotton or wool, or pre-soak the piece for at least 30 minutes in the washing-up liquid solution.

- **Rinse the item** several times in clear, cold water. Make sure you get all the detergent out as it may turn the whites yellow.

- **After thorough rinsing,** place the piece on a cotton towel and roll it up to remove excess water; unroll.

- **Pin the piece facedown** on a blocking board at its original measurements so that it will return to square as it dries. You can make your own blocking board by using a cork notice board: cover it with muslin and secure the muslin with staples.

Don't dry-clean
When cleaning needlework, don't dry-clean – the fluids used contain chemicals that may damage the piece. This is especially true if you're unsure of the fabric of your piece. In addition, the steam machines used by dry cleaners will take the sizing out of the piece, making it difficult to block again.

Outdoor toys

When the time comes to clean your outdoor toys, it's a good idea to do a safety check as well. Tighten up any bolts that have become loose or moved out of the ground.

- **To clean frames,** use a bucket of sudsy water and a sponge. Most play equipment is made of aluminium or steel (if metal) or toughened plastic. Both respond well to basic cleaning.

- **Shift stubborn stains** – bird droppings or mould from leaves that have pooled in crevices over the winter – using concentrated washing-up liquid on a pad. Dry off thoroughly, using old towels.

- **During the summer,** keep a pack of multipurpose wipes in the shed, so that you can regularly clean stains from the fabric tops of climbing frames and swing seats.

Ovens

Proper cleaning improves your oven's efficiency, extends its life and, most importantly, reduces the risk of fire. Even if you have a self-cleaning or continuous-cleaning oven, neither of which is entirely self-sufficient, some of the tips that follow will help you to clean it properly – and they don't involve hours of scrubbing.

- **Wipe the exterior surfaces of your oven** to remove food spills every time you wipe down worktops. All you need is a moist sponge. Make it a habit and you'll save time in the end, because even the exterior surfaces get warm enough to bake food on very quickly.

- **To clean the interior,** start by removing all oven racks and grill pans. Wash them by hand in the sink. Use a solution of warm water and washing-up liquid. Scrub with a nylon-bristled brush or other gentle,

Ovens

non-metal scrubber. Anything abrasive, such as steel wool, will scratch the metal's finish, which can lead to rusting and will make food stick even more the next time.

● **To loosen baked-on deposits** in a conventional (non-self-cleaning) oven, fill a glass bowl with about 100ml of full-strength ammonia. After making sure the oven is completely cool, put the bowl in the oven, close the door and let it stand overnight. The fumes will release the bond between the crusty food and the oven interior. The next day, open the door and let the fumes dissipate. Then remove the bowl and wipe away the loosened food with a cloth or sponge.

● **To remove stubborn food** that remains after the ammonia treatment, try scouring with a non-abrasive scrubber dipped in a solution of warm water and washing-up liquid. As with the racks and grill pans, avoid scratching the oven's finish. On flat surfaces, such as the door glass, try scraping with a plastic ice scraper – the kind you use on your car windscreen.

● **A commercial oven cleaner** is a last-ditch solution when cleaning a conventional oven. Follow the directions carefully and wear protective rubber gloves when applying. These products are strong and harmful to humans. Never spray a commercial oven cleaner on a hot oven, electric elements or oven lights. Heat can make the cleaner even more caustic.

● **Self-cleaning ovens** break down food spills with temperatures as high as 480°C. But the high heat doesn't reach all parts of the oven and in areas such as the frame around the oven opening and the edge of the door outside the gasket, the self-cleaning cycle can actually bake food on even more. So clean those parts first with a non-abrasive scrubber dipped in a sudsy solution of hot water and washing-up liquid. Rinse well, using a sponge and a bucket of clean water. Once the

Put a stop to greasy ovens
No matter what kind of oven you have, you can slow down the build-up of grease by periodically wiping the interior of the oven with a cloth soaked in vinegar.

Ovens

self-cleaning cycle is complete and the oven has completely cooled down, wipe out the ashy residue with a damp sponge.

- **The interior of a continuous-cleaning oven** is coated with a chemical mixture that lowers the temperature at which heat will dissolve foods. So whenever you cook at a temperature above 180°C (gas mark 4), you are breaking down food that has splattered on the walls or bottom. But major spills, especially those involving sugar, can cancel out the effect, so clean these up at once. Wipe out the entire oven occasionally using a non-abrasive scrubbing pad and warm water. Then run the oven empty for an hour or so at 240°C (gas mark 9) to break down any grease or food that hasn't been dealt with by the oven's normal cooking and cleaning cycle. Never use abrasive cleaners or cleaning tools in this type of oven.

- **You can only clean an Aga** or a traditional range cooker while it is turned off for its annual service. In the meantime, be scrupulous about keeping the enamel front and top clean; use a non-abrasive cleaner safe for enamel. Take even more care of the steel tops: a microfibre cloth, just dampened, is best. For the cooking plates, use a stiff wire brush to remove burnt food.

  When the oven is serviced and so is cold, clean out the inside using a cloth dipped in a sudsy washing-up liquid solution.

Expert **ADVICE**

You should never use commercial oven cleaners in a self-cleaning oven. When heated to those high temperatures, the chemical residue grows dangerously caustic. Nor should you use commercial oven cleaners, cleaning powders or metal scrubbers to clean a continuous-cleaning oven. These products may ruin the chemical mixture that allows the oven to clean itself.

P

Paddling pools

Since small children – and generally small children with muddy or grassy feet – are the main users of paddling pools, these tend to get dirty rather quickly.

- **After each day's use,** empty the pool and hose it out to prevent it from incubating germs. Store the pool under cover, upside down or propped up on its side, so that there is no risk of rainwater filling up inside – and creating a potential drowning hazard in your garden.

- **To remove scum,** clean with a sponge or cloth dipped in a solution of 4 tablespoons bicarbonate of soda in 4 litres warm water. Or wash with a solution of 1 tablespoon washing-up liquid in 3 litres water. Rinse with a hose.

Cleaning up after toddler accidents

If someone has an 'accident' in the paddling pool, first get all the children out of the water. Then scoop out anything solid and flush it down the toilet. Empty out the water and then wash the pool with a solution of 40ml chlorine bleach to 5 litres water. Leave the pool to air-dry in the sun.

Painted surfaces

Paint is not only decorative – it's also a protective coating. But even though paint is made to stand up to considerable wear and tear, you must take care when cleaning it.

- **Strong chemical cleaners** or too much scrubbing can dull the paint's finish, creating uneven patches or removing paint altogether. Since touching-up paintwork, even with a colour match, tends to look splotchy, a cleaning mistake could lead to a complete repainting, which is not what you want to happen.

- **Dust painted surfaces regularly** to keep dirt and grime from staining the surface when smeared or moistened. For painted furniture, shelves, door and window trim, or knick-knacks that are coated in a gloss paint, use a clean dust cloth, either dry or slightly dampened with water. Wet-dusting entire walls is not feasible, since many are covered with emulsion-based paint, which wet-dusting could actually remove.

Painted surfaces

- **To remove stubborn stains** from gloss paint, first try a gentle wipe with a cloth dampened in a sudsy solution of warm water and washing-up liquid. If that doesn't work, try an all-purpose cleaner, but only after testing it on an inconspicuous spot. Clean from the bottom up so that your solution doesn't drip down and pick up grime, leaving dirty streaks.

- **Rinse with a clean, moist cloth** or sponge. Dry well with clean towels to prevent water from damaging the paint.

- **To remove marks from surfaces** coated with emulsion, first try rubbing with a white rubber. If that doesn't do the trick, try gently wiping the marks with a water-moistened cloth. Blot dry soon afterwards with a clean towel. But be warned: water can stain or even remove emulsion paint.

Painting equipment

The best painters will tell you that a good clean-up at the end of the day is essential. Not only does it keep their tools in good shape, which means easier application and a better finish, it also prolongs the life of rollers, trays and paintbrushes.

On the other hand, the professionals will also be the first to tell you that there are times when you don't have to completely clean your gear and in these special cases that will save you valuable time and energy. If you dread dealing with the messy aftermath of painting, read on to discover a simple, environmentally friendly clean-up technique.

- **Start by putting the excess paint** from roller trays back into the paint tin. Squeeze as much paint as you can from your brushes (wrap them in newspaper and press with your hands)

Painting equipment

and scrape paint off your rollers with the curved scraper on a 5-in-1 painter's tool, available at paint and DIY stores. Then wipe off as much of the remaining paint as possible using something disposable, such as an old rag, newspaper or piece of cardboard. Let the rag or paper dry, then throw it away.

Supple bristles
To keep the bristles on a clean brush used for oil-based paint soft, rub a little petroleum jelly into them. Before use, rinse it in paint thinner or turpentine. Never rinse a brush used for oil-based paint in water – it tends to make bristles turn dry and brittle.

● **Use a two-bucket system** to keep things tidy. Whether you're using water-based or oil-based paint, use 2 large buckets (plastic 15 litre buckets work well) to contain your mess: one for washing and one for rinsing. The system is economical (because you can reuse solvents), it's friendly to the environment (you reserve rather than throw out paint or used solvent), and it keeps things neat and tidy.

● **Use one bucket for washing.** If you're cleaning up after using water-based paint, mix warm water with a squirt of washing-up liquid in the bucket. If you've been using oil-based paint, put a small amount of paint thinner or turpentine into the bucket – 6cm in the bottom should be enough. Then, wearing disposable latex gloves, immerse the brushes and use your fingers to gently work the paint out of them. Use a brush, comb or an old fork to clean between the bristles.

● **To remove paint from the metal band** on the handle, scrub gently with a wire brush. Use a roller spinner, available at paint shops, to remove paint from the rollers, either spinning it in the wash bucket or, better yet, in a third, empty bucket. (The paint will really fly around.) Wash the roller pans over the wash bucket using a soft-bristled brush. Leave the dirty water or solvent in the bucket, cover the bucket with cardboard or newspaper to prevent evaporation and let it stand.

● **Use the second bucket for rinsing,** after you've removed the bulk of the paint from your brushes or rollers. For cleaning up water-based paint, use clean water; for cleaning up oil-based

Painting equipment

paint, use fresh paint thinner. When the water or solvent squeezed from the brushes or rollers comes out clear, you'll know you're finished. As with the wash bucket, cover the rinse bucket containing water or solvent and let it stand.

- **Let the paint solids settle** to the bottom of both the wash and rinse buckets overnight. The next day, carefully pour the water off the top of the solids. Using a putty knife or paint stirrer, scrape the paint off the bottom of the buckets onto newspaper and discard it.

  Paint thinner or turpentine used for cleaning up after oil-based paint can be reused. Carefully pour the relatively pure liquid on top back into its original container. (Never store solvents in plastic, because solvents will damage plastic containers.) Again, scrape the solids up and discard.

- **If you are using an oil-based paint** again the next day, you don't need to thoroughly clean out your brushes and rollers. Just give them a cursory cleaning (squeeze and scrape off the excess paint back into the paint tin), then wrap them tightly in aluminium foil or cling film. This will keep them from drying out – and will save you the hassle of cleaning up twice. You can save the thorough two-bucket clean-up routine for the end of the decorating project.

- **If a brush or roller** that you've been using just won't come clean of water-based paint, it may be because many of today's water-based paints contain resins, similar to those used in oil-based paints, to improve adhesion, gloss and durability. After cleaning and rinsing the brush or roller in water, try a second rinse in paint thinner or turpentine to completely clean it. Then wash with clean, soapy water to remove the thinner.

Panelling

Panelling comes in two main varieties: real wood and simulated wood. Real wood panelling is usually either sealed with a hard surface coat, such as varnish or polyurethane, or it contains a penetrating stain or oil finish. Simulated wood is a product made to look like real wood and is often coated in plastic.

- **To remove dust** from raised moulding, carving or other features on either type of panelling, vacuum regularly using your vacuum cleaner's brush attachment, or wipe with a cloth. For simulated wood, you can use a moistened dust cloth, but avoid using water on real wood. Moisture can damage wood.

- **To clean real wood** that has a surface coat, such as polyurethane, you may have to use water, but begin by trying a spray-on furniture polish, such as Pledge. These products remove dirt and dust while adding a hard wax finish. For heavier cleaning, try a cloth lightly dampened with a neutral cleaner, such as Pledge Soapy Wood Cleaner.

- **If cleaning wood panelling** with a penetrating finish, such as oil, use a cloth just dampened with methylated spirits. Wipe gently back and forth in the direction of the wood grain. But work quickly and with care: methylated spirits will lift dirt and grease but will also remove the oil finish. When you've finished cleaning, you may well need to reapply the panelling's finish. If you regularly wipe over with a just damp cloth, you should avoid needing to take this more drastic step.

- **Wipe down simulated wood panelling** with a cloth using a solution of warm water and washing-up liquid. If you need something stronger, try an all-purpose cleaner, but only after testing it on an inconspicuous spot. Rinse it with a clean, moist cloth or sponge. Then dry well with clean towels so that the water won't damage the compressed wood beneath the coating.

Patios

Patios can often end up stained by grease drippings from the barbecue, rusty metal furniture and decaying plant matter. The good news is that as your patio is outside, you can use heavy-duty cleaners – and, if worst comes to worst, blast the dirt off with a pressure washer.

- **To reduce staining** in the first place, sweep the leaves and other debris off your patio regularly. Use an outdoor-quality bristle broom or a leaf blower.

- **Give your patio** a more thorough cleaning, using a cleaner that is biodegradable and won't harm the surrounding plants, such as Swarfega Path and Patio Cleaner. Use a stiff-bristled brush (a long-handled one will be easier on your back and knees) to scrub the dirt and grime away. Hose down the patio with plenty of clean water.

- **To deep-clean a patio** made of stone, brick or concrete, use a pressure washer. Take care not to etch your patio material or injure yourself and never hold the jet too close to the patio surface. If you rent a power washer instead of buying one, be sure it comes with detailed safety instructions.

SIMPLE solutions

If you get a rust stain on your patio there is a simple trick you can use to cure the problem. First wet the area and cover the stain with a solution of 1 part lemon juice to 4 parts water. Take care not to get the surrounding area wet if you have coloured paving slabs – lemon can bleach out the colour. Cover your solution with a piece of plastic sheeting (to prevent the moisture from evaporating) and hold it down with something heavy. Let it stand for 10 minutes or so. Scrub with a stiff-bristled brush and rinse with the hose. Repeat if necessary.

Pearls

Unlike hard, crystalline gemstones, pearls are as sensitive as they are beautiful. Perfume, cosmetics and hair spray can stain them and the acids in your perspiration can eat away at their fine coating – known as nacre. And since a pearl's value is largely determined by its colour, lustre and the thickness of the nacre, cleaning your pearls is essential to maintain their value.

Fortunately, cleaning is also easy and harmless to the pearl, as long as you stick to the following simple methods.

Products to avoid

Pearls can be harmed by many common cleaning substances and methods, including ammonia, commercial jewellery cleaners with ammonia, ultrasonic cleaners, steam cleaners, detergent, bleach, powdered cleansers, baking soda, vinegar, lemon juice and most types of washing-up liquid.

● **Wipe off your pearls** after each wearing. Use a barely damp, very soft cloth (a chamois leather is best). This removes harmful substances, such as perspiration, perfume and make-up that can penetrate the pearls' porous surface. As a preventive measure, always apply any perfume, make-up and hairspray before you put on your pearls.

● **Occasionally, clean pearls more thoroughly** to restore their natural finish and lustre. Use a bar of mild hand soap, such as Pears, and lukewarm water to create light suds. Dip a soft cloth in the suds and gently wipe the pearls. Rinse with clean water and dry with another soft cloth. Never soak your pearls – you don't want the string to get wet.

● **To be completely sure that your pearls** and the string on which they are hung are dry, try this simple technique. Lay the pearls out on a slightly damp cloth and set aside. When the cloth is dry, the pearls and string will be too.

● **It's important that the string** doesn't get wet. If you wore your pearls when the string was at all damp, it might stretch and attract hard-to-remove dirt between the pearls.

● **Never hang pearls up to dry,** since that may also stretch the string.

Pet equipment

Keep your pet's things clean. Cleaning will prolong the life of the equipment, keep your pet healthy and reduce pet odours.

- **Wash food and water bowls daily** to avoid the growth of bacteria. Put them in the dishwasher, if they are dishwasher safe. You can include them with your own dishes – the high water temperature will disinfect everything. Or hand-wash using hot, soapy water. (Do this separately from your dishes.) Keep two sets of dishes for your pet and rotate them. Stainless-steel bowls are usually easiest to clean.

- **Clean leads periodically** to remove dirt and salt, which can corrode the metal parts. Soak non-leather leads in a sink full of warm water with a squirt of washing-up liquid and a dash of liquid fabric softener, to keep the lead soft. Rub clean with a sponge. Rinse in a sink full of clean, warm water. Hang up to dry. Clean leather leads using an appropriate technique – see Leather, pages 249–250.

- **Hand-wash dog coats** with the same care you'd use on your own clothes – unless the label instructions say otherwise. Fill a basin with lukewarm water and add a gentle fabric wash, such as Woolite, or a squirt of mild washing-up liquid. Soak and then gently rub out any stains. Rinse thoroughly in clear, lukewarm water. Wring gently, then wrap in a clean towel to remove moisture. Reshape the garment and leave to dry.

- **Wash pet toys regularly** to keep them clean and bacteria-free. Wash rubber and plastic toys in a sink full of hot, soapy water with a dash of bleach. Scrub with a nylon-bristled brush. Stuffed toys and rope toys can go in the washing machine and tumble dryer. When they grow old, throw them away.

- **To wipe dribbles off pet toys,** use a wet wipe. Take along a portable carton of wipes when you're out for a walk.

Pewter

Did you know that pewter is the fourth most precious metal after platinum, gold and silver? An alloy of tin and varying amounts of antimony, lead and copper, pewter has long been prized for its lasting value. It does not rust and tarnishes only slightly or not at all (depending on the alloy's metal content).

Antique pewter, which is usually high in lead, can look dark and dull, but that patina is part of its appeal and value as an antique. Before cleaning pewter, first determine whether your pewter piece is an antique or of more recent vintage.

● **To remove dirt and grime** from antique or newer pewter, wash it in a sudsy solution of warm water and washing-up liquid. Gently wipe the surface with a sponge or soft cloth. Rinse with clean water, then drip-dry in a dish rack or on a folded towel. Never put pewter in the dishwasher. If your piece is an antique, stop here. Because of its metal content, polishing it won't necessarily make it shine – but it may decrease its value.

● **To make bright, modern pewter shine,** use a silver or brass polish or a mildly abrasive scouring powder, such as Ajax, and a soft cloth. For severe corrosion, try applying the metal polish with ultra-fine steel wool. Use grade 0000 only – a coarser steel wool would scratch the finish. Buff with a soft cloth after using the steel wool.

Photographs, slides & negatives

Photographs, slides and negatives are easily damaged and your options for cleaning them are quite limited. So keeping them out of harm's way is your best bet. How much you're willing to do for a photograph probably depends on whether it's a family heirloom or just one of many old holiday snaps.

- **The ultimate protection** for a photograph is a glass covering and a frame. This way, the only thing that gets dirty is a hard surface that's easy to wipe clean. A frame will enhance the photograph's value and help it last longer. But don't hang the photo where direct sunlight will reach it.

- **To clean the framed photo,** take it off the wall and lay it flat. Spray some glass cleaner onto a soft, clean cloth and wipe off the dust. Never spray directly onto the glass – the cleaner could drip behind the frame and damage the photo.

- **For valuable unframed photos,** acid-free paper and plastic envelopes, and acid-free storage boxes offer good protection; another option is an album made of high-quality materials.

- **Remember that high temperatures,** high humidity and direct sunlight are all damaging to photographic materials.

- **Handle photographic materials** very carefully. The salts and oils from your skin can damage them easily, so never touch the image area directly. Ideally, handle photographic material while wearing white cotton gloves. If you must use bare hands, handle your photos, slides and negatives by the edges only.

- **If your photograph has dirt on the surface,** see if it will come off with the gentle swipe of a soft brush. If not, stop there – anything more will put the photo at risk. You'll have to take it to a professional lab to be washed.

> **Protect precious memories**
> Handle photos, slides and negatives only by the edges, preferably using white cotton gloves. Never touch the image area and limit exposure to heat, humidity and sunlight. Frame important photos under glass, using acid-free materials, or store in acid-free conditions, using special envelopes, sheaves, album pages and boxes.

Photographs, slides & negatives

● **If your photo has fingermarks** around the edges or on an unimportant part of the image, you may be able to simply wipe it away. Dip a cotton bud in distilled water and wipe at the mark very gently. Don't go over the mark again and again, because you'll soften the emulsion and damage it. Let the photo dry before you store it.

● **To clean dust from slides and negatives,** buy a can of compressed air from a camera shop. Test the can by spraying your skin first. If the can has been exposed to high temperatures or has been shaken, water may spray out with the air – not something you want to get on your photographic materials. Wearing white cotton gloves, hold your slide or negative by the edges and position the nozzle to the side, 9cm from the surface. Spray in several quick bursts to remove any dust.

● **An antistatic cloth can remove dust** from slides and negatives – provided you use a light touch. Antistatic cloths are available at camera shops. Hold the slide or negative in one

hand, and by the edges only. With the other hand, fold the cloth around the film so that it touches both sides. With as little pressure as possible, draw the cloth down the surface, moving only in one direction. The more pressure that you apply, the more likely you are to drag any dust across the fragile surface and scratch the slide or negative.

● **To protect your negatives** from dirt and dust, slip them into the sleeves of clear plastic sheets that are sold at camera shops. Do this the moment you get the negatives home. These sheets fit into ring binders and are an excellent way to mark and catalogue your negatives.

Pillows

Pillows can be a big source of sneezes – particularly for allergy sufferers. Dust, body oil, perspiration and dead skin particles gather on (and inside) pillows. That combination is bad enough, but pillows also harbour the dust mites and microscopic organisms to which many people are allergic.

And if you have goose down, dust and dirt act as abrasives and shorten the life of the down. So give your pillows – which are usually stuffed with either a synthetic fibre, goose down or feathers – a good cleaning at least twice a year.

- **Most fibre-filled pillows** can just be put in the washing machine. While you should always follow the instructions on the pillow's care label, generally you can use the cold-water cycle for a fibre-filled pillow and tumble it in the dryer on low heat. Or you can dry it on a clothesline. Hang the pillow in the sun by one corner. Make sure it is completely dry before using.

- **Down and feather pillows** should be machine-washed or dry-cleaned depending on the manufacturer's suggestion. Some recommend dry-cleaning only, claiming that machine-washing down and feathers reduces their natural resilience. If you do decide to dry-clean your pillows, take them to a cleaner with experience of cleaning down. If there are any lingering dry-cleaning solvent fumes, air the pillows until they are all gone.

- **If you machine-wash down pillows,** the big problem is drying them afterwards. Most are fine in the machine – as long as you have checked the care label – but it is not very safe to dry them in the tumble dryer as it could overheat. Also, it's expensive: it may take four hours of tumbling to completely dry a pair of pillows. Waiting for a hot day and drying them outside may be your best option.

> **For fluffy pillows**
> A quick way to freshen pillows is to tumble-dry them on low heat for 10 minutes. It's much easier than a complete washing, and it removes some dust. Do it twice a year, in between washings.

Plastic containers

Plastic is the miracle product – tough, resilient and easy to clean. Easy that is, until certain foods, most notably tomato-based sauces, etch their way into its pores and cause what seem to be permanent stains. But don't give up hope. Where there is a cleaning will, there is a way.

- **Nearly all plastic food containers** are dishwasher-safe. This includes the Tupperware brand. You also can hand-wash them in hot, soapy water, using a sponge or nylon-bristled brush to scrub away stuck-on food.

- **To remove light stains,** mix a paste of bicarbonate of soda and warm water and scrub with a nylon-bristled brush.

- **For heavier stains,** scrub with a solution of 4 tablespoons dishwasher detergent mixed with 250ml warm water. Rinse well. Wear gloves to do this – dishwasher granules and powder are an irritant.

- **Alternatively, soak in a solution** of 50ml bleach and 1 litre water. (Wash in soapy water afterwards and rinse well.)

- **You could also try** leaving the plastic container to stand in direct sunlight for a day or two.

- **To clean large plastic storage containers** not meant for food, wipe out with a moist cloth. For stubborn stains, scrub with a sponge or nylon-bristled brush in a solution of warm water with a squirt of mild washing-up liquid.

Porcelain

Porcelain is one of the most fragile of all ceramics. Fired at very high temperatures, it is glass-like, so treat it with care.

- **To wash porcelain,** use a washing-up bowl or a sink lined with a towel or rubber mat to protect against breakage.

- **To remove dirt and grime,** use a mild solution of warm water and washing-up liquid. Wipe with a cloth or scrub gently with a soft, nylon-bristled brush. A toothbrush is useful for nooks and crannies. Rinse well using clean water and air-dry in a dish rack or on a folded towel on the worktop.

- **To remove coffee or tea stains** from the inside of porcelain cups or a porcelain teapot, scrub the stain gently with a cloth or soft-bristled brush and a paste made from bicarbonate of soda and a little water.

Pots & saucepans

Cast-iron and copper pans should not be put into the dishwasher and manufacturers of nonstick cookware also advise against this. Dishwashers are harsher on pots than soapy water and hand-washing in the sink.

Besides, dishwasher detergents generally rely on alkaline-heavy cleaners to cut grease and extremely alkaline cleaners can mar cookware just as badly as acidic cleaners can.

- **Hand-wash pots and saucepans** that can't be put in the dishwasher. Remove and discard any food residue first. Fill the sink with moderately hot water and add a squirt of washing-up liquid. Slide the pot into the soapy water and let it sit for a minute. Then gently scrub it in a circular motion, using a sponge, brush or dishcloth. Many nonstick surfaces – especially older ones – are easily scratched, so pay attention to

Tough job
Traditionally, steel wool has been used to remove baked-on food from pans. However, steel wool can damage some surfaces, and when it scratches something, it creates a layer that attracts stains and rust. Use steel wool only as a last resort or on things that you don't mind scratching.

Pots & saucepans

the manufacturer's directions for cleaning. Clean the saucepan all over. You'll know it's come clean when it's smooth to the touch. Rinse in clean, hot water and dry with a tea towel.

● **Removing burned-on food** can be done without working up a sweat – but you do need patience, lots of hot water and washing-up liquid. Squirt some washing-up liquid in the pot or pan, fill it with hot water and leave it to soak for a couple of hours, or even overnight.

Pottery

There is everyday pottery, such as jugs, plates and vases. And then there is fine antique pottery that requires a light touch when cleaning – and possibly a professional's care. There are two types of everyday pottery: glazed and unglazed. The thicker the glaze, the easier the pot will be to clean.

● **To clean glazed pottery,** proceed much as you would with your dishes. Hand-wash fragile or expensive pieces in the sink with warm water and washing-up liquid; a scrubber sponge will be fine for most hand-washing.

● **To remove heavy dirt and grease,** first dampen a cloth in methylated spirits, wipe it over the glazed pottery, then wash as usual in the dishwasher or sink.

● **To clean unglazed pottery,** just wash in the sink with warm water and washing-up liquid. It is porous and it may take a day or two for the pot to dry out, but the water won't hurt it.

● **Fine antique pottery** should simply be dusted or wiped gently with a damp cloth or damp cloth with a little washing-up liquid. For more extensive cleaning, consult a professional.

Spray-on glaze
Some pottery is painted with acrylic, followed by a spray-on glaze that is not kiln-fired. This kind of glaze will not stand up to washing in water. To clean it, wipe it down with a damp cloth.

Power tools

If you don't clean your power tools periodically, they'll let you down – by malfunctioning or even stopping all together. Dust, sawdust and rust can seep into the motor and accumulate, eventually bringing the tool to a standstill.

- **How frequently you clean** your power tools depends on how often you use them and how carefully you store them. In general, give them a good cleaning any time you notice a build-up of residue such as sawdust, oil or grease. To keep everything running smoothly, don't store your tools where weather can affect them – a dry, frost-free shed or garage, or even indoors, is best. And remember, if you don't clean them often enough, simple dust clogs can render built-in safety features useless.

- **To clean your power tools,** first unplug your equipment or remove the batteries and wipe out the battery compartment with a soft, dry cloth.

- **Do not, under any circumstances,** spray anything liquid into the motor of any tool you're cleaning. Instead, use the professional gadgeteer's favourite cleaner – a can of compressed air (which you can buy at a camera shop). Hold the can level before you point the extension straw and hit the spray button. If you don't hold the can perfectly level, you may end up spraying liquid into the motor and that would be disastrous. Spray a blast of air into the air vents. If you see a cloud of dust puff out of the motor, you know you've waited too long to clean your tools.

- **If you're fussy** about the appearance of your tools, you can clean the exterior. Don't use abrasive cleaners. Simply squirt some glass cleaner onto a piece of kitchen paper and wipe away the grime.

> **For sticky situations**
> DIY can often involve the use of glue and, before you know it, your power tools are smeared with adhesive. To remove glue, just apply a dab of petroleum jelly and rub at it with a dry cloth.

Printers

Before cleaning your printer, first remove any paper from the paper-feed tray and, if the tray comes off, remove it completely from the printer. Using a dry cloth, wipe off the sides and bottom of the tray to get rid of dust, pet hair, pollen and general dirt. Never use even a slightly damp cloth: you don't want water anywhere near the printer's interior.

● **Clean the paper rollers** to prevent paper from sticking to them. There are two kinds of rollers: plastic and rubber. Clean plastic rollers with cotton buds dipped in white spirit. For the rubber variety, use latex-paint remover – available from DIY stores. Avoid getting the remover on plastic parts, because it will damage them. Don't touch the printing mechanism unless your owner's manual gives cleaning advice on this.

● **Cleaning the printer's insides** shouldn't be necessary. Many printers work using a laser system and moving things inside can damage this permanently. If you spot a toner spill in a laser printer, don't ever try to clean it with compressed air – toner can be toxic, so you don't want a cloud of it billowing up in your face. Instead, wipe it up carefully with paper towels.

● **Cleaning the printer's outer casing** is a simpler matter and it can be treated like any toughened plastic. Use a cloth, dipped into a solution of sudsy washing-up liquid and tightly wrung out until it's barely damp.

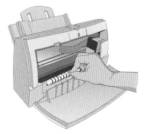

Quilts

New quilts are almost always washable – just check the care label and follow the instructions. But old or handmade ones need special care. Those quilts that have been handed down have character that comes from having been cherished. Unfortunately, that character often appears in the form of water rings, dye bleeds, stains of unknown origin and tears – all of which will dictate how you wash it.

- **Test the fabrics of your quilt** to see if they are colourfast. Mix 1 tablespoon each of ammonia and liquid laundry detergent with 3 tablespoons water. Dampen a white towel with this and dab it on a corner of the quilt. Leave for 30 seconds, then blot with a dry white cloth. If colour comes away on the cloth, the quilt is not colourfast and you can't wash it in water.

   If your quilt is colourfast, you could put it in the washing machine on a hand-wash programme. If the quilt has weak spots in the seams or fabric, put it in a mesh laundry bag first.

- **If you don't want to machine-wash,** use your bath. Fill it with enough water to cover the quilt by 6-10cm. Swirl in detergent, using one with bleach if your quilt is yellowing. Spread the quilt out in the water and then agitate the quilt for about 10 minutes (wear rubber gloves) to release the dirt. If you notice that the colour is starting to run, drain the bath immediately and rinse the quilt with cold water.

   When it's time to rinse, pull out the plug and bunch up the quilt at the other end of the bath. Leave it until all the water has drained out, then squeeze out any excess water. Rinse in cold water, agitating the quilt as you did when washing. If you used bleach, rinse it twice. Squeeze the quilt again.

- **To dry the quilt,** try tumbling it in the dryer with cool air, if you think the quilt can stand it. If not, hang it on a clothesline.

> **Test of strength**
> If you want to clean a vintage or heirloom quilt you need to check whether there are any tears or deterioration of the fabric before you begin. If you find a weak patch of material, tack it down with needle and thread or consider replacing that area.

R

Radiators

A dusty radiator can be worse than ugly – it can also be costly. Layers of dust can compromise the ability of a radiator to do its job and because heat attracts dust, your radiator will be dustier than most other things in the room. A weekly dusting with a feather duster or a dust cloth will keep accumulation down. Twice a year is often enough to do a major radiator cleaning, unless your environment is particularly dusty.

The best times to clean radiators are in the spring or early summer, when you're no longer using them and in the autumn, before you turn the central heating on again. That way, there will be no danger of burning yourself.

● **First, remove as much of the surface dirt** as possible using a hand vacuum or the brush attachment of your vacuum cleaner. The brush can actually go some way towards getting in between the tubes, but the thin nozzle attachment goes further. You won't get everything out with a vacuum, but there are more effective ways to clean inside the crevices.

● **To reach the dust trapped between tubes,** there are a couple of common kitchen items that you could use. Wrap a sheet of paper towel around the broad end of a kitchen spatula and secure it tightly with a rubber band. Then slide the spatula up and down both sides of each tube of the radiator. For hard-to-shift substances and especially sticky spills, spray some all-purpose cleaner on the paper-swathed spatula and then have another go at the area.

Moveable heat
To clean a portable electric radiator, unplug it and then follow the directions given here for fixed radiators. When you put it away for the summer, store it in a large plastic bag so that it doesn't get dusty.

● **Deal with rust spots** as soon as you see them. You can get the larger chips off with a wire kitchen brush, followed by some medium and then fine-grade glasspaper. Be sure to get rid of all the rust so the corrosion will stop after painting. Once you've smoothed the surface and there is no visible rust residue, spray the spot with special radiator paint, available from DIY stores.

Records

With CDs having made records obsolete, it's increasingly hard to track down old copies. Clean the records that you still have, to make them last longer and sound better.

- **Velvet record brushes** are the favourite of many who do clean their records. They have a handle for gripping and a velvet-grained fabric on the bottom. They come with a liquid, which is mostly water with a dash of mild soap. Harsher chemicals will damage record vinyl. Ask for the brushes at specialist music shops and follow instructions.

- **You can use a very soft cloth** with a fine weave if you don't have a velvet record brush. Don't use anything that creates lint – that's what you're trying to get rid of. Make a mixture of 99 per cent water and 1 per cent baby shampoo. Barely dampen the cloth and hold it lightly on the record as it spins on the turntable. Be careful not to touch the record with a fingernail.

- **If you have heavier, sticky grime** on a record, try again with the baby-shampoo mixture and a little more pressure on your cloth. If that doesn't work, take the record off the turntable, holding it only by the edges. Rest one edge against your body and hold the other in one hand. With your free hand, wipe the record with the cloth, moving back and forth in the direction of the grooves.

Roofing

Moss, algae and mildew can all damage your roof. But you must take care if you plan to tackle roof-cleaning yourself. Only embark upon it if you are very confident about working at height. Clearly, falling from a roof can be fatal, so the roofs that we suggest cleaning here are those on a shed, garage or single-storey extension. Leave the roof of multistorey buildings to the professionals.

● **To clean asphalt roofs** as well as cedar and other wood roofs, first go to a DIY store and pick up a cleaner for treated-wood decks – one that contains oxygen bleach. (Don't use chlorine bleach.) On a cloudy day, when the roof is cool, mix the cleaner according to the package directions and squirt it on the roof with a garden sprayer. (High-pressure sprayers will damage the roof.) Let the cleaner sit for half an hour. Then give it a scrub with a broom or brush. Rinse thoroughly with a garden hose.

● **Tile roofs can attract moss and other growth,** too, but cleaning them yourself is not recommended because wet tiles are delicate and become extremely slippery when wet. Always let a professional do the job.

● **Several kinds of metal roofing,** including painted steel and copper, need little maintenance. Although costly to install, such roofs will last many years.

Expert **ADVICE**

The biggest problem with maintaining a tin roof is keeping it painted. Paint often sheds from tin roofs in sheets. Then you've got big problems, mostly with rust. Choose a sunny but cool day to paint a tin roof. Wash the roof first, using a soapy solution in your garden sprayer. Rinse well and allow it to dry. Then paint the roof with a suitable rustproof, oil-based paint.

Rugs

The best way to keep a rug looking fresh is to keep it from getting dirty in the first place. Remove outdoor shoes when entering the house and you'll cut down on dirt tracked indoors.

- **Give rugs a good, regular shake outside.** Vacuum them often, front and back, against the pile to pick up ground-in dirt. Rugs in high-traffic areas need a more thorough cleaning at least once a year; those in out-of-the-way places, less often.

- **To shampoo a rug,** vacuum it first, then mix 100ml mild washing-up liquid or rug shampoo with 2 litres cool water in a clean bucket. With a long-bristled, soft brush or a firm, non-shedding sponge, brush the pile in the direction of the nap. Wet thoroughly but don't scrub.

- **To wash the fringe of a rug,** first place a plastic or rubber dust sheet under it. Then put a clean white towel on top of that (still under the fringe). Using a brush or sponge moistened with the cleaning solution, brush the fringe from the knots out to the end. To rinse, replace the first towel under the fringe with a dry one and blot the fringe with yet another towel dampened with warm water. Allow the fringe to dry on another dry towel.

shampooing a **RUG**

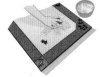

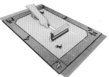

1 Using a sponge, brush the rug with your cleaning solution.

2 After rinsing, squeeze out extra moisture with a window squeegee.

3 Leave the rug to dry: on top of the garden table is ideal.

Rugs

- **To rinse the main part of the rug,** wet clean rags with warm water and press them against it. Squeeze out excess moisture, following the direction of the nap until no more water comes out (a window squeegee works well). Use towels to mop up any excess.

- **If you placed plastic underneath the rug** and it has become wet, replace it with dry plastic. Lay down dry towels on top of the plastic, and lay the rug flat on the towels to dry thoroughly on one side. Then turn it over to dry the other side, replacing the towels again if need be. Or dry the rug on top of a garden table in the shade outside.

- **If the pile feels stiff** once it has completely dried, vacuum or brush the rug gently.

- **To remove a stain on a rug,** first blot it up with paper towel. Scrape up any solids with a dull knife. Work from the outside of the stain inwards, to avoid spreading the stain.

- **If the stain has penetrated the entire rug,** place a clean cloth underneath it to absorb what seeped through. Dilute the stain by blotting with a cloth dampened in clean water.

- **Try using a carpet stain remover.** If that doesn't work use a solution of 1 teaspoon mild washing-up liquid and 250ml warm water; don't saturate. Then blot with a white towel dampened with clear water.

- **Alternatively, mix up a paste** made of powdered laundry detergent and water. Be sure the detergent has no brightening or whitening agents – choose one that's designed specially for colours. Leave the paste to sit for 10 minutes, then scrape off any residue with a wooden spoon. Blot with a clean towel and rinse with another towel wrung out in warm water. Blot the area again to dry.

Satin

Cleaning satin is tricky because this shiny fabric shows grease and other stains so easily. The techniques described here differ according to the type of satin you have.

- **If you get a greasy stain on satin** of any kind, try blotting it first with a clean white rag. Then cover with flour or unscented talc and leave for an hour. The powder should absorb grease. Then gently brush the fabric with a soft-bristled brush and launder washable items according to the care-label instructions. Treat stains first with a pre-wash stain remover. If an item is not washable, take it to a dry-cleaner.

- **Dry-clean or hand-wash** woven acetate or silk-satin bed linen. Wash in the bath using a gentle fabric wash, such as Woolite. Hand-wring gently, wrapping up the sheet in an absorbent white towel and hang out to dry.

- **You can machine-wash** polyester and nylon satin bed linen, although hand washing will keep pilling to a minimum. Machine-wash in warm or cool water and very little detergent. Never use bleach. Put in the dryer on the lowest setting. Never line dry nylon sheets in the sun.

- **To clean satin cushions,** vacuum them using the soft brush attachment. Give greasy stains the flour treatment described above. If stains persist, machine-wash a satin cushion only if it has a removable cover.

drying **satin sheets**

- Shield sheets made of silk and nylon from the sun. Never line-dry nylon satin sheets, for the sun is nylon's worst enemy. If your bedroom gets a lot of sun, choose acetate or polyester satin.
- Never dry woven acetate sheets in a tumble dryer.
- Be especially careful when wringing silk-satin sheets – silk is thin and tears easily.

Scissors

To keep scissors cutting smoothly, it's important to clean them regularly. Keep scissors for different tasks strictly segregated: a pair for cutting paper and craft projects, others for working with fabric or for trimming toe nails.

- **To keep your scissors cutting smoothly,** wipe the blades after each use with a soft rag. This stops lint and other material from getting caught in the blade pivot area, where it can interfere with the performance of your scissors.

- **Oil scissors occasionally** at the pivot area (around the screw head and between the blades), using a penetrating lubricant such as WD-40. Never use vegetable oil or any other oil that will attract dirt and get gummy. Gently work the blades a few times to force the lubricant into the joint.

In the pink
Prolong the life of pinking shears by being sure there is always fabric between the blades when you cut. Only close the blades onto themselves when you're putting them away.

- **If your scissors get dirty,** wash them in washing-up liquid and warm water. Dry scissors thoroughly with a soft cloth before putting them away.

- **If your scissors get rusty,** soak them first in white vinegar. Then use fine glasspaper on the handles and blades, being careful to avoid the cutting edges. Always store scissors in a dry, cool, clean place.

- **To keep the blades sharp,** some scissor makers recommend using sharpeners. Most experts, however, suggest that you take them to a professional for sharpening.

Sewing machines

If you have a modern, computerised sewing machine, follow the directions in your owner's manual. If you have a traditional-style electric or mechanical machine, here's what to do to keep it running smoothly.

- **For a mechanical sewing machine,** be sure you use the right oil. Use sewing machine oil, available at haberdashers and sewing-machine shops. Other lubricants, such as 3-in-One oil and WD-40, dry too fast and will eventually cause the machine to seize up. Put no more than one or two tiny drops of sewing machine oil in each of the oiling holes found on your machine.

- **Remove dust and debris.** Slide the edges of a thin piece of muslin between the tension discs: be sure the presser foot is up to slacken the tension springs. Remove the machine's cover. Using a can of compressed air (available from camera shops) or hair dryer, blast movable parts with a stream of air, from back to front, to remove any loose threads, lint and dust.

- **Take off the throat plate** (sometimes called the needle plate), paying close attention to how it is removed and replaced. The same goes for the bobbin, bobbin case (also called the shuttle) and hook race – watch what you're taking apart or you may not get it together again. Use compressed air, a hair dryer or a small, stiff-bristled nylon brush to clean these parts. At a pinch, a pipe cleaner will extract small fibres from moving parts. So will a dental pick. Don't use toothpicks – they're too flimsy and could break and get stuck in the machine.

- **Dust the outside with a clean cloth.** A mild household cleaner, sprayed on a cloth, will get rid of grimy fingerprints. If the case is metal, sewing machine oil or WD-40, sprayed first on a rag, will give it a shine. Keep your machine covered when not in use.

> **Dry clean**
> Never oil a computerised machine or use any kind of liquid. (Oil and liquids can irreparably damage circuit boards.) Use a hair dryer to blow away lint. If you're unsure about how to clean your computerised machine, take it to a sewing-machine repair shop.

Sheets

Cleaning sheets is an easy job for the washing machine. Simply read the care labels on cotton and polyester-cotton sheets to find the maximum temperature of the wash.

● **For best results,** wash as part of a mixed load: a pair of sheets plus two hand towels and facecloths will fill most washing machines. When drying, to minimise (or hopefully avoid) ironing, remove the sheets when still just damp and fold into eighths. Store in the airing cupboard. If you're doing a turnaround on one set of sheets, you'll need to dry them fully and then iron.

Shoes

To protect new leather shoes, treat them with a water and stain repellent such as Scotchgard before wearing. Use one designed especially for leather and then polish before putting them on and going out for the first time.

● **To give leather shoes and boots** a shine, first remove any laces and brush off loose dirt with a stiff brush or cloth. If the shoes are especially dirty, clean them with saddle soap, following package directions. Rub a clean cotton cloth in polish and then onto the shoes. Let the polish dry for 10 minutes. Buff with a clean cloth.

● **To remove salt stains** from leather shoes, rub with equal parts of water and vinegar, applied with a cotton pad. To erase scuff marks, rub with the cut edge of a raw potato. Then buff.

● **To clean white shoes,** wipe them with a cloth dabbed in ammonia. (This works on canvas, too.) Remove scuff marks with a dab of white (non-gel) toothpaste. Then buff.

Time saver
When you don't have time to polish leather shoes, use baby wipes. This technique will dry out the leather over time, so don't forget to follow up with polish later on.

Shoes

- **To clean patent-leather shoes,** first remove any scuff marks with a clean rubber. Then shine with baby oil, furniture polish, petroleum jelly or cream leather cleaner/conditioner. Buff gently with a paper towel or clean cloth. At a pinch, rub leather or patent shoes with hand cream and then buff. On imitation patent leather, use mild washing-up liquid or a car interior vinyl and plastic cleaner from car-supplies shops.

- **To remove salt stains** from leather shoes, rub with equal parts of water and vinegar, applied with a cotton pad. To erase scuff marks, rub with the cut edge of a raw potato. Then buff.

- **To clean white shoes,** wipe them with a cloth dabbed in ammonia. (This works on canvas, too.) Remove scuff marks with a dab of white (non-gel) toothpaste. Then buff.

Showers

How can the shower – the place where you get yourself clean – get so dirty? With the exception of the kitchen sink, nowhere else in the home shows grime more quickly than in the shower. Soap, shampoo and dirt all combine to make an unsightly scum. However, there are some quick and easy ways to keep your shower sparkling.

- **When you take a shower,** clean the shower straight afterwards. Steam from all that hot water will loosen grime and make the job easier.

- **With tiled shower walls and floor,** if you don't want to use a multipurpose bathroom cleaner (the easiest option) you can use dishwasher detergent (either powder or liquid will do). Mix 4 tablespoons dishwasher detergent with 500ml warm

Showers

water in a small pump-spray bottle and shake to dissolve the detergent. Spray liberally on walls; let it sit for two or three hours, then scrub with a sponge. (Dishwasher detergent is an irritant, so wear gloves and don't get it on your skin. And make sure you rinse away any residue afterwards.) Use a sponge mop to scrub high spots and the floor.

cleaning tile grout

1 Rub bicarbonate of soda and bleach onto grout with a spatula.

2 Leave to dry for an hour. Then scrub with a wet toothbrush.

- **To clean tile grout,** make a paste of bicarbonate of soda and bleach (add bleach to the powder until it's a thick goo). Using a spatula, smear the paste onto the grout. Air-dry for an hour, then scrub with a toothbrush and water. (Never use ammonia nearby – ammonia and bleach don't mix.)

- **To prevent water spots,** rub the shower walls and doors with a squeegee straight after you have taken your shower. Or try using a daily shower cleaner. Mist surfaces straight after you shower, while the walls are still warm and wet. The cleaner will prevent deposits from forming and will wash down the drain the next time you shower.

- **If your shower sprouts mould,** try this trick. Wipe down the walls with a solution of 1 tablespoon ammonia, 1 teaspoon water softener and 1 tablespoon vinegar in 200ml of warm water. Rinse with fresh water. Buff dry.

- **To clean shower doors** and banish soap scum, you can wash the doors down with white vinegar.

- **Alternatively, take leftover white wine** that's rapidly turning to vinegar, empty it into a trigger-spray bottle and squirt this on your shower doors. Rinse well with water and dry with a soft cloth.

- **You can also wipe down** the doors with fabric softener on a damp cloth. Buff with a clean, dry cloth.

Showers

- **Another way to keep soap scum** at bay is to wipe down the shower doors with lemon oil. Baby oil works, too, as does furniture polish, buffed with a soft cloth. (This also works on tiled showers, but don't use these slippery substances on a shower floor – you might slip when you're in the shower.)

- **Scrub shower-door runners** with white toothpaste and an old toothbrush. Brush with vinegar to rinse. Or dip a stiff-bristled paintbrush in vinegar and scrub thoroughly.

- **To keep mildew from growing** on the door runners, run the head of a small sponge paintbrush along the bottom runner channels when you've finished showering.

- **To remove soap film** on a plastic shower curtain, place it in the washing machine with two or three large bath towels. Add 100ml vinegar and wash, removing it before the spin cycle. Hang it up immediately to dry. If the mildew is out of control, use 180ml chlorine bleach instead. To avoid a soapy build-up on the bottom of the shower curtain, rub it with baby oil. Always keep a shower curtain unfurled to give mould and mildew a less inviting place to grow.

SIMPLE solutions

If your showerhead is clogged with limescale deposits, there are many ways you can clean it:
- If possible, unscrew the showerhead and soak it overnight in a bowl of white vinegar. In the morning, remove the deposits with a brush with moderately stiff bristles.
- If you can't unscrew the showerhead, don't worry. Just pour the vinegar into a plastic bag, pull the bag up around the showerhead so that the showerhead is immersed in the vinegar and secure it to the showerhead with rubber bands or twist ties. Leave to soak, as before, then brush off remaining deposits.

Shutters

Used to add character and cut down on strong sunlight, and now often used as a smart alternative to blinds and curtains, shutters can become more unsightly than decorative if you let the dust and grime accumulate.

- **Regular maintenance** will keep your indoor shutter-cleaning chores to a minimum. Dust every month on both sides with the soft brush attachment of your vacuum. In between sessions with your vacuum, go over shutters with a microfibre cloth or feather duster.

- **To clean indoor shutters thoroughly,** remove them from their hinges and put them somewhere level and clean – a workbench topped with a white towel, for instance. Spray the shutters with a gentle all-purpose cleaner, taking special care  to penetrate the cracks and crevices. Allow the cleaner to sit on the shutters for five minutes. Wearing rubber gloves, start cleaning at the top of shutters and work towards the bottom. Clean the slats with a towel, your rubber-gloved fingers or a small soft-bristled brush for nooks and crannies. Use a spray bottle filled with warm water to spray away dirt and other grime from the slats. Using a dry cloth, dry the slats one at a time. Reach hard-to-dry areas with a rag wrapped round the handle of a wooden spoon.

- **Cleaning outdoor shutters** is basically the same operation – with a few refinements. Remove the shutters from the outside walls and lay them flat or prop them against a secure support. Wet down the shutters with an all-purpose cleaner or a spray bottle of water with a squirt of washing-up liquid added. Leave the cleaner on for a few minutes. Then use a screwdriver, wrapped in a towel, to attack hard-to-reach spots. Rinse with a garden hose, using as much water pressure as possible. Dry the slats with a towel. Let them finish drying in the sun.

Silk

Take care when cleaning silk – many silk garments are washable if you are careful, but don't assume that they are. Check the fabric-care label carefully to avoid disaster.

- **Treat stains from spills** and other marks before you wash silk. (See below for special ways to treat perspiration and deodorant stains.) On a hidden spot, apply a paste of powdered laundry starch, such as Dylon Easy In-Wash Starch, and cold water, to make sure the silk is colourfast. If it is, apply the paste to the stain, let it dry and brush it away.

- **To wash a silk garment,** you can either do it by hand or use the delicate cycle and cool or warm water in your washing machine. A mild detergent, such as Woolite, works best.

- **To dry a silk garment,** carefully roll it up in an absorbent white towel to blot up excess moisture. Then either lay the garment out flat or hang it on a padded hanger.

- **Perspiration and deodorant stains** can discolour and weaken silk. (The salt in sweat and aluminium chloride in deodorants can stain.) Dry-clean or wash clothes promptly.

- **To treat perspiration or deodorant stains** on washable silk, try one of these remedies, but first test it on a hidden spot to see if the fabric dye holds. Try soaking the stain in warm water and a paste of table salt and white vinegar. If that doesn't work, make a paste of cream of tartar and warm water and apply it to the stain. Allow it to dry, then brush it off and launder the garment as usual. Alternatively, apply a mixture of warm water and water softener to the stain and then rub with laundry soap. Brush it off and then wash. Or dissolve 2 aspirins in 100ml warm water and apply this to the stain. Let it dry for hours, then brush it off and launder.

> **Silk safety**
> Never use chlorine bleach when cleaning silk – it can irreparably damage the fabric. Don't leave silk to dry in direct sunlight because it will fade. And never wash silk ties; both the silk and its lining are prone to shrinkage. (The lining will usually shrivel first.) Instead, take them to a dry-cleaner.

Silver jewellery

Air and light are the two biggest enemies of silver jewellery. So how you store your silver jewellery makes a big difference to how much it will tarnish.

Jewellery care
If you're cleaning silver pieces decorated with gems, avoid using anything remotely abrasive near the stones. And don't soak silver pieces set with stones for longer than a few seconds, since water can dissolve any glue that holds the stones in place. Silver hates chlorine, so take off silver jewellery before jumping into a swimming pool.

● **Always store clean silver jewellery** in a cool, dry place, wrapped separately in a soft cloth and then enclosed in a re-sealable plastic bag to prevent the jewellery from getting jostled about and scratched by other pieces – silver is a fairly soft metal and marks easily.

● **Clean your silver once a month** if you wear it frequently. The best cleaner is silver paste or liquid polish. Apply with a soft cloth according to the package directions and then buff with another cloth. Rinse the piece gently in warm water.

Another method is to rub the silver with a soft cloth dipped in bicarbonate of soda, using a frayed toothbrush to get into any hard-to-reach areas. Rinse well in warm water and buff dry with another cloth.

Alternatively, line a small bowl with a piece of aluminium foil, with the shiny side towards you. Fill the bowl with hot water and mix in 1 tablespoon bleach-free powdered laundry detergent (not liquid) – try one especially for colours. Put the jewellery in the solution and let it soak one minute. Rinse completely and air-dry.

● **To clean badly tarnished** or dirty silver jewellery, fill a small plastic bowl with warm water and add a few drops of dishwasher powder. Soak the jewellery in the solution overnight. Should the dirt persist on your silver after its overnight soak, clean the piece with an old toothbrush. Then rinse and dry carefully with a soft cloth.

● **Specially treated anti-tarnish cloths,** available at most supermarkets and hardware stores, may also be used to touch up dirty silver jewellery.

Silver serving pieces

Though most people save them for best or let them sit on a sideboard, silver serving dishes, whether plated or sterling silver, actually benefit from being used frequently. Rotate your pieces so that they will age uniformly.

- **Clean your silver twice a year** with a high-quality silver polish and a soft cloth. Apply the polish in a circular motion and use warm water to rinse.

- **If there is candle wax on your silver,** don't scrape it off – you could scratch the surface. Instead, soften the wax in a warm oven or with a hair dryer on low and then peel it off. Or dribble on a little turpentine or methylated spirits to dislodge the wax.

- **To clean ornate silver pieces,** sprinkle on bicarbonate of soda and rub gently with a soft dry cloth.

- **To wash silver,** do it by hand in mild washing-up liquid and warm water and dry immediately with a soft cloth. Water left on silver can pit and corrode it. As a general rule, don't wash silver in the dishwasher; it's simply too soft to withstand the jostling and abrasion. If you must use the dishwasher, keep silver pieces well away from metals such as copper and stainless steel. They will mark each other if they touch.

- **To restore the shine** between cleanings, use polishing gloves and cloths or a jeweller's rouge cloth (a special flannel treated with a red polishing powder). Both are sold at hardware stores.

- **To store a silver serving piece,** slip it into an anti-tarnish bag or cloth. Acid-free tissue paper, sold at craft shops, also works. Then place it in a plastic bag. (Don't use newspaper, because its carbon can eat into silver.) Silica-gel packets placed inside will keep moisture at bay. Don't use rubber bands to close the bag – they contain sulphur, which damages silver. Store away from sunlight.

> **Check the menu**
> Silver reacts badly to mustard, salt or ketchup, so clean it at once if it touches these foods. Eggs and mayonnaise will also tarnish silver. So if you eat any of these foods for dinner, be sure to wash up your cutlery as soon as possible.

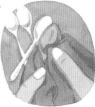

Sinks

With all the soap and water that flow through your sink, you'd think it would be clean all the time. But soapy deposits, food stains, rust and water spots have a way of accumulating quickly and creating a dirty scum.

● **For general cleaning of any sink,** use a squirt of washing-up liquid and scrub the sink with a soft sponge. Rinse away residue. Don't use an abrasive cleaning agent or applicator, because it will scratch. A non-abrasive cleaner, like Astonish, will work on more stubborn staining.

● **For a lightly stained porcelain sink,** rub a freshly cut lemon around the sink to cut through the grease. Rinse with running water. You could also sprinkle bicarbonate of soda in the sink and then rub it with a damp sponge. Rinse with vinegar or lemon juice to help neutralise the alkaline cleaner and then rinse with running water. Or make a paste the consistency of toothpaste with bicarbonate of soda and water and gently rub the sink with a sponge or soft nylon brush. Polish with a paper towel or soft cloth.

● **To remove rust marks** from stainless steel or iron sinks, squirt some WD-40 onto a cloth, then rub the rust mark with it. Rinse the sink thoroughly.

SIMPLE solutions

Sink taps pick up white mineral deposits from the water but these can be easily removed with white wine vinegar:
● Soak a paper towel in the vinegar, squeeze out the excess and wrap the towel around the fixture. After 10 minutes, take it off and buff the tap with a soft dry cloth (a facecloth you're about to wash is ideal).
● For brass or gold-coloured taps: omit the vinegar, which may damage the surface. Just do the best you can and buff off with a soft cloth.

Sinks

- **To remove water spots from any sink** – be it ceramic or metal, use a cloth dampened with vinegar.

- **For a sparkling white ceramic sink,** place paper towels across the bottom and saturate them with household bleach. Let it sit for 30 minutes and rinse with running water. However, do not use bleach in coloured porcelain sinks, because it will fade the colour. Clean these sinks with mild liquid detergents, vinegar or baking soda.

- **For a sparkling metal sink,** use a specialist chrome and metal cleaner. Apply and then polish dry, using a clean old tea towel.

- **Stains in Corian-type sinks** can be removed with toothpaste or a paste of bicarbonate of soda and water. Gently scrub the paste on with a white scrubbing pad. Your last resort is scrubbing very gently with very fine wet-or-dry glasspaper. Scrubbing too hard could wear a groove in the Corian. Polish the cleaned spot with a special polish made for Corian surfaces.

- **Water spots that have etched themselves** into a sink's porcelain are extremely difficult to remove. Buff such spots out with a polishing compound, such as jeweller's rouge, as soon as you notice them.

- **To cover a chip or scratch** on a white porcelain surface – including sinks, tubs and appliances – pick up a container of white enamel paint at DIY shops. Following the package directions, paint over the mark with a small artist's brush, let it dry, rub with fine glasspaper and paint again. Repeat the process until the painted area is even with the surrounding surface. You can also buy a porcelain repair kit, which will include filler, hardener, cleaning spray, glasspaper and more.

Skirting boards

Skirting boards take a huge amount of punishment. Though they're usually coated with a gloss paint to make them hard-wearing, they are kicked by children and bashed with the vacuum cleaner on a regular basis. Scuff marks can be tough to remove, so follow these tips to keep skirtings pristine.

● **To remove scuff marks and dirt** from gloss-painted skirting boards, use a sponge and a grease-cutting all-purpose spray cleaner. Spray the cleaner onto the sponge not the skirting board, to prevent streaking.

● **For really tough stains,** you can try a scouring powder and a plastic scrubbing pad, but test an inconspicuous corner of the skirting board first. If it doesn't affect the finish, you can apply the method to the entire surface. A general cleaning rule of thumb comes into play here: use the least aggressive cleaner initially and then resort to more aggressive tactics as the scuffs dictate.

● **Skirting boards that are painted** with stain or emulsion paint require a more gentle cleaning method (water, washing-up liquid and a facecloth).

● **To clean vinyl or rubber skirting** – more properly called cove moulding – spray on a wax stripper and let it soak in for a few minutes to loosen old wax and grime. Then scrub with a nylon brush and rinse.

● **Prevention can save you a lot of work.** While you may think it's the kids who are scuffing the skirting board, it's more likely to be the vacuum (check the bumper at the front is in place) or your floor mop (avoid mops that have sharp swivel heads). And if you use a strong cleaner on floors, quickly wipe up spills and splashes that could discolour your skirting boards.

Skylights

What better way to let natural light into your home – while maintaining your privacy – than with a skylight? But so you don't lose out on that light, maintain a cleaning routine. The materials depend on whether you have glass or acrylic skylights.

● **To clean the exterior of glass skylights,** treat them as you would any other window-cleaning task. But remember to use extra caution as you are far higher up. By using a long-handled squeegee, it can be possible to clean the outside of your glass skylight; use a commercial window cleaner that doesn't need rinsing or drying off.

● **A twice-a-year cleaning of your skylights** and frames is sufficient; if you clean more often you may wear out the silicone seal around the skylight and cause leaks.

● **Remove dust and cobwebs** around the inside of the frames by using a barely damp mop. Wooden frames can be cleaned with a furniture polish if you can reach them.

● **If your skylight is made of acrylic,** take care as strong cleaning solvents – even glass cleaner – can damage the acrylic. Use a solution of 1 tablespoon washing-up liquid in 4 litres warm water. Dip a soft cloth into this, wipe over the window and rinse well. If stubborn stains remain, use any plastic cleaner. Spray the cleaner on a cloth and wipe over the acrylic pane. You can also use the plastic cleaner to remove marks on vinyl frames.

● **If your skylight has a screen,** you will need to remove it to clean the inside of the window. If this is too difficult, open the window and clean the inside at the same time that you clean the outside. To clean the screen, vacuum it using the brush attachment. If the screen is really dirty and you can remove it, wash it with a soft brush dipped in a solution of washing-up liquid and warm water. Then rinse thoroughly.

Slate

Whether you have slate flooring, a slate mantelpiece or a slate kitchen worktop, light cleaning is a simple task, especially if you have sealed the slate carefully beforehand.

- **To remove dust on slate,** just use the vacuum cleaner or wipe it with a damp cloth or a damp mop.

- **To remove floor dirt,** mix 100ml ammonia in 6 litres water. Apply the cleaning solution with a sponge mop. If you dust weekly, you can do a thorough cleaning with ammonia once a month or every other month.

- **To protect slate floors** from staining, apply a stone sealer – either gloss or satin – after it's installed. Slate is especially susceptible to oil stains (from salad oils, for instance). So sealing a slate floor in a kitchen or eating area may be a good idea. If you wish, follow the sealer with a wax finish that can protect the sealer and make it last longer. The sealer and the wax work together to make slate easier to clean.

- **To clean a slate worktop,** scour the surface using a multipurpose cleaner and a damp sponge. Do not use abrasive pads, which may remove some of the stone.

- **To clean up oil stains,** sprinkle a liberal amount of flour on the surface and let it sit for 10 minutes. Then scrub the surface with a grease-cutting cleaner, such as Flash, or use warm water with a squirt of washing-up liquid.

- **To protect a slate kitchen worktop,** oil it with a 50-50 mixture of boiled linseed oil and turpentine. Wipe the solution onto the slate with a cloth, then buff it with a soft cloth or old towel until it's dry. Oil your kitchen worktop once or twice a year. Oil other non-floor surfaces – mantelpieces or hearths, for instance – every two years.

Sleeping bags

Sleeping bags come with one of three types of insulation: natural (down, or down and feather); synthetic fibres (usually nylon); or fleece. But whatever type of sleeping bag you have, if you use it only a couple of times a year and treat it well, you might be able to go for 10 years without giving it a thorough cleaning.

- **To keep a sleeping bag in good shape,** always use a washable cotton liner inside it or always wear nightclothes when you're using the bag.

- **Spot-clean any stains** after a camping trip with a sponge and soapy water. And when you get home air the sleeping bag for a couple of hours or place it in the dryer for 10 to 15 minutes to get rid of any moisture.

- **Store your bag** in a large breathable storage sack – not the stuff sack you use to take it away – or a plastic bag.

- **To hand-wash a sleeping bag** – which is the best way to do it – fill a bath with warm water and just a little soap. For down bags, select a down liquid soap (available from camping-supplies stores). You can also safely use a mild detergent, such as Woolite. Don't use any detergent containing bleach on a down bag (but it's safe for nylon bags). Check the package directions

SIMPLE solutions

When hand-washing a sleeping bag, try this simple trick to prevent the compartments formed by baffles (those stitched partitions that keep the fill evenly distributed) from inflating and floating to the surface. Keep the bag in its stuff sack (the bag you squeeze the sleeping bag into, to keep it small when you're on a trip) and immerse both bag and sack in the tub of water. You've already forced the air out of the bag when you put it in the stuff sack. Once both are immersed, you can remove the sleeping bag from the sack and work the soapy water into the bag.

Sleeping bags

to determine the amount of detergent to use. Remember that using too much will mean more rinsing later on. Gently knead the bag to help the soapy water penetrate the material. If your sleeping bag has a waterproof outer shell, turn it inside out first so the soapy water will be able to penetrate.

- **Rinse your bag twice** – several times if necessary – with clear water. Don't cut corners on this step, particularly if you're working with down. It's very important to remove all soap before the down has dried. Do not wring water from your sleeping bag. Instead, squeeze out the water by rolling up the bag tightly and carefully.

  - **To machine-wash a sleeping bag,** you may want to use a self-service launderette if your bag is too heavy or can't fit easily within the drum. Follow care-label advice for the correct wash programme.

- **Your bag must be thoroughly dry** before storing. It's often better to dry it at a self-service launderette, where you can use a large dryer. In a home dryer, the sleeping bag may take up so much room that it won't tumble well and any filling that has formed clumps will not be broken up during drying.

- **When you go to the self-service launderette,** use the largest dryer set to high heat. Melting the nylon shell is not a danger because the bag has room to tumble, but if you're in doubt, use a lower setting. Once the nylon shell is dry, set the dryer on medium heat so that the filling can dry. Throw in a couple of clean tennis balls to help break up clumps of down. Remove the bag as soon as it's finished tumbling.

  Even if your bag feels dry, the down insulation may not be. Check for lumps – a sign the down is still wet. After drying a sleeping bag with fibre-pile insulation, gently fluff up the fleece with a comb or brush.

Sliding doors

Your sliding glass doors can collect a lot of sand, dust and debris in their tracks. How you clean the doors depends on the frames – wood, aluminium or, more common in newer constructions, vinyl.

- **Vacuuming the sill tracks** is the first step in cleaning any sliding door. Run the vacuum over the tracks at least once in the spring and autumn, then weekly in summer, when you use the door frequently. When you do your general room-vacuuming, paying extra attention to the carpet just in front of the door will help to reduce the amount of dirt that gets dragged into the tracks.

- **To keep your door sliding smoothly,** spray silicone on a soft, dry cloth and wipe it onto the track. Don't allow the silicone to come into contact with wood surfaces or the weather strip. Lubricate rollers with a light oil, such as 3-in-One.

- **To clean the outside of a vinyl frame,** use a mild washing-up liquid solution – just a couple of squirts to 3 litres hot or warm water is fine – and apply this with a soft sponge or cloth. Rinse with clear water. Make sure you clean the frame before you wash the window so that you won't get your sparkling window wet and smeary again. Start at the top of the frame and work down.

- **To clean the inside of a vinyl frame,** wipe with a damp cloth at the time that you clean the window. Don't use anything abrasive in an attempt to buff or shine the vinyl frame or to remove marks. You'll simply create scratches.

- **To clean wood-framed sliding doors,** fill a spray bottle with warm water and a squirt of mild washing-up liquid. Very lightly mist the door frames and wipe off any dirt with a soft cloth. Finish by gently drying with another soft cloth. Never

Sliding doors

use a hose or any high-pressure washer on the door, because you may also saturate the wood. Likewise, if your wooden door frame is painted, never use abrasive cleaners, as they can soften emulsion paint. A few will even soften oil-based paint. If stubborn grime won't come off with water or a mild detergent, consider lightly sanding it and then refinishing.

Streaky clean
Don't clean aluminium frames in direct sunlight or very hot or very cold temperatures – the cleaning solution may dry too quickly and streak the surface, making it difficult to restore the frame's original appearance.

● **To clean aluminium-clad sliding doors,** again use washing-up liquid and water, made up as above and applied with a sponge or soft brush from top to bottom. Rinse immediately. Air-dry or wipe with a soft, dry cloth. For a protective coating, apply car wax to the aluminium. All exterior aluminium frames should be cleaned annually.

● **Next, clean the glass, inside and out.** Any window cleaner will be fine for this job, but avoid getting the cleaner on the window frames, because ingredients in some glass cleaners may damage the frame materials.

Smoke alarms

You'll already know to check and test the batteries in your smoke alarm each week. But did you know that you should also clean them every other month? Cobwebs, dust and even spiders can cause your smoke alarm to become less sensitive and so work less effectively.

● **Clean the outside and inside of the alarm** using a vacuum cleaner and a brush attachment. Flip open or unscrew the casing to get inside. If you can't reach the alarm with your vacuum's extension tubes, stand on a ladder. A can of compressed air (available from camera shops) can also be sprayed on the casing and inside the alarm to clean it.

Smoke alarms

- **Test your alarm, once you've cleaned it,** to see that it's working properly. Stand by the smoke alarm, light a candle or strike a match and then blow it out. The smoke should activate the alarm. Or, if your system is activated by light (it should say so on the box), shine a torch into the alarm to set it off. Simply pressing the button on the alarm casing is not a test. That only indicates the horn is working, not the smoke-detection mechanism.

- **Cover the alarm** whenever you're doing major work in the house that could send dust into the air. Don't forget to remove this covering promptly after you've finished. You should also protect the alarm if you're painting around it – and never paint the alarm casing.

Sofa covers

Removable covers on your sofa are fairly straightforward to machine-wash (but check care labels first). It's taking them off, then stretching them back on again that is time-consuming.

- **To remove dust and debris,** go over the covers with your vacuum cleaner, using the upholstery attachment. For cushions, use the vacuum nozzle without any attachments.

- **To clean sofa covers,** remove them and give them a good shake outside. Most can be washed, with the exception of rayon, which often requires dry-cleaning. Consider washing curtains at the same time if they're made of the same fabric, so if they fade slightly, it will be consistent and not noticeable.

- **Covers will sometimes shrink** the first time they're laundered, but it shouldn't be by very much. If hard-to-remove

Sofa covers

stains mean you decide to wash them twice, remember to put the curtains through a second time as well.

- **Tumble-dry sofa covers** if this is indicated on the care label. If not, don't peg them out on the line: the wet weight of the cover is so great that it may pull the fabric out of shape. Instead, dry flat; put some old dry sheeting on a garden table, then lay the cover on top, holding it down with a couple of books or bricks (wrapped in clear plastic) so that it doesn't blow off.

- **You're ready to get them back** onto the sofa while they are still marginally damp. (Too dry and it will be impossible to fit them back on again.) Pull all seams and cording into place before you start. Save your hands and nails by using a wooden spoon to help tuck the corners of the cover back into place.

Soft toys

Stuffed animals tend to spend a lot of time with children, who unintentionally rub whatever food and grime they have on their hands into the fake fur. Because of the variety of stuffing materials and accessories they have, cleaning soft toys can be trickier than simply throwing them in the washing machine.

- **Periodically dust stuffed toys** using the vacuum cleaner brush attachment. Be sure not to suck up any loose buttons or clothing accessories. Go over fake hair with a clean hairbrush, and then vacuum again to lift whatever the brush has loosened. To remove pet hair and lint, use a lint roller.

- **To remove light dirt,** just wipe the surface with a damp cloth, trying not to get moisture into the stuffing.

- **To remove juice and other spills,** shake the toy straight away – outside or in a bath, to keep the liquid from splashing

---

Tumble toys
For a quick and easy way to dust and freshen soft toys, toss them into a dryer and tumble on the lowest setting for about 10 minutes. To remove odours from a stuffed animal, add a scented dryer sheet when you tumble them in the dryer.

Soft toys

onto anything else. This will remove some of the liquid without smearing it into the fur or stuffing. Blot up as much remaining liquid as you can with paper towels – never rub. Wet with a cloth or sponge and blot again. Rinse the cloth or sponge and repeat until the spill is gone.

- **If your toy needs deeper cleaning** and it isn't machine washable, rub gently with a cloth or sponge dampened in a solution of warm water and mild washing-up liquid, being sure not to soak the filling. Rinse off the solution by wiping with a cloth or sponge dampened with clear water.

- **If it is machine washable,** place the stuffed toy in a pillowcase (to protect the fur) and wash in cold water using a mild detergent on a gentle cycle. Don't use bleach or fabric softeners. Put the whole bag in the dryer and tumble on low.

Sprinklers

Clean your lawn sprinkler once at the beginning of the watering season and once at the end, and you can help prevent the blockages that make it malfunction.

- **Remove sprinkler spray heads** (if possible) and rinse in water. Scrub lightly with a toothbrush to remove sediment. Use your hose to force high-pressured water back through the holes. If that fails, try gently pushing a wire into the nozzle as water flows out. If you have a mineral build-up, wipe it with or soak in a solution of 1 part vinegar to 3 parts water.

- **Take valves apart and clean them** the same way you would the spray heads. Rinse clogged screens in clean water.

Stainless steel

Stainless steel is hardy and rust-proof, but that doesn't mean you don't have to clean and care for it. Without attention, stainless steel will dull over time and pick up oily fingerprints as well as mineral spots from hard water. The biggest problem, however, is scratching. Scratch it and you remove the oxide coating that makes it stainless, and it will rust like any old steel.

- **Clean stainless steel appliances** and sinks with a solution of warm water and a squirt of washing-up liquid, using a soft cloth or sponge. Always rub the solution in the direction of the stainless steel grain. Rinse with a cloth or sponge and clear water. Polish the stainless steel dry to avoid spotting, using paper towels or a cloth. For more cleaning power, use a solution of 1 part white vinegar and 3 parts water or scrub with a paste made of bicarbonate of soda and hot water.

- **Wash stainless-steel cutlery** and pots in hot, soapy water or a dishwasher. Scrub off stubborn food with a cloth, sponge or nylon-bristled brush, but avoid abrasives. To remove baked-on food, scrub with a paste of bicarbonate of soda and water.

- **Polish stainless steel with a clean, dry cloth** to remove hard-water spots. For stubborn spots, wipe with a cloth soaked in straight vinegar. Or use a stainless-steel polishing product; follow the package directions.

---

preventing **corrosion and rust**

- To avoid corroding stainless steel, rinse acidic, salty or milk-based foods off stainless-steel utensils that won't be washed right away.
- Never use abrasive scrubbers, such as steel wool, on stainless steel. They will dull the finish and may even cause it to rust.

Stairs & steps

You're vacuuming away, getting through room after room and then you hit the stairs, which can be a bit of a struggle, especially if they are carpeted. What should you do?

- **Clean stairs from bottom to top.** That way, you don't grind dirt into the carpet. After cleaning the broad stair treads, use a vacuum crevice tool to get into the cracks along the wall and where the vertical riser meets the tread. Periodically, vacuum the carpeted risers.

Stone

Stone is one of the most durable materials there is. Most of it has been here for millions of years. But durable is one thing; clean and scratch-free is another. Even tough stone can be scratched by everyday grit and damaged by some of the most common household substances, including that old cleaning friend, vinegar. Take care of your stone and it will outlast you.

- **Sweep or dust stone often** to remove sand and dirt from flat surfaces, where it can be ground down by shoe soles, furniture or the base of pots and pans. The grit can scratch the stone. Dust using either a vacuum cleaner or dry dust mop (for floors) or a clean, dry rag (worktops and tables). Wipe up spills immediately to avoid staining.

- **To clean a stone worktop,** first try using only warm water. Wipe it off with a soft cloth or sponge. Let caked-on food soak for a while before wiping. You should be able to remove spills, crumbs, sauces and other substances this way. If not, add a little washing-up liquid to the water. Rinse well with clean water, because leftover soap can leave a film or cause streaking. Avoid stronger cleaning products, such as bath and tile cleaners

Stone

and scouring powders. These can stain or scratch your stone. Never use vinegar, lemon juice or other acidic cleaners on marble, travertine or limestone. The acid will eat away at the calcium in the stone.

● **To remove stains from stone,** keep it simple and be patient. Most stains are solid residue jammed in between the crystals of the stone after the liquid that carried it there has evaporated. To remove it, you need to combine the solid residue with a liquid again. First, determine whether your stain is water-based (for example, from apple juice) or oil-based (mayonnaise, for instance).

● **If it is a water-based stain,** pour hot tap water on it and leave it to stand for a few minutes. Wipe away the excess water and then place a 1cm pile of paper towels on top of the stain and saturate this with hot tap water. Cover with a piece of plastic and place a flat, heavy weight, such as a cast-iron frying pan, on top. Leave it for about 10 hours. (Do it overnight and you won't have to worry about anyone moving it.) Discard the paper towels, which by now should have soaked up the stain.

● **If the stain is oil-based,** follow the same procedure and use acetone (but don't heat it) instead of hot water. After the 10 hours is up, throw away the paper towels and wash the stain. In both cases, let the spot dry and then have a look at it. If some of the stain remains, repeat with hot water or more acetone.

● **Sweep stone patios regularly** to remove leaves and sticks, which can stain and hold mould-growing moisture. Once a year, give your patio stones a more thorough cleaning using a patio cleaner, available from DIY stores. Use a stiff-bristled brush (a long-handled one will be easier on your back and knees) to scrub the patio. Rinse the stones with a garden hose.

Suede

Suede, which is leather with a soft-napped finish, is one of the trickiest materials to clean. It can be one of the most expensive materials as well. As tough as suede seems, you will get it dirty – and since you're reading this entry, you probably already have – but there are a few tricks you can use to help with cleaning it. Above all, be careful and be patient.

- **Brush suede regularly** to remove any dirt that may have accumulated in the pile. This will also help to restore the nap. When you are going to put a suede item away for a while, brush it with a suede brush first – these are available at stores that sell leather goods or shoes, and in shoe-repair shops. Do it gently and in a slow, circular motion. If you don't have a suede brush, use a clean, dry kitchen sponge instead.

- **If you stain a suede item,** blot up as much of the stain as possible and then take the item to a professional cleaner who has experience with cleaning leather and suede.

- **However, there are some things** you can do at home to try to deal with certain stains. With grease or oil stains, you can cover these with a small pile of talcum powder and leave to stand overnight. The powder may absorb the stain.

- **For dried-in water marks,** try brushing these lightly with a suede brush or clean dry sponge.

Expert **ADVICE**

If you use perfume, hairspray or any other alcohol-based cosmetic products, don't apply them when you're wearing a suede coat or any other suede garment. They can make the colours run. For the same reason, never use a liquid or solvent-based spot remover on suede shoes, clothes or bags.

Table linens

Because of the food stains they so easily accumulate, most tablecloths and fabric napkins need to be, and are, machine washable. But simply throwing dirty or stained table linens into the machine may not be enough to keep them looking crisp and fresh under your fine china, crystal and silver. A few tricks of the trade will help.

Wine wise
If you get wine on a washable tablecloth, soak it for half an hour in a solution of 1 teaspoon biological laundry detergent to 2 litres warm water. Then machine-wash using the hottest water that's safe for the fabric.

- **Wash table linens before stains set.** After any spillage or big, messy dinner parties, put linens in a washing machine as soon as possible, following the manufacturer's washing recommendations on the care label. Pre-treat stains with a commercial spot remover. For best results, don't let the pre-treatment dry before washing.

- **If your table linens have lace trim,** make sure the lace is machine washable. Some lace is not and may shrink considerably when washed in water. If the lace is not washable, have the item dry-cleaned.

- **If the lace trim is washable** – and luckily, most table-linen lace is – wash it gently. The safest technique is to hand-wash it in a sink or bath full of warm water, mixed with a squirt or two of washing-up liquid.

- **If the lace is machine washable,** wash the tablecloth in a mesh bag tied at the top to prevent the lace from snagging.

- **To keep the lace from creasing,** which it will do in a tumble dryer, air-dry it, laying it as flat as possible.

- **When ironing tablecloths,** cut down on the creasing by placing a table next to your ironing board. Let the cloth hang over the table but don't let it drag on the floor.

- **When ironing a lace trim,** make small, gentle circular motions with your iron to avoid stretching the lace.

Tapestries

Tapestries are like fine rugs hung on walls except that, fortunately, they are not subject to the abuse that rugs get. But tapestries still need regular care and cleaning. Antique tapestries can be extremely valuable – and fragile, since age deteriorates textile fibres. If you have an antique tapestry that needs cleaning, play it safe and take it to a professional – a textile restorer or a dealer in antique tapestries or oriental rugs who has cleaning experience.

- **Periodically dust your tapestry** using the upholstery attachment on your vacuum cleaner. If possible, leave the tapestry hanging and carefully vacuum it in place. This will save the time and hassle of having to take it down and re-hang it. Depending on the conditions in your home (how much dust you have), do this once or twice a year.

- **If you need to spot-clean a tapestry,** make a suds shampoo by mixing ½ teaspoon washing-up liquid in 1 litre warm water. Squeeze a sponge in the solution to whip up a head of suds. Test for colourfastness by rubbing a cotton bud dipped in the suds on an inconspicuous corner of the tapestry. If the colour holds, continue.

  Using as little water as possible, scoop the suds off the top, applying them sparingly with a sponge to the tapestry surface. Rub gently. Before the suds dry, lightly rinse each area as you go with a clean, damp sponge. Be sure to remove all the suds, or the residue will cause the textile to soil faster.

- **For a deeper cleaning,** have the tapestry dry-cleaned by a professional. Make sure the dry-cleaner has experience cleaning the type of tapestry you own.

- **To remove wrinkles or creases,** iron the back of your tapestry with a steam iron on a medium setting. If you must iron the front, lay a thin towel on the tapestry to protect it.

Telephones

You use it every day. So do the other members of your household – and guests. As well as fingermarks, there's also the issue of germs: especially if anyone using the phone has a cold.

- **Simply spraying it with disinfectant won't do.** Your phone is an electronic instrument with intricate wiring and receiver and speaker holes that you don't want to gum up. Follow the rule for cleaning all electronics – always apply cleaner to a cloth and use the dampened cloth to wipe it clean.

- **To clean and disinfect a phone,** use an anti-bacterial product, such as those made by Dettol. Spray sparingly onto your cloth, then wipe the phone.

Televisions

Dust is likely to be your biggest challenge when cleaning your television. However often you clean, it seems always to come back, thicker and more static.

- **Unplug the television before you clean it,** particularly if you need to use a wet cleaner.

- **To clean a TV screen,** first identify the type of screen you have. Only standard tubes and plasma screens can be wiped with a wet cleaner as described below for the TV casing. Liquid crystal display screens, which include not only LCD TVs but also projection TVs with digital light processing (DLP) screens, should be wiped clean with a dry, clean cotton cloth. Consult your owner's manual. If the TV came with a cleaning kit, use its cleaner and cloths.

- **To clean a TV's case** – or a tube or plasma screen that allows liquid cleaner – slightly dampen a soft cotton cloth with your

Tube tactics
Always follow these rules when cleaning your TV. Pull the plug before you start to clean and identify the type of screen you have. Some don't take well to liquid cleaners. Never spray any liquid directly onto any type of television or its screen. Spray cleaner onto a cloth to slightly dampen it and then use the cloth to wipe it.

Televisions

chosen cleaner. (Pick a non-fraying fabric to avoid having any ragged ends catch in the ventilation slits.) Glass cleaner makes the best cleaner, because it evaporates quickly. Or use a solution of 1 part liquid fabric softener to 4 parts water as your cleaner. Wring out the cloth so it's barely damp, never dripping, and wipe down the television. Never apply liquid cleaner directly to your screen or casing – the drips could damage the electronics. Buff the screen afterwards with a dry cloth.

- **Dust the body of the box** with a dry cloth, or clean it with a solution of 1 part neutral-pH cleaner (such as liquid hand soap) to 3 parts water.

Tents

After every camping trip, shake out loose dirt and wipe the floor and door flaps of your tent. Use a soft sponge and warm tap water. Let it dry completely before storing.

- **Grit and sand can wear down** the inside of the zip, causing it to stick. To keep zips running smoothly, run a candle up and down the teeth every now and again.

- **Occasionally clean your tent more thoroughly.** Set it up outside and lightly spray with a garden hose. Mix water with a gentle fabric cleaner, such as Woolite or a tent soap (sold at camping stores), and use a sponge or soft cloth to wipe the tent clean. Rinse well, but don't saturate the tent. Let it dry in indirect sunlight (UV rays can weaken tent materials).

- **To clean off mildew,** wash the tent with soapy water (as above) and then wipe it out with a solution of 1 cup salt, 1 cup concentrated lemon juice and 3 litres hot water; don't rinse. Leave to air-dry. Always store your tent in a cool, dry place.

> **A useful barrier**
> To keep your tent clean, always use a ground sheet beneath it. The ground sheet will help keep the tent's floor – and you – drier, too.

Ties

Ties are more complicated than they appear – and often made in special silks and elaborate weaves. It's all too easy to ruin a tie if you don't know the correct techniques.

Tie marks
Never put water (or mineral water, or any other liquid) on a tie while trying to remove a stain. You might create a larger water mark that is hard to remove. And many of the stains normally found on a tie are oil-based, such as gravy or salad dressing, which can't be removed with water.

● **Have a tie professionally cleaned** once or twice a year, depending on how often you wear it, but clean a stained tie immediately. Look for a cleaner who's experienced in cleaning silk ties and ask how they 'finish' the tie: ties should not be pressed, they should be rolled and reshaped with steam. If you're trying a new cleaner, don't give them your best ties first.

● **If you spill something on your tie,** blot away the excess using a clean white cloth or napkin and then take the tie to a dry-cleaner as soon as possible. Stains, especially food stains, tend to set after 24 or 48 hours. Never try to rub the stain out. You might rub the colour from the fabric, especially if it's silk.

Tiles

While they are two dramatically different materials, ceramic and vinyl tiles are both relatively low-maintenance, easy-to-clean surfaces. Both can scratch, however, so keeping them dirt-free reduces the risk of particles rubbing against the tiling and turning into a scratch.

● **For regular cleaning of floor tiles** – both ceramic and vinyl – sweep with a broom or vacuum. Trapped dirt and sand are highly abrasive and can cause lasting damage to matt and glossy finishes. If you vacuum, avoid using the machine's beater bar, which can permanently damage tile finishes.

Tiles

- **Once a week, clean floor tiles** by going over them with a damp mop. Again, this goes for both ceramic and vinyl tiles. Damp mopping removes stubborn, smeared-on dirt. Never use excessive amounts of water with vinyl tiles, since the water can seep under them and damage the glue. Avoid soapy or oily cleaners, as they can leave a dull film. If anything, add a splash of vinegar to the mop water. Or use a special tile-floor cleaner, such as HG Superfloor Shine Cleaner, sold at tile stores. Follow directions on the package.

- **For ceramic wall tiles,** wipe them regularly with a damp sponge. As with floor tiles, avoid soapy or oily cleaners. Add a splash of vinegar to the water, or use a commercial bathroom cleaner. Never use abrasive scrubbers or cleaning products, such as scouring powders. These can scratch glazed tiles, dulling the finish and making them more susceptible to dirt.

- **To keep grout clean,** it's best to do it regularly so that scum and mildew don't have a chance to get a foothold in the porous surface. In the bathroom, do it after you've had a bath or shower; the steamy, moist conditions will loosen the dirt. Or run some hot water until the room is steamy. Mix together 4 tablespoons vinegar with 3 litres water and scrub the grout with a toothbrush or nylon scrub pad.

  For more cleaning power, go over it once with a degreaser, such as HG Grout Cleaner, which will loosen the germ-harbouring soap scum, then rinse. Let your cleaning products do the work for you – too much scrubbing will grind the grime in more deeply. Spray or wipe each product on and let it stand for several seconds. Wipe it down with a clean, wet sponge to rinse off the cleaning solution. If you must scrub, use a long-bristled brush that is not too stiff (you don't want to wear down the grout) or use an old toothbrush – steel wool is too abrasive.

> **What a heel**
> To remove black heel marks from tiled floors, rub with a clean white cloth dipped in methylated spirits.

Tin

Tin, silvery white with a brilliant lustre, is used as a decorative plating and to protect metals from rusting. You see it often on Mexican crafts and inexpensive kitchenware. Be careful not to scratch it when cleaning. If you do, you'll invite rust.

- **Dust decorative tin regularly.** Use a feather duster for detailed pieces. Or wipe with a dry or slightly damp rag.

- **Wash tin items** in a solution of mild washing-up liquid and warm water, using a soft cloth. Don't use abrasive scrubbers or cleaners – they may scratch through tin plating or paintwork.

- **To remove rust on unpainted tin,** rub it with extra-fine (0000) steel wool and then wash as above. Rinse well and dry completely. To prevent rust, apply a thin coat of car wax.

Toasters

Toasting bread makes crumbs and you need to get these out of the toaster. Fortunately, most toaster makers are aware of this and design their appliances for easy cleaning.

- **Empty the crumbs out of your toaster** once every week or so, depending on how much you use it. Always unplug the toaster before you start cleaning it. If you can't get all the crumbs out, try disintegrating them with heat. Run the toaster empty on the hottest setting two or three times.

- **For hard-to-remove crumbs,** loosen them with a clean, dry toothbrush. Again, be sure the toaster is unplugged. Turn the toaster upside down and shake the crumbs out.

- **Wipe down the outside** of the toaster with a damp cloth. Add a dash of vinegar or squirt of washing-up liquid to the cleaning water for more cleaning power.

Toilets

We all have to clean toilets. There's no getting around that. But most people are not very efficient at cleaning their toilets. And many are stumped by the stubborn rings that seem to get left around the bowl.

- **To clean a toilet,** work from the top down. Start with the tank, move to the seat, clean inside the bowl and then clean the base. Doing it this way will help you focus. Moreover, the dirtiest part of the toilet – and therefore the last place you want your rag to touch – is the base. For everything but the bowl, use a dry cloth and a spray-on bathroom cleaner. Spray the cleaner on the toilet surface and wipe it off with the cloth. Keeping the cloth dry makes it easier to wipe everything up. Wet it and you'll be chasing that moisture around and have to wring out the cloth, too. Avoid sponges, which work quite well but can absorb – and transfer – micro-organisms.

- **Clean the bowl** with a rounded bowl brush and cleaner. Avoid brushes with metal wire, since they may scratch the bowl. (For rings around the bowl see right.)

- **To clean around the hardware** that holds the seat to the toilet and the toilet to the floor, use an old toothbrush.

> ### Stone cleaner
> For stubborn rings around the toilet bowl, use a pumice stone. Keeping the stone wet, rub it on the ring until it's gone. This works for old rings as well. It will not scratch white vitreous china, which is what most toilets are made of, but it will scratch glass fibre, enamel, plastic and other materials.

Tools

In the old days, toolmakers dated their tools – carving the year into the wooden block of a plane, for example – in the expectation that the tools would last for generations. Back then, a tool would last a long time if its owner took care of it. The same is true today.

- **The most basic goal with hand tools,** especially those made of wood and metal, is to keep them dry. If a tool gets wet, wipe it dry. If it gets sweaty or dusty, clean it with a damp cloth, then wipe it dry with another cloth. Water can rust a saw blade and warp a wooden level.

- **Keep retractable measuring tapes** free of dirt, sand, dust and other debris. These foreign objects can scratch the coating. Once it is scratched, the metal tape will rust. Wipe the tape clean with a dry cloth frequently. Don't use a wet cloth – and don't let your tape get wet. Moisture will find its way into the spring mechanism and will rust it. To remove tar and glue from the tape, use methylated spirits.

- **All tools should be kept** in a clean, dry environment, so make sure you store hand tools in a cupboard or in a sealed box, if they're stored outdoors in a shed or garage. And always keep sharp and bladed tools away from small children.

Expert **ADVICE**

Avoid oiling most tools (garden tools are the exception), since the oil may get on the handle, causing the tool to slip dangerously.

Toys

The main issue in cleaning toys is to never use anything toxic. Even if your children no longer chew on their toys, their hands will end up in their mouths at some point – hands that have been holding their toys.

- **Wash toys regularly** to keep them clean and bacteria-free. Wash rubber and plastic toys with warm water combined with a squirt of washing-up liquid. Wipe clean with a soft cloth or sponge. Be careful of painted-on features, such as faces, numbers or other designs, as these could rub off. Dry with a cloth or leave to air-dry. For larger plastic toys, use a hose, a bucket of soapy water and a soft-bristled scrubbing brush.

- **Wipe down metal toys,** such as tractors and cars, using a damp cloth. Water leads to rust, so avoid soap (since suds require rinsing) and don't submerge such toys. If a metal toy or toy with metal parts gets wet, dry it quickly with a hair dryer to avoid rusting. If there are batteries, beeping sounds or blinking lights, don't wet the toy. Water will ruin the circuitry.

- **Clean wooden toys** with a mild solution of a neutral cleaner, such as Pledge Soapy Wood Cleaner, and water. (Follow the manufacturer's directions for amounts.) Use a cloth or soft-bristled brush. Don't soak or submerge the wooden toy. Instead, dip the cloth or brush in the soapy water and wipe the toy clean. Rinse with a clean cloth and plain water. Dry with a clean, dry towel. If the toy is scratched splintered, or chipped, or if the water has raised the grain (making the wood feel rough), lightly sand it with fine glasspaper once the toy has dried.

- **If a wooden toy** has a natural, oil-based finish, reapply oil to keep the wood conditioned. Since toys often end up in children's mouths (wooden baby chew toys are

Toys

expressly meant for this purpose), use a food-grade vegetable oil. Allow the oil to penetrate for about an hour and then wipe off the excess. It is especially important not to clean wooden toys with harsh chemicals, because wood absorbs and harbours such chemicals which could harm a child if ingested.

- ● **Clean Barbies and similar dolls** by wiping with a cloth and water mixed with a little washing-up liquid. Wash hair with baby shampoo. (A drop of hair conditioner will soften the hair.) Don't use any heat source, such as a hair dryer, to dry the hair, as that will turn it frizzy. Instead, comb the hair out gently, starting from the bottom and working up to remove tangles. Let the doll air-dry.

Trainers

Trainers can get very dirty and smelly, but whether you clean them in the washing machine or not depends on a variety of factors. Many shoe manufacturers discourage machine-washing because their trainers are made of leather and use adhesives. But some simple canvas or all-synthetic shoes can safely take a spin in the machine.

- ● **Before cleaning any type of trainer,** check the care label. If they are older and you have no label, you have to decide whether it's worth the risk. Take out the laces and wash these too. Put them into a mesh bag and into the machine.

- ● **For leather trainers,** it's best to use a regular leather cleaner and conditioner.

- ● **To clean canvas or synthetic trainers** in a washing machine, spray them first with a stain-removal spray, especially

Trainers

if they are grass stained. Wipe the spray around the shoe, let it sit for a couple of minutes and then put the shoes in the wash. Include light-coloured towels in the wash. The rubbing action of the towels will not only help clean the trainers, but will also keep them from bouncing around in the drum.

- **To clean canvas and synthetic trainers** by hand, rinse in clear water and then use a soft brush to scrub the shoes with a neutral cleaner, such as a non-scented liquid hand wash. For scuff marks, scour with a white, nylon-backed scrubbing pad. Rinse and then air-dry. Stuff the shoes with white paper to retain their shape.

- **As an alternative for canvas trainers,** squirt on some foam shaving cream, let it sit for half an hour and brush off what remains. Then wipe the surface with a clean, damp cloth.

Tumble dryers

When cleaning a dryer, the most important task is to clean the filter. Dryers work by heating air, drawing it across your wet clothes to sop up the moisture, and pushing the soggy air outside through a vent or condensing it into water and storing this in a tank that you empty regularly.

- **The most modern tumble dryers** have alerts to remind you to clean the filters that collect lint before or after every load of clothes. Look in your manual for how to pull out the removable metal or plastic filters. Hold it over the bin, while scraping the little blanket of lint off the filter with your hand. If some of the lint won't come free, you might take the filter to a sink and clean it with warm water and a mild washing-up liquid or get those bits next time round.

Clean ducts
If your filter is clean but the dryer isn't as efficient as it used to be, the duct taking the air outside may be blocked. Detach it from your dryer and clean it out. (Do this once a year as a matter of course.) Make sure the vent cover on the outside of your house is in place.

Umbrellas

Umbrellas don't get very dirty, which is fortunate, because they've got to be among the most awkward things in the world to clean – like trying to bathe a stork. But while personal umbrellas usually get along without attention, you may need to clean large patio umbrellas, especially those left permanently outside through the summer months, which may collect tree pollen, wet leaves and bird droppings.

● **To clean a personal umbrella,** just let the rain do the job the next time it showers. After your umbrella's got wet in the rain, open it up and let it dry thoroughly before you put it away; this will help to prevent mould and mildew developing on the fabric.

● **For a more thorough clean,** open up the umbrella, spray it with a hose, and scrub gently with a sponge dipped in warm water with a squirt of washing-up liquid. Rinse and dry thoroughly before storing it.

● **To remove dirt, pollen and bird droppings** from a patio umbrella – which is usually made of either vinyl or a coarse fabric – spray it with a garden hose. Then scrub it with a nylon-bristled brush dipped in a bucket containing a sudsy solution of warm water and washing-up liquid. Rinse by spraying the umbrella with the hose.

● **Protect a patio umbrella's metal rods** by polishing them with car wax. Wax also makes the metal easier to clean in the future. Following the manufacturer's directions, lightly wax the metal. Take care not to get the wax on the umbrella covering, as it can stain fabric and gunk up vinyl mesh.

Shady coating
To avoid stripping away the protective coating often found on vinyl patio umbrellas, don't scrub it with anything abrasive, or use bleach, bleach-based cleaning products or solvents. This coating protects the material from damaging UV rays. Removing the coating can cut the life span of vinyl in half, making it weak and brittle.

328

Upholstery

Upholstery poses a cleaning challenge, since it almost always covers some sort of padding – be it cotton batting or foam rubber – and because it's often not removable. Even when upholstery material can be removed from the padding, as in the case of zip-up seat cushions, some experts warn against removing and washing it.

- **Sofas sold as having loose covers** are, of course, different: for most, you can simply use the washing machine to clean the covers. Just follow care instructions on the labels. The danger of taking off cushion covers from fixed upholstery is that they may not fit back on the cushions afterwards. There may also be some fading, which could make your sofa arms look very dark in contrast. Assuming you're leaving everything in situ, the most basic aim with most upholstery cleaning is to clean without soaking the padding beneath.

- **Vacuum upholstery regularly** to remove dust and dust mites. Use an upholstery attachment with a gentle brush end, so you don't damage the upholstery material. Use a crevice tool attachment for nooks and crannies. If your upholstered piece is stuffed with feathers, do not vacuum it unless it is lined with a down-proof ticking fabric. You might suck the feathers out. If you have no vacuum-cleaner attachments, brush the dust away with a soft-bristled brush at least once a month. Dust, when moistened or ground in, can stain upholstery.

- **For more thorough cleaning,** or to remove stains, your upholstery will need washing. First, check the upholstery manufacturer's suggestions, usually tagged to your item. This tag will tell you whether you should use a water-based shampoo, a dry-cleaning solvent or neither of the two. Next, pick an inconspicuous spot on the upholstery and pre-test whatever cleaning technique

Upholstery

is recommended. If there is any shrinking, bleeding or the colours run, contact a professional cleaner. If not, proceed.

● **If shampooing is safe,** use as little moisture as possible. It is important not to wet the upholstery's stuffing, because it dries very slowly and can attract dust mites and mould. Clean, using suds only. The easiest method is to use a foaming commercial shampoo in an aerosol can. Follow the directions on the can, which typically will tell you to allow the foam to stand until dry and then to vacuum it off.

● **To make your own upholstery shampoo,** mix ½ teaspoon washing-up liquid per 1 litre warm water. Make suds by squeezing a sponge in the solution. Scoop the suds off the top, applying them sparingly with the sponge to the upholstery. Rub gently in the direction of the fabric's grain. Rather than letting the suds dry as you would with a commercial shampoo, work on a small area at a time, lightly rinsing each area as you go with a clean, damp sponge. Again, avoid soaking the fabric. Be sure to remove all the suds or the residue will cause the fabric to become dirty more quickly.

● **If the fabric calls for dry-cleaning only** and the upholstery is portable, have it professionally cleaned. However, if you are cleaning a stain – or if the upholstery is part of a large piece of furniture – you can do it yourself, using a commercial dry-cleaning solvent.

Don't pour the solvent on the stain. Instead, moisten a clean, white cloth with the solvent and use the cloth to draw the stain out. Blot repeatedly – never rub. Rubbing can stretch or damage the texture of the fabric. Always use solvents sparingly and in a well-ventilated area. And don't use them on upholstery filled with latex foam-rubber padding, because the solvent can dissolve the padding.

Drying out

To dry upholstery that has been rinsed with water, lay a pad of paper towels on the spot and place a weight, such as a brick or a hardback book on the pad. (Put the brick or book in a plastic bag or on a piece of foil to prevent colour transfer to the upholstery.) Let the upholstery dry, then remove the paper towels.

Vases

Dirty vases not only look unattractive, but they also reduce the lifespan of the cut flowers you keep in them. The residue in vases, including growth such as algae, plugs up the stems and causes the flowers to dry up more quickly.

- **The easiest way to clean vases** is to scrub them with hot, soapy water and a bottle brush. Rinse well and let them dry completely before storing.

- **To remove white mineral-deposit stains** from the inside of vases, swirl a mixture of sea salt and vinegar around inside the vase. The salt will gently scour the surface while the vinegar breaks down the deposits.

> **Narrow necks**
> If you can't get inside a vase with a bottle brush, fill it with hot water and add a couple of denture-cleaning tablets; let it stand overnight. Rinse well and dry.

VCRs & videotapes

As with any electronic gear, the cleaner you keep your VCR, the better all the small parts will work – and the longer the equipment will last. That said, don't open up your VCR for interior cleaning. You can cause more harm than good. Luckily, the insides rarely need cleaning if you keep the outside clean. The only interior part you need to keep clean is the playback head – but you can do that with a head-cleaning tape.

- **Clean the front panel** with a soft cotton cloth and glass cleaner. (First, turn off the VCR.) Don't use paper towels as they can tear and shed lint. Don't spray the glass cleaner directly onto the unit. Instead, spray it on the cloth and gently wipe the cloth on the panel. For sensitive areas, such as around the panel-control knobs and buttons, dust with a small, dry paintbrush. Don't apply cleaner to these areas, since liquid could seep into the controls. This way, you won't accidentally change your control settings, either.

VCRs & videotapes

- **To clean the chassis of the VCR** – that is, the sides and top – use a soft cloth either dry or lightly misted with glass cleaner. Don't wet the cloth, since any residue left on the chassis may collect dust and lead to corrosion. Never spray anything directly onto the chassis. Wipe away from the vent holes (not towards them) to avoid pushing dust into the workings of the VCR.

- **Dust the back of the unit,** where the cables plug in, with a dry paintbrush. Don't use cleaner around this sensitive area. If you must remove the cables to access the back, be warned; many units store information for user settings, clock and timers, and this memory can be lost when the unit is unplugged from the electrical outlet.

- **Wipe cables down** with a cloth misted with the same cleaner you used on the panels. Be careful not to pull the cables out.

- **Clean the playback head periodically** – once every few months, depending on use, or when the playback quality indicates a problem. If you rent a lot of videotapes, you may need to clean more often, since rental tapes bring with them dirt picked up from all the other VCRs they've been played in.

- **Use a good-quality dry head-cleaning cassette** – 'dry' because the liquid that sometimes comes with head-cleaning cassettes may not evaporate completely before another tape is inserted, which can worsen the situation by attracting grime from the tape to the playback head. Always read your owner's manual. If your VCR incorporates an automatic head-cleaning system, head-cleaning tapes may not be recommended.

- **If you need to clean a videotape,** carefully wipe it with a damp cloth. Make sure you don't wet the tape itself or the tape path. Remove any labels or adhesives that are coming off; labels that have fallen off are one of the biggest causes of tape jams.

VCR cleaning frequency

You should clean the outside of the VCR whenever you dust your living room – electrical equipment can attract a lot of dust. Clean the playback head every few months, depending on how often you use the VCR – or whenever playback quality indicates you might have a problem.

Velcro

When Velcro gets 'dirty' – meaning the two sides get clogged up with lint and fuzz – it stops working. When that Velcro is attached to a pair of sandals or a handbag, you might be tempted to get rid of the items. Don't; it's easy to freshen up Velcro so that it works as good as new.

- **To remove lint from the bristly side** of Velcro, use a fine-toothed comb. Gently comb out the lint and hair and stray threads. If possible, submerge it in water while combing.

- **To remove lint from the soft side** of Velcro, use the sticky side of gaffer tape the way you would use a lint roller.

- **To keep Velcro fresh,** seal the two parts together when it's not in use or while washing. If you need to, buy extra Velcro tape and use that to seal the Velcro. You can always replace old Velcro with new; it's available from most haberdashery stores.

Vents

Located in floors, walls and ceilings, vents typically have angled louvres to keep large debris from getting into the house, while still allowing in air. These louvres also collect lint and dust.

- **Vacuum the outside** of the vent frequently. Make it part of your regular vacuuming routine, and you'll cut down on dust and lint build-up considerably. Use a brush attachment, which helps loosen dust.

- **At least twice a year,** remove registers and returns and clean both sides. Use the vacuum, but if that does not completely remove the dust, wipe them with a moist cloth. If you replace filters behind your returns more often than twice a year, clean the return vents every time you remove them.

Vinyl

Vinyl exterior surfaces are often advertised as being maintenance free. But that doesn't mean you don't have to do some cleaning, even if you do have a conservatory or window frames made of this tough, water-repellent coating.

Vinyl care
When cleaning vinyl, avoid harsh solvents and cleaners. They may cause the vinyl to become brittle.

● **To wash exterior vinyl** use a garden hose attached to a long-handled car-brush attachment (Flash Home Car Wash System, for instance). If you don't have one, make up buckets of water, squeezing a dash of washing-up liquid into each. Use a sponge or, for speed – a kitchen sponge mop – and water. If mildew is a problem, use a solution of 50ml chlorine bleach per 5 litres water, applying this with a squeezed-out kitchen mop for speed and accurate coverage. Rinse off thoroughly.

● **Exterior vinyl may need to be washed** every 12 to 18 months, depending on the climate and the level of pollutants in the air locally to you.

● **For a more thorough wash,** use a pressure washer, which you can hire from HSS Hire Shops for the day or weekend. Remember to wear safety goggles. Move methodically from side to side from the bottom up, and reverse the direction for the rinse cycle.

● **To clean articles made of vinyl,** there are a couple of cleaners you could try. At the most basic level, you could mix a little liquid washing-up liquid with some warm water. If mould and mildew are a problem, then try a solution of 1 part white vinegar to 2 parts water.

● **To keep vinyl soft and pliable,** rub a little petroleum jelly into the surface and then buff with a soft cloth. Or use a vinyl cleaner/conditioner, which you can buy at hardware and car-supplies stores.

Wall coverings

The most common wall covering is washable wallpaper, which is treated with vinyl for easier cleaning. But many other coverings exist, such as silk, linen, hessian, hemp and cork. These generally are not washable, although some gentle cleaning methods won't hurt them.

- **To determine whether wallpaper is washable,** wet an inconspicuous area with a solution of a little washing-up liquid and water. If the paper absorbs water or darkens or if the colours run, it's not washable.

- **When cleaning washable wallpaper,** don't flood the surface with water, over-wet the seams or edges or leave water on for more than a minute.

- **Don't scrub unless** the manufacturer says the covering is scrubbable. Don't use harsh, abrasive cleaners.

- **To clean other wall coverings,** vacuum regularly, using the small brush attachment. Some people also swear by using white bread. Simply ball up a slice until it is doughy in your hand, then roll it onto the dirty area. This should pick dirt up off the wall covering. Keep going, with fresh pieces of bread, but making sure an already dirty surface never touches your wall.

Smudge away
Remove smudges and fingerprints with an art rubber. To remove greasy spots, make a paste of plain flour and water. Apply to the spot, let it dry and vacuum up. To remove wax, heavy crayon or grease, hold a double thickness of greaseproof paper on the spot and press it with a warm iron.

Walls

There are two major sources of the dirt that gets on walls: the kind that comes off people's hands and the type borne on the air. How often your walls need washing will depend on the hands and air that touch them. If you have a smoker, a wood-burning stove or fireplace in the house, your walls will show it. If you have children, they will add their own special grime.

Walls

- **To dust walls,** a lamb's-wool duster works well. Or wrap a microfibre dust cloth or clean white cloth around a broom and dust with that. It's especially useful on the highest parts of the walls and the ceiling.

- **To remove spots,** rub gently with a white art rubber, available at arts and crafts and office supply stores, or with a paste of bicarbonate of soda and water. Use white spirit on grease and WD-40 (both available at hardware stores) on crayon marks. Use methylated spirits on ink or marker spots.

- **Apply cleaners to the cloth,** not the wall, and test on an inconspicuous area first. There is a big danger that, with the alcohol, you will also pull paint off the wall. So try to go just along the stain line. You want to be using just enough solvent to dissolve the stain, yet not have enough solvent left over to dissolve the painted wall beneath.

- **To wash down walls that are painted** or covered with washable vinyl paper, use a mixture of 200ml ammonia, 1 teaspoon washing-up liquid and 4 litres water. Or use sugar-soap cleaner, made up as directed.

- **Keep the cleaning solution** in one bucket and plain water for rinsing in another bucket. To protect the floor, use a dust sheet. To keep water from running down your arms when they're raised, wrap rags around your wrists and hold them on with rubber bands or elasticated hair ties.

- **To clean the walls,** wash with one of the solutions mentioned above, using a natural sponge or a white cloth. Working from the bottom up, wash a small area using circular strokes. Rinse with plain water and dry with a towel before moving onto the next section of wall. Use a sturdy stepladder to get to those areas too high to reach from the floor.

Bottoms up

Almost everywhere you clean, you're advised to start at the top and work down. However, some professional decorators don't do this with walls. They start at the bottom and go up. The logic is that dirty water running down a dirty wall leaves worse streaks than dirty water running down a clean wall. Either way, if your wall is filthy, you'll still do an awful lot of mopping up.

Washing machines

Every now and then you have to give back – that is, clean the washing machines and tumble dryers that do so much cleaning for you. Fortunately, it's easy to do – and these machines even help to clean themselves occasionally.

- **Cleaning the exterior of your washing machine** or dryer is very easy. The most common spots are blotches of spilled laundry detergent, fabric softener or bleach. They're all designed to respond best to warm water, so wipe them up with a cloth dipped in a solution of warm water and mild washing-up liquid, which will vanquish dirt and accumulated dust, too.

- **To clean inside your washing machine** open it up and wipe down the inside of the door using the same solution of warm water and mild washing-up liquid on the cloth that you used on the exterior. Use an old toothbrush to clean the crevices of the moulded frame around the door. If you have a removable detergent cup, take it out to clean it. If it's built in, clean it as thoroughly as you can, using a pipe cleaner, if necessary. The rest of the interior of your washing machine gets a pretty good cleaning every time you use it.

- **To cure residual musty odours,** run the washing machine through a wash cycle without any clothes in it. Use the hottest temperature setting available and a medium or high water level. While the machine is filling pour in 200ml bleach. As a preventive measure, follow this routine once a year.

Waste-disposal units

These small, but extremely useful kitchen appliances have their own built-in scrubbing action. You can keep your waste-disposal unit smelling fresh and running properly, with just a few common household items.

- **To keep food waste from building up** inside your disposer, grind only small amounts of food at a time.

- **After you've finished grinding food,** run a steady, rapid flow of cold water for up to 30 seconds. Even if instinct tells you that hot water cleans better, stick to cold water. It solidifies fatty and greasy wastes so they will be chopped up and flushed down the drain.

- **Don't pour oil or grease** through the disposer. Don't grind large bones (small bones are safe and even help break up grease deposits) or bulky, fibrous materials like sweetcorn kernels.

- **Never put caustic soda** or chemical drain cleaners into your disposal unit.

- **To remove any fatty wastes** that build up inside the disposer, periodically grind a handful of ice cubes mixed with 100ml bicarbonate of soda. Together the powder and cubes (which of course are cold) will safely scour the inside of the unit. To eliminate odours, grind lemon or orange peel through the unit every so often.

SIMPLE solutions

If you're going on holiday, or even if you know that you won't be at home for several days, make sure no food wastes that might start to smell are left in the disposer. To flush any residue, plug the sink, fill it with around 6cm of water and run the disposer while the water drains.

Waste-paper baskets

The details of cleaning waste-paper baskets vary according to the materials they're made of. However, always take the waste out of the basket before you start any cleaning.

- **To clean a waste-paper basket** made of a natural material, use a vacuum cleaner with the small brush attachment. If the basket becomes soiled, wipe it with a damp cloth or sponge. Don't use harsh cleaners.

- **To clean a plastic or metal** waste-paper basket, wash it with a solution of 4 tablespoons bicarbonate of soda in 4 litres warm water. Use a cloth, a sponge or, for more challenging dirt, a stiff brush. Rinse and dry with a soft cloth.

- **Clean the kitchen waste bin** at the same time you're mopping the kitchen floor – mix up your cleaning solution in the bin instead of a bucket. During the time it takes to mop the floor, the dirt in the bin will be loosening. When you pour out the mop water, clean the bin with a stiff brush, rinse with running water and dry with a cloth.

> **Less wasteful waste handling**
> Using a liner makes cleaning a waste-paper basket easier. But don't always buy brand-new plastic bags to line your waste-paper baskets; it's cheaper and greener to re-use the plastic shopping bags you're given in supermarkets and other stores. For bins in bedrooms and living rooms used paper bags also work.

Watches

The salt in sweat is one of your watch's biggest enemies. Other contaminants include skin oils, dirt and substances such as lotions and insect repellents. Clean only the band and the outside of the watch, leaving the inner workings in the hands of a professional watch mender.

- **For regular cleaning,** wipe the band and watch with a damp cloth, then again with a clean, dry cloth.

- **For more extensive cleaning,** remove the band by releasing the pins on both sides of the watch. Clean a leather

Watches

band with saddle soap and buff with a dry cloth. Wash a cloth one with a little washing-up liquid and water, rinse in clean water and lay flat to dry. Clean a metal band by soaking it in a solution of washing-up liquid and water. Use an old toothbrush to scrub. Rinse in clean water and dry with a soft cloth.

- **To store your watch,** keep it in an individual compartment in a jewellery box or wrap it in a piece of soft cloth.

- **To clean the inner workings,** take the watch to a professional. Mechanical watches (the kind you wind up) need an overhaul about every two years and analogue quartz watches (with hands and batteries) need one every three to five years, which is just about when you need to replace the battery anyway. Digital watches, which have no mechanical workings, don't need an internal cleaning, although you will eventually need to replace the battery.

Wheelchairs

With regular cleaning and careful maintenance your wheelchair will run far more smoothly and last much longer.

- **Wash the wheelchair frame,** wheels, tyres, seat and back with warm water and a little washing-up liquid. Apply with a cloth or sponge, rinse with plain water and dry with a clean cloth. Don't get water in the wheel or caster bearings.

- **Remove the caster axle bolts,** wipe away dirt with a cloth and put back the bolt. This spot tends to collect hair, string and other debris that will make the chair harder to propel.

  - **To clean the axles,** remove the wheels and wipe the axles with a clean cloth containing a few drops of oil (whatever oil is recommended by your owner's manual).

Whirlpool baths

Whirlpool baths have two elements that require cleaning: the external surfaces and the unseen circulation system.

- **To clean the bath surfaces,** wipe with a cloth after each use. Clean periodically with a solution of hot water and washing-up liquid and rinse. Don't use abrasive scrubbers or cleaners, which harm the glossy finish.

- **To clean the circulation system,** follow the instructions that came with your unit. Or do the following: adjust the jets so they are not drawing air; leave the water in the bath after using and add a large bottle of white vinegar (or 2 teaspoons powdered dishwasher detergent and 300ml chlorine bleach). Run the whirlpool system, following the operating instructions, for 5 to 10 minutes; drain and refill with cold water. Circulate for five minutes; then drain and wipe dry with a clean cloth.

Wicker, rattan & bamboo

Wicker is not a single material. It's a term for something made of any of several materials that are bent and woven together. The most common are rattan, cane, reed, bamboo, willow and twisted paper fibre (the kind used in Lloyd Loom furniture).

Wicker comes in many finishes, ranging from natural to oil, varnish, shellac or paint. There are also synthetic versions of wicker made from resin, plastic or glass fibre. And when it comes to cleaning, the materials aren't all the same.

- **Synthetic wicker is the only wicker** that should be allowed to remain outdoors. Clean it with a garden hose and plain water, using a cloth or sponge, or scrub with a stiff brush and a solution of a little washing-up liquid in water. Rinse with the hose and dry with a clean cloth.

Wicker, rattan & bamboo

- **To clean natural-fibre wicker,** keep furniture free of dirt with a vacuum cleaner, using the brush attachment. Other useful tools are a toothbrush, a stiff paintbrush and a pencil-sized dowel sharpened in a pencil sharpener. Wipe the wicker with a damp cloth or sponge, but undertake more extensive wet cleaning cautiously. Consult an expert before doing any major cleaning or refinishing of antique pieces. To find an expert, check with antiques dealers or on the internet.

- **To wash most natural-fibre wicker,** use a solution of a little mild soap – Carex handwash, for example, or a squirt of washing-up liquid – in warm water. Wipe with a cloth or sponge wrung out in the solution. Rinse with a garden hose and dry quickly – in the sun or with a hair dryer or fan. Don't sit on the furniture for two or three days, as you could stretch the fibres and cause them to sag.

- **There are some exceptions** to this. Don't hose down bamboo or twisted paper wicker. Clean these with a sponge dampened with soapy water, followed by a sponge moistened with clear water. Wipe dry.

- **To treat wicker for dryness and cracking,** use 1 part turpentine to 2 parts boiled linseed oil on natural-fibre wicker, except for bamboo. Apply with a paintbrush, using as much as the wicker will absorb. Wipe off any excess with a cloth and let it dry for three or four days. For bamboo, apply a thin coat of liquid or paste wax periodically.

- **To clean an unfinished wicker basket,** a gentle vacuum is all that's required, since too much moisture will damage the basket. Don't use the vacuum cleaner on fragile baskets though – its suction may be too powerful. Instead, dust a delicate basket with a damp cloth.

New life for an old basket

To rescue a worn-looking basket, give it a coat of spray paint. First, check whether any small pieces of broken wicker are sticking out. If they are, use wire cutters to trim them off. Then hang the basket on a metal coat hanger, attach it to a tree or clothesline and spray-paint it. Let it hang there for several hours to dry out thoroughly.

Wicker, rattan & bamboo

- **Clean a varnished or painted basket** with a gentle vacuum. Then use a spray bottle filled with water and a tablespoon of vinegar. The spray allows you to penetrate the small areas between the wickerwork. Wipe the basket dry with a very soft cloth such as an old T-shirt, which is less likely to get caught on rough edges. Use a cotton bud to get to the tight places. Air out the basket in the sun, but keep it away from direct heat sources like radiators, which can warp the basket.

- **Clean most other baskets** with a vacuum cleaner, followed by a solution of water and a drop of washing-up liquid on a soft cloth. Apply with a soft brush in problem spots. Avoid cleaners with phosphates, which can cause the basket to disintegrate.

Windows

So much has been printed about the fastest and best way to clean windows that you'd think it was an Olympic event. In fact, lots of things work: choose the one that's best for you.

- **Clean the windowsills** and frames before the glass. Vacuum to remove loose dirt before wiping with a damp cloth.

- **Start at the top** and work down to avoid dripping onto clean windows.

- **Don't clean windows** in direct sunlight or hot weather. The cleaner will dry before you can wipe it off, creating streaks.

- **Make your drying strokes go up and down** on one side of the window and back and forth on the other. That way you can tell which side the streaks are on.

Windows

- **The cheapest way to clean a window** is to use plain water and newspaper. However, this can get messy. So you may prefer to use paper towels or a soft, lint-free cloth for the final wipe down. Dip a cloth or squeegee into a bucket of water, picking up just enough water to wet the window without drenching it. Then wad up the newspaper a little and rub the window until it's dry. Paper towels also work but are expensive and wasteful. A chamois cloth works as well.

- **Using a squeegee to clean windows** is often preferred by professional window cleaners. If it's your choice, buy a squeegee with a removable blade so that it can be replaced as it wears. The main disadvantage of a squeegee is that it's impractical on small panes of glass – although you can buy smaller ones. When using a squeegee, adopt the following technique.

1 First, wet the squeegee and draw it across the top of the window pane.

2 Start the squeegee at the bottom of that swath and draw it down one side of the glass to about 4cm from the bottom.

3 Repeat this step, overlapping each stroke as you work your way across the whole window. Draw the squeegee across the bottom of the pane. Wipe the squeegee on a cloth between strokes. Use a clean cloth to wipe the window edges, if necessary. On very large windows, wash and dry the top half, then move on to the bottom half.

- **For grease or hard-water deposits,** use 100ml white vinegar in 2 litres water plus a squirt of washing-up liquid. With really stubborn hard-water spots use straight vinegar.

- **For grime, grease or smoke,** use 100ml clear ammonia in 1 litre water.

Windows

- **For tough jobs,** use 250ml methylated spirits with 40ml clear ammonia and a drop of washing-up liquid in 2 litres water. This solution needs rinsing off afterwards, so only do this if all else fails.

- **For scratches in glass,** rub a little toothpaste into the scratch and polish with a soft cloth.

- **To peel off paint and stuck-on adhesives**, scrape with a razor blade. Don't use a putty knife, however, because it's duller and can damage the glass.

- **For the ultimate dirty window,** get a specialist window-clean product from a car-supplies shop. This is pricy and will need rubbing in, then rinsing off. So it's just for a small area.

Woks

A well-seasoned wok is practically nonstick and needs only light cleaning. Follow our instructions for seasoning and caring for your wok and it will last for ages.

- **To clean a new wok made of carbon steel** (the authentic kind), begin by removing the temporary protective coating applied by the manufacturer. Scrub the wok inside and out with washing-up liquid and steel wool, rinse with hot water. If some coating still remains, fill the wok with water and boil it until the coating dissolves. Empty the water and scrub again thoroughly with steel wool and soap.

- **To season a new wok,** after washing it as described above, first set it on a burner and heat on high until a few drops of water sprinkled into the wok do a mad dance. As it heats, the wok will change colour, becoming darker.

Quick cooking
When you cook with your newly seasoned wok, avoid using it for dishes that require long simmering – this can remove some of the seasoning. It's ideal, of course, for stir frying; however, it's also perfect for deep frying food and this cooking method can actually add to the layers of seasoning.

Woks

When the wok turns black, dip some wadded-up sheets of paper towel into sesame oil. Hold the wad in a pair of tongs and wipe the oil over the inside of the wok. Turn the heat down to low and let the wok sit on it for 15 minutes. If the surface looks dry, wipe with another thin coat of oil. Turn the heat off and let the wok cool. Repeat the oiling and heating process once more before using the wok for cooking.

- **To clean a wok after cooking,** wipe it out with a paper towel or damp cloth. Scrubbing a seasoned wok or using a detergent will ruin the seasoning, but if you do need to do this, then simply re-season, as above. Similarly, if a wok gets rusty, just follow the steps for cleaning and seasoning a new wok.

- **To clean an electric wok,** follow the manufacturer's directions, which will vary depending on what kind of surface the wok has and whether it is immersible in water.

seasoning a **new wok**

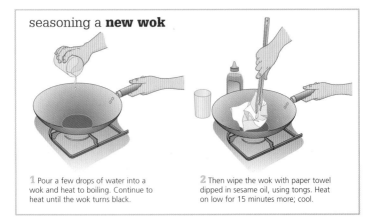

1 Pour a few drops of water into a wok and heat to boiling. Continue to heat until the wok turns black.

2 Then wipe the wok with paper towel dipped in sesame oil, using tongs. Heat on low for 15 minutes more; cool.

Wood-burning stoves

A clean wood-burning stove is a safer one – every year wood-burning stoves are responsible for many fires. One common cause of these fires is the improper disposal of ashes.

● **To dispose of ashes safely,** use a metal shovel and transfer them to a tightly covered metal bucket; don't use plastic shovels, paper bags or cardboard boxes. Take the bucket outside and leave it for a couple of days to ensure that all embers are gone. For final disposal, add to garden soil or sprinkle on the lawn. Clean out the ashes when they are around 10cm deep.

● **To clean a stovepipe,** disconnect it from the chimney and from the stove when the fire is out. Take it outside and shake it into a metal bucket to remove the soot and creosote. If there are stubborn clumps of residue, use a stiff-bristled brush.

● **To clean the outside of the stove,** vacuum when there is no fire, using the small brush attachment. For dirt this won't remove, wipe the surface of enamelled stoves with a damp sponge. Use stove polish on stoves made of cast iron, plate steel, sheet metal or a combination of these materials. Rust or other heavy dirt may be cleaned from a cold stove with fine steel wool and WD-40.

● **To clean glass doors on a wood stove,** follow the directions in your owner's manual. A mixture of water and a little ammonia works well to remove smoke, but check your manual first to make sure the glass doesn't have a special protective coating, which might be harmed by the ammonia.

● **Other stove parts** that need periodic cleaning are baffles, smoke shelves and catalytic combustors. These devices increase the efficiency of your stove and reduce pollution. Your owner's manual will tell you if your stove has one or more of these parts and will explain how to clean them.

Woodwork

Woodwork usually gets dirty faster than walls because it's the edging around doors and windows that most often comes into contact with hands and dirty fingers – and little children are often the worst culprits. Woodwork will probably need cleaning more often than walls, but fortunately there is usually a lot less of it to clean.

- **For routine woodwork cleaning,** vacuum around skirting boards, chair rails (if you have them), dado rails and casings (the framework around doors and windows), using the small brush attachment. Dust the top surfaces of this woodwork periodically with a microfibre cloth. Use a long-handled duster for hard-to-reach areas.

- **To wash woodwork,** use a solution of a little washing-up liquid mixed with warm water. Apply this with a wrung-out sponge or cloth and then rinse with plain water, using a clean sponge or cloth. If the woodwork's gloss coating has been dulled, follow by rubbing with a cloth that has a tiny amount of furniture polish on it. This works on both painted and polyurethane surfaces.

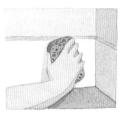

  - **To clean heavily soiled areas,** apply a little undiluted washing-up liquid directly onto the sponge or cloth. Rub the dirty area and rinse thoroughly with plain water.

- **To prepare the surface for new paint,** wash with a solution of sugar soap. Wear rubber gloves and rinse afterwards.

- **To clean any woodwork** that has a varnish or shellac finish, use a solvent-based (not water-based) wood cleaner, available at home-improvement stores and hardware stores. It is both a cleaner and wax in one product. Apply it with a clean, soft cloth and buff afterwards.

Worktops

Since your kitchen worktop is where most food preparation takes place, keeping it clean helps to cut levels of bacteria and so reduces the risk of possible contamination and sickness.

Worktops have come a long way since Formica, a plastic laminate, reigned supreme. Today, the most common type is a solid-surface synthetic (Corian is one popular brand). Other popular types are marble, granite and engineered or synthetic stone – and wood. It's worth reading the manufacturer's directions for cleaning your kind of worktop.

- **For day-to-day cleaning,** remove the equipment on top first, then clean up surface dirt and crumbs with a soft-bristled brush or handheld vacuum. Wet a nylon-backed sponge with soapy water (use washing-up liquid in warm water) and use the soft side of the sponge to wash the counter, backsplash included. Let the soapy water sit on the surface a few minutes to soften any spots. Switch to the scrubbing side to remove any intransigent spots. Rinse with warm water and buff dry with a clean, lint-free towel. Or squirt with a multipurpose kitchen cleaner and wipe clean with a sponge. Most will not need rinsing.

- **Plastic laminates, such as Formica,** should not be cleaned with abrasives. Mop up spills immediately with a sponge, then use a soapy sponge or all-purpose kitchen cleaner. For obstinate stains, sprinkle the worktop with bicarbonate of soda and rub with a soft, damp cloth. Rinse and dry with paper towels or a cloth. Alternatively, spread a paste of lemon juice and cream of tartar on the stain and let sit for 15 minutes. Rinse and dry.

- **Solid-surface synthetics, such as Corian,** can withstand light abrasion. Wet a scrubbing sponge or sprinkle a mildly abrasive cleaner, such as Cif (without bleach), onto a damp

> ### Oil splatters in the kitchen
> To clean up cooking-oil splatters from your hob and worktops, start by wiping up the oil with paper towels. Then wipe down the surfaces with a moist sponge and a solution of washing-up liquid and warm water, or use a 50-50 solution of vinegar and warm water.

Worktops

sponge and apply with gentle pressure. Rinse with water applied with a sponge and dry with a soft cloth.

- **To clean stone worktops,** first blot up spills at once with paper towels. Don't wipe – that will only make it worse. Flush the spot with warm water and mild soap, rinsing several times before drying with a soft cloth. Remember, acid will etch into marble and anything greasy stains granite.

- **To clean marble and granite worktops,** start with the don'ts: never use anything abrasive. Instead, wash with a few drops of plain or anti-bacterial washing-up liquid on a damp sponge. Rinse the surface completely with clean water and dry with a soft cloth. Or buy a cleaner formulated for stone from your kitchen-unit supplier.

- **Use coasters, trivets or place mats** under glassware and dishes to protect stone surfaces from scratching. Heat damages marble, so never set anything hot on it.

- **Stone worktops** are sometimes sealed with a penetrating commercial sealant. Make sure that wherever you prepare food, the sealant is non-toxic. Vegetable oil is an effective non-toxic and homespun coating for food-preparation areas.

- **Engineered stone** usually resembles granite but requires no sealant and little extra care. Wash with soap and water and an all-purpose kitchen cleaner.

- **Most wooden worktops** will be treated with a tough laminate layer. But if you have untreated wood, go easy. To avoid scratching, do not use abrasive cleaners. Instead, use a soapy liquid cleaner that is especially for wood or dilute washing-up liquid. Always dry scrupulously afterwards. You will do the most damage if you leave wood wet. Regularly treat the wood with wax to prevent cracking.

Paper towels

Using paper towels for all your kitchen cleaning would be expensive and wasteful. But for emergency messes paper towels are still the top choice. They are perfect for liquid spills, pet accidents and wiping up anything (such as wet paint or cooking grease) that might ruin a rag. But don't get ones with decorative prints, since the inks can occasionally bleed.

Zips

There are times when you should clean a zip independently of the item it fastens – in particular, those with a heavy-duty function. For example, the zips in tents, sleeping bags, luggage, wetsuits, fishing gear, jackets and boots may need separate attention now and then.

- **To clean zips in washable items,** wash the item with water and detergent that is suitable for the fabric. Close the zip before putting the article into the washing machine. When ironing, protect the zip by closing it and covering it with a cloth. Excessive heat can damage or destroy nylon, plastic and polyester zips.

- **To make the slider work more smoothly,** rub a candle along the zip teeth and move the slider up and down several times to work in the wax. A white candle works best, so you don't smear dye around. Wipe off any excess. This treatment will counteract the damage done by detergents and bleach to the factory-applied coating that keeps zips slippery.

- **To clean the zips on large articles** – such as tents, backpacks, wetsuits, suitcases and boots – first unzip the zip. Remove any loose dirt from the teeth with a toothbrush. Dip the toothbrush in a solution of a little washing-up liquid and warm water. Rinse with plain water and leave the zip open until it has dried. Lubricate the teeth with a candle, as above.

> **Drawn shut**
> If your zip sticks and you don't have a candle handy, then try this trick. With the zip closed, run the lead of an ordinary hard pencil up and down the teeth. Then open and close the zip a few times. Rub your finger along the zip to wipe off any graphite (which is what pencil lead is made of) that remains, and which might mark clothes.

Dealing with household

CLEANING CRISES

DEALING WITH HOUSEHOLD CLEANING CRISES

Here's a fast-find guide to the most likely of household disasters. If something messy has just happened, don't despair – chances are we've got advice on how to deal with it right here.

Animal accidents on floors

If you've a pet that frequently messes, keep a crisis kit to hand. Include paper towels, plastic bags (for disposing of solids and used paper towels) and an enzyme-based cleaner (available at pet shops). Start by removing any solids. Then blot up as much liquid as possible, using paper towels. You'll soak up maximum liquid if you stand on or press the paper towels. Soak the accident site in the enzyme cleaner. Let sit for a few minutes and then blot. Rinse the residue with water to prevent smells that might draw the pet back to use the same spot.

Baby sick or nappy contents on fabric

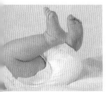

First try cold water; don't use hot water, since it can 'cook' the proteins. Soak washables in cold water for half an hour, run the stain under cold tap water, and gently rub the fabric against itself to loosen the stain. Then launder in warm water. For carpeting or upholstery, spray with cold water and blot. Repeat until the stain is gone. If residue remains, soak the accident site in enzyme cleaner: wash and rinse according to directions.

Berry stains on clothing or linens

Berry stains – raspberry, blackberry, strawberry and more – are considered dye stains and they're tough. For washable clothes and towels, pre-treat the stain with a commercial stain remover. Or apply liquid detergent directly to the stain. Work the detergent in well. If the stain doesn't lift out, rinse off, then soak the fabric in a diluted solution of oxygen bleach (4 teaspoons to 2 litres water). Clean in the washing machine, using the maximum temperature that the item will take.

For dry-clean-only clothes, try a solvent. Methylated spirits is good at lifting off fruit stains, but you need to take extreme care, as there is also a risk that this could also take the colour out of your clothes or linens. Using a cotton bud with a dash of methylated spirits, dab at the stain. With a second, dry cotton bud, blot it up. Or use Stain Devils Instant Wipes, which are suitable for dry-clean items.

Blood on fabric or carpeting

If it's a fresh bloodstain, cold water should be all you'll need to remove this protein stain. Don't use hot water, since hot water can cook the proteins, causing the stain to coagulate between the fibres in the fabric. Soak washable fabric items in cold water for half an hour, then run the stain under the cold tap, and gently rub the fabric against itself to loosen the stain. Launder in warm water.

For carpeting or upholstery, spray the stain with cold water and blot with a clean white towel (white, so there's no chance of dye transfer), repeating until clean.

Rubbish spills on the carpet
Quickly pick up large solids and put them in a bag or bin. Clean up small solids, such as coffee grounds, with a vacuum cleaner. Blot up liquids with paper towels. If stains remain, work out what they are and address each using the correct stain-removal technique. For large spills, work from the outer edge to the centre of the stain to contain the spill.

Candle wax on fabric or carpeting

If the wax is still soft, blot up the excess with paper towels. If it is hard, gently scrape the excess with a dull knife. Next, lay a plain brown paper bag or white paper towel (something with no dyes or printing ink) over the wax and run a hot iron over the paper. The heat will melt the wax and the paper will absorb it. Continue by moving the bag or paper towel around to unsaturated sections until all the wax is absorbed. Remove residue by blotting with a dry-cleaning solvent. Be sure to test the solvent first on an inconspicuous spot.

Chewing gum on fabric, carpeting or hair

Rub an ice cube on the gum until it freezes and hardens. To avoid water drips, put the ice in a plastic bag first. Scrape away the hardened gum with a dull knife. If residue remains, remove it by blotting with a dry-cleaning solvent; be sure to test it first on an inconspicuous spot. For gum in your hair, apply vegetable oil or peanut butter to the gum and knead until it's soft. Pull away bits of gum. Then shampoo.

Coffee on clothes

For washable fabrics, soak for half an hour in a solution of 1 teaspoon biological liquid detergent per 2 litres warm water. Then launder with the hottest water safe for the fabric. Don't scrub the coffee stain with soap: natural soap makes tannin stains harder to remove. For stubborn stains, you may need to wash the item with bleach.

Cooking smells filling the house

Open the windows and turn on the extractor fan, if you have one, to get fresh air circulating. Next, put any tea towels and cloths in the washing machine. Smells cling to the cooker and the worktops around it, so wipe off greasy residue and you are wiping off the smell. Use a multipurpose kitchen cleaner. If the smell is still there, clean the walls and cupboard doors near the stove. Because heat rises and is drawn to cool areas, concentrate on windows and windowsills, light fixtures and upper cabinets. If the smell is still there, wash the curtains. Or mix 4 tablespoons vinegar in 2 pints water and boil. The rising warm air will carry odour-neutralising vinegar particles to the surfaces on which smoke and grease have settled.

Kitchen odours

Here's how to handle a few common kitchen odour problems:
- To get the smells out of your bin, grind up lemon or orange peel and drop this into it.
- To keep the fridge smelling sweet, throw old food away, wipe down the interior with damp paper towels, and place an open box of bicarbonate of soda inside.

Felt-tip pen marks

First, try wiping the marks off with paper towels or a dry cloth. Depending on the surface, if the felt tip is still wet, you may be able to remove the mark. If not, try wiping with a clean cloth moistened with methylated spirits.

Fleas in the carpet

Vacuum all carpets and upholstered furniture, concentrating on areas frequented by your pet, and under seats and sofas. Empty the vacuum. Wash removable rugs or pet bedding. Apply a specialist flea-killing product; the most effective are those that 'fog' the room, rather than sprays that you have to direct onto areas you suspect fleas might have moved to. Treat your pet at the same time.

Lipstick on clothing

Lipstick contains both an oily/waxy base and dyes. You must first remove the oily/waxy part and then you can try to remove the dye. For washable fabrics, begin by applying a dry-cleaning solvent, such as Spotless Dry Clean Liquid. Next, rub with a liquid detergent and scrub in hot water. This should remove the oily/waxy part. Then wash in the washing machine with a detergent that contains an oxygen or all-fabric bleach.

Mud tracked in on a rug

Let the mud dry first and you'll have a better chance of getting it out. If the mud is ground in, wait until it dries. Then brush it to the surface and get up as much as you can with a dull knife. After that, vacuum. If you still see muddy prints, mix a few drops of washing-up liquid in 200ml warm water and blot the solution onto the rug with a clean white towel. Use another damp towel to rinse and remove soap residue.

Nail polish on wooden furniture, floors or rugs

Blot up the excess with a paper towel. Then blot the mark with a cloth moistened with acetone-based nail-polish remover. Don't let nail-polish remover seep into a rug's latex backing. To remove the nail-polish remover, mix one squirt of mild washing-up liquid (containing no bleach or lanolin) with 1 litre water. Wipe the wood or work the solution into the textile with a clean towel. Draw the solution back out by blotting with a dry paper towel. Rinse by lightly spraying with clean water and then blot up the water with fresh paper towels.

Oil & grease on clothes

Blot up as much as you can with paper towels or carefully scrape up solids with a dull knife. For clothes that can only be dry-cleaned, blot the grease with paper towels dampened with acetone-based nail-polish remover. (Don't use acetone on acetate, because it will dissolve the fabric.) For washable clothes, spray with a pre-wash stain remover or use a liquid laundry detergent. Work the detergent into the stain. Immediately after pre-treatment, wash the item in your washing machine using hot water (if that is safe for the fabric and colours).

Suntan lotion

Blot excess lotion with paper towels or scrape it up with a dull knife. On washable clothes, spray the stained area with a commercial pre-wash stain remover, such as Vanish. Or apply liquid detergent to the stain and work it in. Machine-wash in hot water (if that is safe for the fabric and colours). With dry-clean-only clothes, blot with a paper towel dampened with acetone-based nail-polish remover.

Paint drippings on floors or carpeting

Blot up as much of the paint as possible with paper towels. If it is latex paint, spray with clean water and blot. If it is oil-based paint, blot with a clean cloth or paper towels moistened with paint thinner or turpentine, refreshing cloths or paper towels repeatedly. If vestiges of the paint remain on the carpet, moisten the tufts with 3 per cent hydrogen peroxide and let that stand for an hour. Blot with clean paper towels.

Pen-ink stain on your pocket

Place the stain face down on white paper towels. (Put plastic underneath to protect your work surface.) Blot with a cloth moistened with methylated spirits, forcing the stain into the paper towels. If that does not work, try white spirit. Test it first in an inconspicuous corner of the material. Rinse with water and machine-wash.

Smoke from fireplace

If smoke from the fireplace comes into the house instead of up the chimney, first make sure there is no chimney fire; if there is one, call the fire brigade. If not, then your chimney is probably not drawing well. Check the direction of any wind and open doors or windows on the side of the house exposed to the wind. Open more windows and doors to help to blow existing smoke outside. If the smell lingers, wash the curtains and clean the upholstery. Wipe all exposed metal in the room with a degreaser, since smoke seeks out cool surfaces.

Tar on good shoes

Remove as much tar as possible by gently scraping with an old spoon. Remove further residue by blotting with paper towels. Then rub gently with paper towels moistened with methylated spirits. Repeat several times using clean paper towels and freshly applied alcohol. If any tar remains, try wiping with a sudsy solution of warm water and a squirt of washing-up liquid. Put a small amount on a cloth and gently blot or rub. Rinse by spraying lightly with clean water and wiping dry.

Water or alcohol stains on fine wood furniture

On fresh spills, soak up any excess liquid with paper towels, then rub the spot vigorously in the direction of the grain with the palm of your hand or a cloth dipped in furniture polish. If the stain is old and dry, you'll need an abrasive/lubricant combination. Using extra-fine (0000) steel wool, gently rub in a paste wax, following the grain of the wood.

Wine on the carpet

Blot up what you can with paper towels; work from the outside in to contain the spill. Apply a solution of ¼ teaspoon mild washing-up liquid and 2 pints of water and work into the affected area. Blot with clean paper towels. Rinse by lightly spraying with water; blot again. Do this until all suds are gone. Then spray lightly with water and cover with a pad of paper towels; weigh them down and leave to dry. If the stain persists, moisten with 3 per cent hydrogen peroxide. Let it stand for an hour. Finally blot thoroughly with clean paper towels.

Wine on table linen

If the fabric is washable, soak it for half an hour in a solution of 1 teaspoon biological laundry detergent per 2 litres warm water. Machine-wash using the hottest water that's safe for the fabric. Don't use soap: natural soap – including soap flakes, hand soap and detergent containing soap – makes tannin stains harder to remove. For stubborn tannin stains, you may need to wash the item with bleach.

SIMPLE solutions

If you've had a party, then wine spills won't be all you have to worry about: there can be a lot of mess left after a big bash! But if you follow this simple routine when the party's over, then you'll soon have your home spick and span again:

● Gather up cups, bottles and glasses. Look for spills and address them straight away.
● Fill your dishwasher and start the first load.
● Next, gather up the party rubbish, starting in the outer rooms and working your way towards the kitchen. The goal is to centralise the clutter.
● Dust and vacuum, again working your way towards the kitchen. Clean the kitchen last. Take the rubbish out as soon as bags are filled and tied.

Tools of the
CLEANING TRADE

CLEANING PRODUCTS

The following is a mini-encyclopedia of cleaning compounds and solutions. We explain the uses of different types of similar products and show how to save money by making your own.

Abrasive cleaners

With abrasive cleaners, fine, scarcely visible particles add friction to your cleaning. The finer the particle, the less abrasive the cleaner; the coarser the particle, the more abrasive the cleaner. The disadvantage of using abrasive creams and powders is that they need to be rinsed off. So using them takes longer than non-rinse spray cleaners.

Use a full-strength abrasive cleaner – a scouring powder, such as Ajax – to wear off dirt, stains, tarnish and hard-water deposits. Rub across the surface of the hard-surface item with a sponge or brush and then rinse.

Use a mild abrasive cleaner, such as Cif cream, for sinks, tiles, showers, baths, toilets and worktops. Be careful not to rub too hard; even mildly abrasive cleaners can scratch surfaces.

A pumice stone will help remove a particularly stubborn toilet-bowl stain. Keep a piece especially for this purpose.

Scrubbing pads, ranging from nylon mesh to steel-wool soap pads, also work by abrasion and are a quick way to clean metal saucepans.

Toothpaste can remove water marks in sinks and tarnish on silver. Coat the silver with toothpaste, run it under warm water, work it into a foam and rinse it off.

Salt is very useful if you have a spill in the oven. With the oven still warm, dampen the spill lightly and sprinkle on some salt. When the oven cools, scrape away the spill and wash the area clean.

Bicarbonate of soda is a mild abrasive. Sprinkle it on or make a paste by adding water. Use it to scour cooking dishes, saucepans and ovens without special surfaces.

Acidic cleaners

Acid is the opposite of alkali on the pH scale, with 0 indicating extreme acidity, 7 neutrality and 14 extreme alkalinity. Some common acids include lemon juice (citric acid), vinegar (acetic acid), hydrochloric acid and phosphoric acid.

Common uses for acid cleaners include removing rust stains, mineral deposits, stains on concrete and stains on grout, as well as unclogging pipes. Read product labels and use extreme caution when using acid cleaners. Otherwise, you risk damaging finishes and injuring yourself. Acid burns skin and the fumes can damage your lungs.

Hydrochloric acid (pH0) is the strongest acid and is used in extreme cases of hard-water deposits, lime and rust, most often in the toilet bowl. A cleaner with 9 per cent hydrochloric acid has a significant amount of acid in it and could etch surfaces and burn skin. Wear gloves and eye protection and follow directions. If the label says the product merely 'contains' hydrochloric acid, it's likely to be fairly diluted and mild.

Phosphoric acid (pH2 to 4) is milder than hydrochloric and can be used on baths, sinks and tiles to dissolve mineral deposits, rust stains and mildew. Cleaners with phosphoric acid are safe to use on the metal trim on shower doors and on taps if you rinse thoroughly after cleaning. Be aware that phosphoric acid doesn't really 'clean'. It etches surfaces and if you use it too frequently, you could dissolve the grout around your tiles.

> **Acid test**
> Take these sensible precautions when using acidic cleaners:
> • Don't use vinegar if you add chlorine bleach to your rinse water. The mixture will produce a harmful gas.
> • Don't use vinegar on wooden floors.
> • Don't let acidic cleaners sit too long on metal fixtures, or they'll damage the finish.
> • Don't use acid on stone (such as granite and marble) or concrete – both are alkaline and will dissolve with acid.

Vinegar and citric acid (pH2 to 4) and other acids in this category work well for frequent cleaning. They're often used on glassware, kettles and other kitchen items. Be aware however, that if you boil up vinegar to make a concentrated solution, you are also increasing its acidity, so you will need to wear gloves and take care. You can use vinegar in the final rinse when washing clothes to eliminate soap residue; pour 200ml white vinegar in the fabric-conditioner drawer.

Lemon juice is good for removing stains in clothing, such as fruit juice or berry stains. It acts like bleach, which also makes it good for cleaning cutting boards and worktops. To remove a stain on a worktop, squeeze on fresh lemon juice, let it sit for 45 minutes, sprinkle on bicarbonate of soda and rub with a sponge or soft cloth. Then rinse out the sponge or cloth and wipe again.

Alcohol

Alcohol used for cleaning comes in several forms. It's a colourless liquid, has a mild odour and is highly flammable. The most common is methylated spirits – it's particularly good at getting rid of stains. However, its unpleasant smell makes it a poor choice for general cleaning. So if using methylated spirits is suggested, this is generally a last resort. Your cleaning will be more pleasant if you can get good results using commercial cleaning solutions. White spirit is commonly used to thin or remove paint and varnish and to remove greasy smudges.

Alcohol-based cleaners evaporate quickly so they are especially suited to cleaning glass because they clean and quickly vanish without leaving streaks. They are also useful for cleaning telephones and the keyboards of computers, calculators and similar electronic goods. Apply alcohol to electronic items with a cotton bud.

Alcohol aware
A word of warning: keep these alcohols stored safely and out of the reach of children. They are toxic: drinking even just a moderate amount can cause unconsciousness, blindness and even death.

Alcohol is also useful for eliminating oil-based stains in carpet and upholstery, for removing hair spray from mirrors, and dissolving ink, lipstick, crayon and other difficult stains.

Alcohol can soften plastic and paint, so don't let alcohol-based cleaners remain on such surfaces long.

Alkali cleaners

Alkali cleaners are at the opposite end of the pH scale from acidic ones. Any cleaner above pH7 (neutral) is considered an alkali. Multipurpose cleaners usually have an alkali base because such cleaners neutralise acid and most stains are acidic.

Common uses for alkali cleaners include degreasing and removing heavy soiling. They're also good for windows and dealing with coffee and tea stains. Alkali cleaners include washing-up liquid (not the mildest ones – these will be pH neutral) mild detergents such as Woolite, and all-purpose cleaners such as Cif Active Gel with Baking Soda. The more aggressive degreasers, oven cleaners, lye drain openers and wax strippers are also alkali-based products.

The mildest alkali cleaners (pH8 and pH9) include washing-up liquid and bicarbonate of soda. In a solution with water, bicarbonate of soda cleans hard surfaces such as glass, tiles, porcelain, stainless steel, chrome and glass fibre.

Moderate alkalis (pH9 to pH11) include all-purpose degreasers, washing detergent, ammonia, soaps, scouring powders and window cleaners.

The strongest alkalis (pH12 to pH14) include lye (used in drain openers and oven cleaners), garage-floor degreasers, carpet shampoos and caustic soda (for extra cleaning power for unblocking drains).

Alkali care
Some cautionary notes about using alkali cleaners:
• Strong alkalis can damage skin and fabrics. They also corrode and darken aluminium. Wear hand and eye protection when handling the stronger alkalis.
• Most alkalis, except bicarbonate of soda, are toxic if swallowed.
• To remove an alkali residue from a surface you have cleaned, rinse with a solution of 2 tablespoons vinegar in 1 litre water; wipe dry.

All-purpose cleaners

The big advantage of all-purpose cleaners is that you don't have to keep a lot of special cleaners round the house. Don't assume, however, that your all-purpose cleaner disinfects. Check the label if you need to get rid of germs as well.

You can use all-purpose cleaners safely on most surfaces and fabrics – worktops, cabinets, walls, floors and patio furniture. They will even remove fingerprints. It's best to test an all-purpose cleaner on an inconspicuous part of the item you're cleaning before you squirt it over the entire object. Because many all-purpose cleaners have a relatively high pH, they may cause colours to run. They also can damage wood.

Use citrus-based cleaners on clothes, carpets, grout, shower curtains, rubbish bins, patios and hardwood garden surfaces, toilets, the kitchen and stains. They remove gum, tar and grease and they leave a pleasant smell behind.

Ammonia

Ammonia, made up of nitrogen and hydrogen, is a gas that is suspended in water. Ammonia is an alkali booster (by itself, it's not a cleaner) that helps detergents work.

Many common cleaners use solutions that are 5 to 7 per cent ammonia. Household ammonia is actually mostly water and the ammonia content is 5 to 10 per cent.

Sudsy ammonia has a detergent added and works well on hobs, floors, ceramic tiles and stainless steel. A bowl of ammonia left in the oven overnight will loosen burned-on grease – just wipe it off in the morning. Ammonia is also found in commercial window cleaners.

Ammonia alert
Take extra care when working with ammonia:
• Keep the area well ventilated. Evaporating ammonia fumes can cause nausea.
• Never mix ammonia with chlorine bleach, which creates poisonous chlorine gas. If inhaled, this combination is potentially deadly.
• Ammonia can darken and discolour fabrics, so proceed carefully.

Bathroom cleaners

Bathroom cleaners are designed to eliminate soap scum and mildew on baths, sinks, tiles, showers and grout. It's a good idea to use bathroom cleaners that disinfect – that is, kill germs. To do this, you must leave the cleaner to sit for the time instructed on the label. If you wash it off more quickly, your surface may be clean but not disinfected. In general, these are tough cleaners for a tough job, so always protect your hands by wearing rubber gloves.

All-purpose cleaners, such as Cif Bathroom Mousse, are the best choice when you're cleaning the whole of the bathroom. Look for any product that will deal with germs and soap scum at the same time.

Acidic bathroom cleaners, such as Bathroom Power, are good for getting rid of soap scum. Watch out for ones that are not safe on enamel, such as Flash Bathroom Spray. If you have an enamel bath, confine these to the sink only. For a homemade alternative, try white vinegar mixed in equal parts with water. Apply the solution with a damp sponge or cloth and rinse thoroughly.

Commercial toilet-cleaning products, such as Toilet Duck Active Fresh, are numerous and widely available. Bleach does not remove limescale, it merely whitens it. So if scale in the toilet bowl is a problem, always choose a limescale-killing product. Among the most effective are those you leave in overnight, such as Harpic Power Tablets.

Toilet wipes are a new and speedy way to give a daily clean. Just wipe a product such as Parazone Flushable Toilet Wipes around the seat and rim of your bowl – then throw the used wipe into the bowl and flush.

Bicarbonate of soda

This venerable white powder is still the most versatile cleaning substance around. Made of non-toxic fine crystals, bicarbonate of soda acts as a chemical cleaner and doubles as a scouring powder. It also neutralises odours, keeps drains clog-free and is handy for putting out grease or electrical fires – sprinkle it on dry.

For regular cleaning on hard surfaces, pour a little bicarbonate of soda on a damp sponge or cleaning cloth and wipe. Follow up with another clean, damp sponge or cloth.

To remove surface stains in the kitchen or bathroom, pour out enough bicarbonate of soda to cover the stain and add just enough water to make a paste. Let the paste stay on the stain for several minutes, then scrub with a sponge and wipe it away.

To help remove oil and grease stains from clothing, add 100ml bicarbonate of soda to the wash.

To keep your kitchen sink clog-free, pour 100ml soda down the drain each night, followed by warm water. Do the same thing for other drains in your house once a week.

To kill odours in carpeting, rugs and even car mats, sprinkle on bicarbonate of soda, let it stand for 15 minutes and then vacuum.

When you're changing cat litter, sprinkle some in the bottom of the cat box and then a little on top of the new litter.

Add it to ashtrays to control the stench of cigarette ends.

Bicarbonate of soda also soaks up odours when it's dissolved in water. Pour 4 tablespoons bicarbonate of soda into 1 litre warm water. Use the solution to rinse your mouth to get rid of garlic breath, deodorise a stinky plastic container and soak washable nappies that smell strongly of ammonia.

Best buckets
When you need to mix up a cleaning solution – of bicarbonate of soda and warm water, say – then a bucket will be your best bet. Make sure it's got a sturdy handle, so you can carry the solution to where it's needed. And if you want to clean floors with your solution, make sure the bucket is wide enough for a mop to fit inside. Pick one that has a compartment on the top for wringing out the mop.

Carpet deep-cleaners

Once, buying your own deep-cleaning carpet machine was a risky option. It was easy to over-wet your carpet with them, running a risk of encouraging mildew, while some models didn't heat the water hot enough to do a good cleaning job.

Now, there are some excellent models around. But you need to be sure you have enough storage space available, before buying a bulky piece of equipment that's only likely to be used a couple of times a year.

Renting a deep-cleaning unit is economical, but ferrying the equipment from the hire shop to your house and back again is a hassle and it's hard to know what condition your rental unit will be in.

If you buy a unit, the higher-end home machines, such as Bissell PowerWash ProHeat, include such features as dials that automatically adjust the amount of cleaner dispensed based on whether you're cleaning a low or high-traffic area; an on-board heater that gets the water about 25 degrees hotter than hot tap water; and a powered hand-tool attachment made especially for cleaning small spaces, such as stairwells and around toilets.

Deep-cleaners work by forcing a heated cleaning mixture into the carpet, then sucking about 90 per cent of the liquid back out – and with it grime and embedded dirt. (They are sometimes called steam cleaners, but they actually use hot water – not steam.) Even the most powerful vacuum cleaners can't reach the dirt at the base of a carpet, so periodic deep cleaning is important. Every 6 to 18 months ought to do it.

Drying times vary from about 4 to 6 hours, depending on the thickness of the carpet and underlay.

Car polishes

There's a big difference between polishing a car and waxing it. Polishing adds brilliance. Wax provides protection. And if you polish your car at least once a month, you'll probably eliminate the need to wax.

Before you polish, the car must be clean, or you'll rub tiny particles of dirt into the finish and create noticeable scratches. Clean the exterior with car-wash solution rather than dishwashing detergent – detergents draw oil out of the car's paint, which accelerates oxidation and makes the paint look cloudy.

Once the car is clean, it's time to polish. The role of polish is to condition and nourish the paint and give it a deep, wet-look shine. Done properly, polishing adds brilliance and makes the bodywork of the car as smooth as glass before you wax. The paint is rejuvenated and unlike the wax build-up you can get from over-waxing, polishing actually improves the finish with each application.

The key to proper polishing is using clean cloths. Have several cloths (100 per cent cotton or microfibre are best) on hand and constantly rotate the area of cloth you use, so you're not pushing the residue you've already removed back into the paint. When there are no more totally unused areas on the cloth, change to a clean one.

Spray-on polishes are the easiest to apply, but there are trade-offs. They aren't as good at rejuvenating an oxidised finish and their shine does not tend to last as long.

Liquid and paste polishes require more elbow grease, but the effect is more durable. And a warning – if the label of a polish tells you to keep the product away from the rubber and plastic trim on your car, take heed. Such polishes will leave permanent, unsightly streaks on the trim.

Cleaning cloths

When it comes to cleaning, 100 per cent cotton cloths are ideal. Soft, old T-shirts are excellent for re-use as cloths. Old socks are also handy, because you can wear them like mittens and just use your hands to dust. Just make sure you wash cotton cloths between uses. And look out for microfibre cloths (see page 383), which can be used to clean a whole host of items.

Dishwashing detergents

When you come to do the dishes you're either going to load them into the dishwasher – if you've got one – or wash them by hand. Therefore, you'll need either a suitable dishwasher detergent or a washing-up liquid.

Hand-dishwashing products are among the gentlest detergents available and can also be used to wash everything from delicate clothing to the family dog. Washing-up liquids work by loosening grime and suspending it until it can be rinsed away. When the suds disappear, so does the cleaning action, so you'll need to add more detergent. If you buy a cheap brand that gives out quickly, you'll just have to use more – and then it's not really a bargain.

Recent innovations include hand-care ingredients, such as vitamin E, aloe vera and aromatherapy-inspired scents added to the liquid. Anti-bacterial washing-up liquid also has the bonus of being able to halt the growth of bacteria on sponges and cleaning brushes. Simply squeeze a little onto your sponge or brush and it should work for up to 12 hours.

Never use washing-up liquid in a dishwasher, because the suds and foam it produces can inhibit the cleaning process in the machine.

Automatic dishwashing detergents come in three forms: powdered, gel and tablet. All are effective, although older machines may not be good at dissolving tablets.

Powdered formulas have been around the longest and are generally the least expensive. The newer products – gels and tablets – offer some added benefits in certain situations, though. Powders can turn to grit if your dishwater doesn't get hot enough (60°C) to dissolve all the powder. Dishwashing gels dissolve more quickly than powders or tablets and therefore can start cleaning dishes faster. Tablets

are convenient because they eliminate the need to measure, since each tablet is formulated to clean one load.

Rinse products prevent spotting and filming by lowering the surface tension of the water, so it can run straight off dishes. They also help items dry faster when left to air-dry or when you use the energy-saving function on your dishwasher. Rinse agents come in liquid and solid forms. Liquids may be used only in dishwashers with a built-in rinse reservoir. Solid forms are made to attach to the upper dishwasher rack, where they dissolve slowly during the various cycles.

Dishwasher salt is essential if you live in a hard-water area and use a budget dishwasher powder.

Disinfectants

Disinfectants are designed to kill germs on surfaces, including bacteria and viruses that can spoil food, create odours and cause illness. Some products also clean as they disinfect, so read the label if you're looking for a dual-purpose disinfectant.

Disinfectants contain microbe killers. Disinfecting cleaners also contain surfactants (surface-active agents) to remove soiling.

When choosing a disinfectant, checking the label is especially important. Depending on the formulation and active ingredients, disinfectants may be designed to kill bacteria that cause intestinal illnesses, such as *E. coli* and salmonella; staphylococci, the kinds of bacteria that cause skin infections; the fungi that cause athlete's foot; and viruses, such as rhinovirus, which is the primary cause of the common cold.

To allow disinfectants to work, follow the package directions to the letter. That usually means letting the disinfectant sit on the soiled surface for at least 10 minutes to kill bacteria. Many people use diluted household chlorine bleach as a disinfectant and stain remover – that's fine. It does the job and very economically, too. Make sure you follow label directions and dilute accordingly.

There's no need to disinfect your entire house. Stick to areas where you prepare food, plus other moist surfaces such as sinks and toilets. Be especially vigilant if someone in the family is sick or especially vulnerable to infection, because they are elderly or suffering from an illness, such as cancer, which reduces their immunity.

Be careful not to reinfect an area you've just cleaned by using a dirty cloth or sponge. If you clean a surface with disinfectant but then wipe with a contaminated cloth, you're simply re-depositing germs on the clean surface. Some people prefer using paper towels after disinfecting, since you throw away the contaminants. This can get expensive of course, so there's no need to shy away from cloths and sponges. Both work as well, if not better, as long as you wash them with chlorine bleach and let them dry thoroughly between uses.

Disposable wipes

Disposable wipes have taken the cleaning world by storm in the last few years, generating the most growth in the household-cleaning marketplace.

The appeal of disposable wipes is understandable. In terms of convenience, it will always be hard to beat any pre-treated product that you just throw away after a single use. The popularity of wipes is driven by what's known as the three Es of consumer product value – they're effective, efficient and expedient.

You can now get disposable wipes for disinfecting surfaces such as toilets, sinks and worktops. (In such cases, disposing of germs along with the wipe is an attractive feature.)

Furniture wipes to clean and shine wood are also available.

Floor sweepers, sold as kitchen-mop systems, use dry and pre-moistened disposable floor wipes.

Dry disposable wipes rely on an electrostatic charge to attract dust. Disposable mitts, also electrostatically charged, make quick work of dusting surfaces like wood, ceramic and vinyl. The dust sticks to the mitt instead of becoming airborne.

Drain cleaners

Drain cleaners come in four varieties – acids, alkalis, oxidisers and enzymatics – and their job is to get rid of blockages in drains, most commonly in kitchens and bathrooms.

Oxidisers are effective on organic blockages. These chemicals react with and combine with the blocking material, breaking it up and disintegrating it (rather than dissolving it).

Enzymatic drain cleaners are slower-acting as they consume or digest waste blockages, but they're easier on your pipes than acids, caustics and oxidisers (which is more of a concern with old plumbing). They're also thought to do less harm to septic systems. However, most commercial drain cleaners are a combination of the two.

To prevent drain clog-ups in your kitchen sink, pour 50g bicarbonate of soda around the kitchen sink drain opening. Rinse this into the drain with 50ml hydrogen peroxide. Do this once a month. The fizzing action helps to clear away the residue clinging to your pipes.

Drain don'ts
Chemical drain cleaners have the potential to harm the user if instructions aren't followed exactly. Some of these drain cleaners, particularly the faster-acting ones, cause bubbling that may splash harmful chemicals back out of the drain. So stand back once you've poured in the cleaner. Never use muriatic acid (a dilute form of hydrochloric acid) to clear blockages. It's highly dangerous.

Enzyme digesters

Enzyme digesters are chemicals, created by micro-organisms that eat away organic matter. So they're effective on organic stains – including unpleasant substances such as urine, vomit, faecal matter, protein stains and the odours associated with them.

Use enzymes around the toilet and flooring to keep your bathroom smelling fresh by digesting soil, spills, bodily oils and bacteria. You'll also find enzymes in drain openers and in carpet, upholstery and laundry products. Enzymes are safe for use in septic systems and can also be used in waste-disposal drains. Enzymes are temperature sensitive, so don't use them with hot water. Disinfectants will also render them ineffective. Remember that once you open an enzyme digester, it has a short shelf life.

Enzyme digesters come as a powder that you activate with warm water, triggering a feeding frenzy on organic matter. If you've ever cleaned spilled milk from a carpet, only to have the mark return days later, you need to use an enzyme product. Most ordinary cleaners mask the odour but can't remove the organic source.

When treating a carpet stain or odour with an enzyme cleaner, first soak up as much of the stain as possible with old bath towels. (Use a wet vac if there's a lot of volume.) Apply the enzyme according to the package directions. Pour it over the stain and make sure the enzyme penetrates to the underlay. If it doesn't, you're wasting your time – the stain and smell will remain. Keep the carpet wet the entire time the enzyme is 'eating' the cause of the odour. It's a good idea to cover the area with a piece of plastic and place weights along the edges until the recommended time is up. Then rinse with 100ml distilled white vinegar per 3 litres water. Rinse a second time with plain water.

Enzyme digesters make a great laundry pre-soak that works away at organic stains before you run garments through the wash. Use warm water in the soak, according to the package directions (the exception being blood, which requires cold water). Be careful: enzymes will eat away at animal fibres, including silk and wool.

You can select proteolytic enzymes for protein stains, such as meat juice, egg, blood and milk, or amylolytic enzymes for starch and carbohydrate stains. Since enzymes are costly and starches and carbohydrates generally do not leave stains, you're probably better off buying proteolytic enzymes.

Floor-care products

Floor cleaners, floor polishes and floor finishes are not interchangeable. Floor cleaners, as the term implies, will remove dirt. Floor polishes remove scratches because they're slightly abrasive and they seal and protect the cleaned surface. As far as floor finishes are concerned, real wax isn't usually used any more on the most popular kinds of modern flooring. It has been replaced by various polymers.

Each floor manufacturer has recommendations for cleaning and protecting its products, so try to check the manufacturer's directions and follow them. As a general rule, you should remove all dirt from the floor before you apply the appropriate protective finish. Otherwise, you'll end up with a shiny, but dirty floor.

If you don't have the cleaning instructions from your floor's manufacturer, here is a general rundown of the products you'll need. Be sure to read any product's label to make sure it's safe for the floor you're working on.

For vinyl floors, start by cleaning with a mild detergent or all-purpose cleaner such as Flash. After rinsing, apply a water-based floor polish and finish, such as Johnsons Klear Floor Shine, according to the package directions. You can find one-step clean-and-polish products, but you probably won't be as happy with the results. This same approach works for asphalt and rubber flooring. Solvent-based paste wax will also add shine to vinyl flooring (it requires buffing) but shouldn't be used on asphalt or rubber.

For wood floors, try not to use any cleaners at all – just a damp mop. When that's not enough (and for laminate floors as well), choose a specialist product like Pledge Soapy Wood Cleaner that won't leave a residue.

For ceramic tile floors, a general household cleaning product such as Cif Liquid will do a good job, or use a specialised tile-cleaning product. Avoid abrasive cleaners. Grout will be easier to clean if it has been treated with a silicone sealer.

Expert **ADVICE**

Mops are used to clean floors in two ways – dry-mopping or wet-mopping. Always keep it dry if you can: it's so much faster. However, to pick up ground-in and wet dirt, you'll have to introduce water and/or cleaning solutions to your mop:

● Cellulose sponge mops are made of open-cell foam and are good at cleaning vinyl. To use, dip the mop in a bucket of cleaner and warm water, wring out the excess moisture and mop. The head of your sponge mop will need to be replaced occasionally – how often depends on usage.

● String mops are usually 100 per cent cotton (although some contain polyester), and can be used indoors or outdoors. They're good for cleaning garage floors and decking, tiled and linoleum floors and granite flooring. But they are not ideal for hardwood or marble floors, because they can hold a lot of moisture, which can damage those surfaces. You can machine-wash cotton mop heads.

● Towel mops use strips of fabric, secured in a holding device. Towel mops can be used wet on all floors, you can replace the mop head easily when it becomes soiled and you can wash and dry it as necessary. In addition to floor cleaning, you can use towel mops to dust cobwebs and clean ceilings.

Furniture waxes & polishes

When you apply a wax or polish to your wood furniture, you're not beautifying the wood itself – you're improving the finish on the wood. Use either polish or wax – not both. If you put polish on wax, it will just puddle. Polishes don't offer as much protection as wax – they are designed as a quick way to add sparkle to a dull-looking finish.

Furniture waxes – whether they are paste or liquid – are made from combinations of synthetic and natural waxes. The synthetic element is paraffin. The natural elements include beeswax and carnauba, a vegetable extract.

Wax provides a barrier against moisture seeping into the wood of your furniture. It also helps speed up cleaning because you'll be able to remove marks and dust more easily. Before you wax, check the manufacturer's instructions. Generally, most gloss or semi-gloss finished furniture can be waxed. If your furniture has a satin or flat finish, wax may give it a random, messy-looking sheen.

To apply wax, rub it on thinly with a clean, cotton cloth. Then let it sit for several minutes (check the label for precise timing) and buff it with another clean cloth.

Furniture polishes often contain vegetable oil, alcohol, perfume and dye. Mineral oil-based polishes, such as Pledge, are sold in bottles or aerosol cans and are easy to apply.

Polishes that act as revivers contain fine abrasive pumice in the polish formula and don't contain oil. They clean and protect the surface and are more like a wax.

Polishes that contain silicone produce a shine but can make refinishing the furniture more difficult in the future. Look for products that say they're silicone-free.

Glass cleaners

Commercial glass cleaners contain either ammonia or alcohol. They clean dirt, smears and grease and can be used on surfaces other than glass, such as Formica and laminate – but not on Corian or marble.

The composition of a glass cleaner, such as Windolene, is a mix of ingredients: detergents or surfactants to dissolve dirt and grime; fragrances; ammonia, an alkaline cleaner; colouring; alcohol to remove filmy residues and prevent streaks; and solvents to dissolve oily films.

Choose a glass cleaner that does not contain phosphorus, which has a tendency to smear glass. Citrus cleaners may not be the best choice for your home's windows either, since they often contain a solvent called limonene, which can damage wood and vinyl frames. Some glass cleaners are formulated specifically to stop them from dripping.

Homemade glass cleaners are cheap, effective and easy to put together. For general cleaning, mix 2 squirts of a mild washing-up liquid in 3 litres of warm water in a bucket.

For cleaning smeary glass, mix 50ml white vinegar with 400ml distilled water (water that's been boiled in the kettle and allowed to cool) in a spray bottle and squirt lightly onto your windows. Then polish using your preferred method.

When you use glass cleaners to actually clean windows, do it in the early morning or early evening – not during the middle of the day when the sun's rays will be heating the glass. The heat of the glass will cause whatever window cleaner you're using to dry more quickly and you're likely to end up with a problem with streaks.

As an alternative, use no cleaning products at all – microfibre cloths (see page 383) clean windows perfectly.

Squeegees
Anyone cleaning windows, mirrors and tiles should use a squeegee. They are quicker and more effective at removing cleaning solutions and the dirt those solutions loosen. They don't streak, they don't leave behind lint and they're not as messy as newspapers. A 20-25cm wide squeegee is the most suitable size – any bigger and it will be unwieldy. Any smaller and it won't cover enough surface.

Hydrogen peroxide

Hydrogen peroxide is an oxidising agent, similar to bleach, that removes colour and cleans surfaces. Many products that promise to brighten or whiten clothes contain hydrogen peroxide. Use it with care.

Peroxide is made of two parts hydrogen and two parts oxygen and it's the extra oxygen molecule that turns plain water into a potent oxidiser. The higher the percentage of hydrogen peroxide, the stronger it is.

Peroxide is a germ killer, as well as a substitute for bleach, and it's an effective way to get rid of salmonella and *E. coli* bacteria. To kill these germs, spray 3 per cent hydrogen peroxide onto your worktops or cutting boards, for example, followed by a spray of white distilled vinegar. Then rinse with fresh water.

For removing carpet stains, 3 per cent hydrogen peroxide is a good choice. Pour the agent on the spot, wait 30 minutes and blot it up with paper towels. Rinse with 2 tablespoons white vinegar mixed with 1 litre water, then blot. Rinse again with plain water and blot once more. Test on an inconspicuous spot first.

Brighten your dingy laundry whites by adding 200ml 6 per cent hydrogen peroxide to your wash.

To remove yellow underarm stains on your clothing, pour 3 per cent peroxide directly onto the stain; let it sit for several hours and then rinse.

To remove red dye stains caused by sweets and ice lollies, use 3 per cent peroxide poured directly onto the spot. Wait for 30 minutes and then rinse.

Metal polishes

Commercial metal polishes remove tarnish (oxidation) and create a burnish or shine when you apply some elbow grease. Read the labels to find a polish suited to the metal you want to clean. (A general-purpose metal polish will give less satisfactory results.) Metal polishes typically do their job through a combination of mild abrasion with chemical cleaners.

Metal polishes come as liquids and creams. Convenient polishing cloths, lightly saturated with polish, also are available.

How often you polish depends on how often your item is handled. Every time you handle a metal piece, you transfer acid from your hands to the item, which causes the metal to oxidise.

To apply polish, use an old cotton T-shirt or lint-free cotton cloth. Then use an old towel to remove any excess and a microfibre cloth to buff the polish. Be sure to remove as much of the polish residue as possible, as the chemicals can damage metals over time. To reach nooks and crannies, use an old toothbrush. Some metal polishes contain strong chemicals, so always wear rubber gloves and work in a well-ventilated area.

Microfibre cloths

Microfibre cloths are very efficient. Made up of interwoven fibres that are ten times finer than silk, they grab and trap dust and pull it off the surface you're cleaning, without scratching. They're great for cleaning computers, CDs and television screens – in fact, any surface that's especially vulnerable to scratching.

Use microfibre cloths for dusting and polishing household surfaces, or combine them with cleansers, polishes or water for an unlimited number of household tasks. Because these cloths absorb several times their weight in fluids, they're particularly adept at streak-free cleaning.

Cleaning microfibre cloths is easy, too. Shake them out when they're filled with dry dust and machine-wash them when they look especially dirty. Remember to choose a hot wash to kill bacteria. Also available as mitts, the cloths can be used and washed up to 500 times (lasting about two years under normal use) before losing their effectiveness. When washing them, avoid using fabric softener or bleach or including softener sheets in the tumble dryer. Also avoid drying them with towels, since lint from the towels will stick to the microfibres. Some microfibres are treated with cleaning solutions and shouldn't be washed at all, such as microfibre jewellery-cleaning cloths that remove tarnish and polish precious metals.

Oils

Oils used on natural wood surfaces or leather keeps them from drying out and makes them look healthy. Most oils for wood or leather are extracted naturally from animals, seeds or the peel of citrus fruits. Oils should never be used on stone, which is porous and will absorb the oil, producing dark spots in the stone. When you're thinking of using oil on wood or leather, always test it first on an inconspicuous spot. Some commonly used oils are listed below:

Citrus oil (orange, lemon and grapefruit), such as Pledge with Orange Oil, will help restore the finish on wood that has been neglected or has faded. Citrus oil penetrates to moisturise and condition wood. They are often combined with a chemical cleaner. Apply lightly, putting the oil on a cloth and then wiping onto the furniture or woodwork. Oil has a tendency to streak if you apply too much, so be very sparing. Allow 30 minutes for the oil to dry.

Pine oil is a general cleaner and disinfectant for floors, counters and bathrooms. It comes from the turpentine family and has a distinct aroma. To use, dilute it in a spray bottle or in water according to the package directions.

Teak and linseed oil are good for natural wood, tabletops, wood panelling and wooden floors. Some brands have dyes in them, so they act like a stain. Linseed oil is also good for protecting outdoor furniture. Both oils can combust spontaneously, so be very careful not to leave oil-soaked rags lying around. Hang these outside to dry thoroughly before you dispose of them in an outdoor rubbish bin. Or dispose in a sealed metal container.

Neat's-foot oil, which is obtained from the feet and shinbones of cattle, is a great conditioner for leather. To use it, apply with a cloth, let it soak in for about 5 to 10 minutes and then buff or polish it dry, using circular motions. Cotton towels and old T-shirts are suitable for this.

Oven cleaners

These are among the strongest – and most toxic – cleaners available for domestic use. Most contain a strong cleaning alkali, usually sodium hydroxide or potassium hydroxide. This caustic soda, or lye, converts fats to soapy water-soluble compounds that will wipe away easily.

Oven cleaners come as aerosol sprays, liquids, pastes and powders and are usually thick so that they will stick onto the vertical walls of an oven. They are highly toxic and can cause deep burns and blindness if they come into contact with skin or eyes. If swallowed, oven cleaners can be fatal. Don't use oven cleaners on self-cleaning ovens, which break down fats and other food with high heat instead of chemicals.

> **Oven danger**
> Be careful with all oven cleaners. Wear rubber gloves and protective goggles and work in a well-ventilated area. Never spray commercial oven cleaner on a hot oven, electric elements or oven lights – heat can make it even more caustic.

Sealants

To prevent grime from taking up long-time residence in our homes, scientists have devised sealants – for textiles, grout, wood, brick and concrete – to block pores, making surfaces less susceptible to staining and easier to wipe clean.

Fabric sealants come in two varieties – fluorochemical sealants, such as Scotchgard and Teflon, and silicone sealants.

Silicone sealants work only against water-based spills, such as juices; any spill containing oil may penetrate the sealant. Silicone sealants can even trap oily stains, making them harder to remove.

Brick and concrete floor sealants, like fabric sealants, add a protective layer to floors, making cleaning easier. Always clean and prepare a floor surface well before applying a sealer. Reapply when signs of wear appear.

Expert **ADVICE**

Spray bottles can be real time and money-savers. They allow you to mix your own cleaning solutions or buy your favourite commercial cleaners in bulk, and they also make applying cleaning solutions easier and more exact than simply pouring them on. Even when you're just using water – for instance, if you need to lightly wet a carpet stain – spray bottles do an excellent job:

● To find good spray bottles – ones that are more durable and have a larger capacity – visit a hardware store or supermarket.

● When using spray bottles, it's important to label them the minute you pour in your cleaning solution – this prevents future confusion and possible safety issues.

● To avoid contaminating nearby surfaces, use the appropriate nozzle setting for the job you're doing. Use a tighter stream for smaller areas, such as toilet seats, and a wider mist for larger areas, such as large bathroom mirrors. If you're using a harmful cleaning chemical, such as bleach, in a spray bottle, avoid making the mist too fine. It will make the chemical much easier to inhale or get in your eyes.

Wood sealants also protect against scratching and water damage. Penetrating sealers seep into the grain of the wood and keep dust and dirt from doing the same. Surface-coating sealers – polyurethanes, shellacs and varnishes – form a protective layer over the wood surface. Polyurethane is the most popular surface sealant because it's durable and relatively easy to use. Polyurethane sealers are either oil or water-based and they come in a variety of finishes, from matt to gloss.

Grout sealants combat what has traditionally been one of the toughest things in the house to clean. This sealant, available at home and hardware stores and easily applied with a sponge paintbrush, prevents oil, dirt and mildew from staining grout lines in tiling.

Soap

The manufacture of soap has changed little over the centuries. Animal or vegetable fats are still treated with a strong alkali, such as sodium or potassium. Soap is not the same as detergent, which is a synthetic product first made in Germany in 1916 in response to a shortage of soap-making fats. But both contain 'surface-active agents', or surfactants, which reduce the surface tension of water and dirt, in effect loosening the dirt, dispersing it in water and holding it in suspension until it is rinsed away.

Soap is used today almost solely for personal skin and body care. For most other cleaning situations, synthetic detergents have almost completely replaced natural soaps, especially for machine-washing dishes and clothes. In hard water, soap is not as effective as detergent and may form a curd or soap scum that can ruin clothes and stain baths and sinks.

Don't use soap on tannin stains, such as those produced by coffee, fruit or jam, if you can avoid it. Soap makes the stain harder to remove.

Solvents

Safe solvents
Always take safety precautions when using solvents:
• Solvents are highly flammable. Never use them near open flames.
• Always open windows to ventilate the area in which you are working.
• Wear chemical-resistant gloves, long-sleeved shirts and long trousers, protective eyewear and, depending on the solvent, a ventilator.

Water is the universal solvent, since it can be used to dissolve many different substances, from dirt to blood to certain paints. In cleaning terminology, however, solvent refers to liquids other than water that are used to get rid of substances that water can't dissolve. Water can't dissolve grease, for instance. Working on the principle that 'like dissolves like', you'd need a no-water-based solvent, such as methylated spirits, to dissolve grease.

Common cleaning solvents include acetone (found in many nail-polish removers), methylated spirits, turpentine, dry-cleaning fluids and kerosene.

Cleaning uses for solvents typically include removing greasy or oily substances, cleaning materials that can be harmed by water, and removing stickers and waxes.

Solvents are a last resort, to be used for the few things that water and detergent won't clean. Solvents can be dangerous to breathe and harmful if they come in contact with your skin and eyes, but they do vary in their degree of toxicity.

Spot removers

You'll see dozens of these on the cleaning aisle at the supermarket. There seems to be a spot remover for every conceivable stain. However, most products fall into two categories: wet and dry.

Wet spot removers, such as Vanish, are water soluble. These typically contain a concentrated laundry detergent and work best on food stains. However, some solutions also contain secondary solvents, such as alcohol and mineral spirits, to boost their stain-removal power and make them more effective on greasy stains.

Dry spot removers, such as Spotless Dry Clean Liquid, contain chemical solvents, including some that dry-cleaners use. (Liquid is still involved. The 'dry' means water isn't used.) These are best for dry-clean-only fabrics, as well as greasy or oily stains that water won't touch.

Carpet and upholstery spot removers are specially designed for use on those materials. They are sometimes foamy, since low-moisture foams that can be vacuumed off are typically better for textiles with pads or cushions beneath.

Be sure to use the right spot-removal product for the right job. To make sure the material you're cleaning is colourfast, pre-test the product in an inconspicuous corner or seam. Always follow the manufacturer's directions carefully.

Toilet cleaners

Commercial toilet cleaners tend to be strong and acid-based. Often they contain hydrochloric acid for eating away at stubborn stains and mineral deposits – the rings that seem cemented to the toilet bowl. Many have a thick consistency, which helps them stick to the wall of the toilet for long enough to dissolve stains and limescale.

For regular toilet cleaning, choose the method that suits you best. Liquid cleaners that you can squirt under the rim will be best in areas where limestone is a big problem. Otherwise, use tablets that can work overnight in the bowl.

Or try using a pumice stone. Keeping the stone wet, rub it on the ring until it's gone. This works for old rings as well as recent ones. Pumice will not scratch white vitreous china, which is what most toilets are made of, but it will scratch glass fibre, enamel, plastic and other softer materials.

INDEX

F

G

PICTURE CREDITS

CREDITS

For Toucan Books
Senior Editor Caroline Smith
Art Editor Dave Jones
Picture Research Jane Lambert
Photographer Michal Kaniewski, Ad Libitum
Illustrators Sue Ninham, Stephen Pollitt
Cartoonist Geoff Waterhouse for *Just for Laffs*

For Vivat Direct
Editorial Director Julian Browne
Art Director Anne-Marie Bulat
Managing Editor Nina Hathway
Picture Resource Manager Sarah Stewart-Richardson
Pre-press Technical Manager Dean Russell
Product Production Manager Claudette Bramble
Production Controller Jan Bucil

Note The information in this book has been carefully researched and all efforts have been made to ensure accuracy and safety. Neither the authors nor Reader's Digest Association Limited assume any responsibility for any injuries suffered or damages or losses incurred as a result of following the instructions in this book. Before taking any action based on information in this book, study the information carefully and make sure you understand it fully. Observe all warnings and Take Care notices. Test any new or unusual repair or cleaning method before applying it broadly, or on a highly visible area or valuable item. The mention of any product or web site in this book does not imply an endorsement. All product names and web sites mentioned are subject to change and are meant to be considered as general examples rather than specific recommendations.

We are committed both to the quality of our products and the service we provide to our customers. We value your comments, so please so contact us on **08701 351 1000** or via our website at **www.readersdigest.co.uk**

If you have any comments or suggestions about the content of our books, email us at **gbeditorial@readersdigest.co.uk**

How to Clean Just About Everything Published in 2011 by Vivat Direct Limited (t/a Reader's Digest), 157 Edgware Road, London W2 2HR

How to Clean Just About Everything is owned and under licence from The Reader's Digest Association, Inc. All rights reserved.

Reprinted twice in 2011

This edition is adapted from **How to Clean Just About Anything** published by The Reader's Digest Association, Inc. in 2006.

Origination ImageScanhouse
Printed in China

ISBN 978 0 276 44582 8
Book code 400-481 UP0000-3